Philip of Spain and the Netherlands

Philip of Spain and the Netherlands

An Essay on Moral Judgments in History

Cecil John Cadoux

The Lutterworth Press

THE LUTTERWORTH PRESS

P.O. Box 60
Cambridge
CB1 2NT
United Kingdom

www.lutterworth.com
publishing@lutterworth.com

Paperback ISBN: 978 0 7188 9676 8
PDF ISBN: 978 0 7188 9678 2
ePub ISBN: 978 0 7188 9677 5

British Library Cataloguing in Publication Data
A record is available from the British Library

First published by The Lutterworth Press, 1947
This edition published 2023

Copyright © Cecil John Cadoux, 1947

All rights reserved. No part of this edition may be reproduced, stored electronically or in any retrieval system, or transmitted in any form or by any means, electronic, mechanical, photocopying, recording, or otherwise, without prior written permission from the Publisher (permissions@lutterworth.com).

Alteri
sed quam Dissimili
Philippo

Contents

Preface   xiii

1 Moral Judgments in History   1

2 Catholic Revaluations in History   18

3 The Character of the Inquisition   41

4 The Spanish Monarchy and the Netherlands   64

5 The Duke of Alva in the Netherlands   93

6 The Personal Character of Philip II   111

7 The Popes of the Period   134

8 The Character of Resistance to Philip in the Netherlands   159

9 The Personal Character of William of Orange   183

10 Conclusion   214

Chronological Table   226

Index   244

Preface

I am anxious to make it clear to readers of the book now offered to the public that its purpose is not to re-tell the story of the revolt of the Netherlands against Spain, but – on the basis of that story – to discuss whether, and if at all, how far, and in what ways it is open to us or obligatory upon us, to form and express moral judgments of approval or disapproval regarding the leading parties in this great historical episode. That most people who take any interest in history at all are, in point of fact, prone to pass moral judgments of this kind on historical characters generally is, I think, a matter of common knowledge: that their right to do so is a much-discussed question is less widely known, as will, I think, be clear from the evidence adduced in my first chapter.

Needless to say, if we are to assess rightly the moral quality of any particular character or movement in history, at least an adequate knowledge of the relevant facts is indispensable. It might occur to some to suggest that no one should attempt an assessment of this kind unless he has studied the bulk of the sources in their original languages. While fully realizing, however, the vital importance of factual accuracy, I cannot but think that to confine all discussion of historical episodes to those who can claim to have fully examined the sources for themselves would be to impose a needlessly severe restriction on debate. How gravely it would narrow the field of disputants, at least in regard to what we call *modern* history, is revealed by the opinion recently expressed to me by a learned scholar, to the effect that the available sources of information concerning any period of history subsequent to A.D. 1500 are so abundant that it is virtually beyond the power of any one investigator really to master them for a longer period of history than twenty years. But, apart from that, we can surely feel that, short of so exhaustive a knowledge, one can derive from the works of modern scholars, representing as they do differing and independent points of view, yet each of them conversant in large measure with the contemporary documents, at least sufficient knowledge of a period to permit of a tentative estimate of certain aspects of it.[1]

I can make no claim myself to have delved into the abundant source-literature, in Spanish, Dutch, French, and other languages, dealing with the revolt of the Netherlands: still less can I produce fresh light from documentary sources hitherto unpublished. But I am confident that enough of the facts for my immediate purpose is available in the works of the numerous modern historians accessible to me: and while a thorough investigation of the original sources might necessitate a minute modification here and there, and might therefore be a really necessary propaedeutic, were one proposing to recount the story in detail afresh, it is hardly a sine qua non for a discussion of the kind I am here proposing.

I have not therefore attempted to quote authorities for every factual statement uttered or presupposed in the ensuing pages. Here and there, for some special reason, I have stated the authority I am depending on for some statement of fact. But for the most part, the documentation is intended to subserve the interests of the controversial evaluation of the facts.

For the sake of any who may be interested to consult the authorities I have quoted, I may say that – for reasons of brevity – I have confined such bibliographical particulars of the works concerned as it seemed needful to give, to the *first* occasion on which each is quoted. Thereafter, abbreviated titles only are quoted. The index will give the page on which the first reference to each work occurs.

Once or twice, as I have been writing, it has occurred to me that the reading of the book might be in places difficult and confusing to one without a sufficient previous knowledge of the story. For the assistance of such persons, I have appended a chronological summary of the main relevant events which occurred during the lifetime of Philip II. Some readers may prefer to peruse that summary before they go further than the end of Chapter II. In any case, I hope that, with the assistance of that appendix, and in the light of the explanations offered in this Preface, the line taken in the main discussion will at least be

---

1. Cf. H. Pirenne, *Histoire de Belgique,* vol. iii (ed. 1912), p. VIII: "Je ne crois pas que l'historien doive attendre avant de prendre la plume que tous les détails de son sujet aient été élucidés."

clear to the reader, even if (contrary to my hopes) it fails to win his complete concurrence.

The manuscript of this book was complete before I could get access to Dr. G.J. Renier's recent work, *The Dutch Nation: an historical study* (Netherlands Government Information Bureau, London, 1944). As the composition of a Dutch scholar with a first-hand knowledge of the authorities, it has a value of its own; and I read it eagerly as a check upon what I had myself ventured to write. The point on which I feel it is most valuable as a corrective is its stress on the non-democratic character of the native government in the Low Countries during the sixteenth and following centuries. Accepting this as in substance true, we may yet note that the oligarchical administration was at least more in line with the popular will than was the rule of Spain, that democratic forces were increasingly at work throughout, and that the popular voice, though debarred from framing official decisions, did make itself heard in the national affairs.

On the particular issue with which my own book deals, Dr. Renier's work is somewhat less helpful. He disallows all concern with Philip's moral character. "To the historian", he says, "it matters little what Philip was: he must know what Philip did or tried to do". He bestows praise on his policy in the Netherlands, because he wanted to substitute an efficient centralized monarchy for the ramshackle disorderliness of the normal institutions of the States. The quality which he emphasizes as good in Philip's rule is, somewhat strangely, the fact that it was "modern". I cannot agree that the ruler's personal character, especially when it affects his governmental measures so closely as it did in Philip's case, is a matter of indifference to the historian. And while I can see the general truth of the statement that centralization is more efficient and possibly more "modern" than unsystematic devolution, I hold that the ethical character of the centralizing monarchy in question must needs affect our judgment in a particular case.

Furthermore, Dr. Renier's book is marked, like that of his friend, Dr. Pieter Geyl, by a tendency to belittle the importance of the religious factor in the great struggle between Spain and the Netherlands. As I have touched on this tendency at the close of my first chapter, and have discussed the particular issue elsewhere in the book, I do not need to deal with it further here. The only comment I wish to make is that, in adducing the Netherlanders' tolerance and dislike of persecution and torture as a ground of their opposition to Spain, Dr. Renier seems *to me* to be a little inconsistent with himself; for their dislike of torture and persecution was itself a religious conviction, and not by any means due to indifference or to their taking religion "as a matter of course". Finally, I am disposed to think that his statement that the Calvinists were as intolerant as the Spanish inquisitors is an exaggeration: but that, too, is a matter which will have to be considered at length in the course of our study.

C.J.C.
Oxford
April 1944

Chapter One

Moral Judgments in History

There must be comparatively few among the students of history, and even among its teachers, who can claim to know their way about that tangled field of human knowledge described as "the philosophy of history". Not only is the literature on the subject enormous, but the arguments are often abstruse in the extreme. How far, for instance, can we be said to possess a real knowledge of the past? In view of the scantiness of our data, can we form any right judgments about it? How exactly do chronicles differ from history properly so called? Where precisely does bare fact end and interpretation begin? How (in view of the personal factor affecting every writer's selection and presentation of his material) can *any* writer's views safely be accepted by his readers as just or adequate? What are the main truths to be learnt from the historical process as a whole, or even from distinct parts of it? Here are samples of the mass of questions with which the philosopher of history has to grapple.[1] It is an exceedingly tall order: and the reader will perhaps be relieved to learn that I am not proposing to make in this book any attempt to solve these basic problems. For though I have been a keen student of history from my youth up, and a teacher of it for the last twenty-five years, I make no claim to a place in the ranks of those rare experts who are capable of dealing competently and adequately with the deeper questions the subject raises.

Yet no intelligent student of history can altogether ignore this difficult field of inquiry. However much he may wish to avoid abstractions, he cannot do without some working rules of his own as to what is credible and what is not, and why, as to how the personal predilections of his informants must be allowed for when he is using their statements, and as to what interpretations are to be placed upon the facts educed. In other words, however

---

1. The perusal of a work like Hilda D. Oakeley's History and the Self: a study in the roots of history and the relations of history and ethics (London), 1934), or M. Mandelbaum's The Problem of Historical Knowledge: an answer to Relativism (New York, 1938), will suffice to convince the reader how wide and abstruse the field is.

little of an expert in philosophy he may be, he must have at his disposal a modus operandi in handling historical material and problems, roughly analogous to the technical ability of the chemist or physicist, who fulfils a useful function, though he cannot claim to be able to answer the ultimate riddles of material existence.

Within the field of the philosophy of history, however, there is one little area with which I do propose to deal, first generally, and then – throughout the bulk of this book – with special reference to a particular phase of the story of Europe. It is that which concerns the moral judgments we are entitled to pass on the dramatis personae of history and on those who have written about them. The task which I thus set myself – apart altogether from the need of rightly selecting and rightly understanding the factual data – is more complex than might appear at first sight. The old assumption that one was entitled to censure and vilify with the utmost severity all whose actions one could not personally approve of, and all whose beliefs one could not personally share, has in these days given place to a milder and more sympathetic approach. The judgments now customarily passed by Christian writers on the non-Christian religions, for instance, by ecclesiastical historians on the so-called "heresiarchs", by historians generally on great aggressors like Alexander and intolerant despots like Louis XIV, tend to be far less censorious than was once customary. And the change is a change for the better. For if it be not quite true that "Tout savoir, c'est tout pardonner", it *is* true that, unless we make some effort to enter into the mind and motives of an historical character, to understand the spirit of the times in which he lived, and to allow for the limitations to which he was inevitably subject, no adverse judgment we may pass on him or his deeds will have in it much justice or value. In other words, sympathy is an indispensable prerequisite of fairness.[2]

---

2. G.F. Bridge, writing in *The Hibbert Journal*, vol. xvi, pp. 50-52, during the first World-War (Oct. 1917), pointed out that, regarding most of the great conflicts of the past, even though our sympathies may be definitely enlisted on one side, we usually have to admit that there was something of value in what the other side was fighting for. Percy Gardner, writing of the sixteenth century, says: "As in almost all the great crises of history, when ideas clash, good and evil, right and wrong were everywhere mingled, and ranged on both sides..." (*The Growth of Christianity* [London, 1907], pp. 225 f.). Similarly, P. Geyl, *The Revolt of the Netherlands* (London, 1932), pp. 15 f.

The question as to whether and how far we are entitled (or perhaps obliged) to express judgments of approval and disapproval on historical characters has, of course, often been discussed: and it may be interesting to glance at one or two of the more recent episodes in the controversy.

Lord Acton was disposed to express strong and indignant disapproval of all acts of persecution and oppression.³ When in 1887 Dr. Mandell Creighton brought out the third and fourth volumes of his *History of the Papacy,* dealing with the Popes of the period 1464-1518, he was vehemently criticized by Lord Acton for judging the Borgias so leniently. An interesting correspondence between the two scholars ensued.⁴ Shortly after this, Creighton delivered a lecture on "Historical Ethics",⁵ in which he explained his principles at length, and offered an elaborate justification of the leniency for which he had been reproached. As an historian, he said, he was more concerned with the results of statesmen's actions than with their personal characters. British historians, in depicting the history of their own country, were apt to suffer from a hypocritical self-righteousness: statesmen have, in the nature of things, to face more complicated dilemmas than private persons have: as trustees, they are not free to do as they like, nor can they disregard public opinion. We cannot in fairness, Creighton urged, disregard the spirit of their age: persecution, for instance, followed inevitably from the universally accepted belief that religious uniformity was absolutely necessary for social well-being. And so on. Yet at the end he confessed himself ready to condemn morally deeds which harm the popular conscience, efface the recognized distinctions between right and wrong, and

---

3. See *Letters of Lord Acton to Mary, daughter of… W.E. Gladstone* (1904), pp. lxxi f., 70, 121 f., 144, 148, 185-187 – mostly referring to what he had written in 1881-1884. Motley, needless to say, had already judged similarly: "And because anointed monarchs are amenable to no human tribunal,… it is the more important for the great interests of humanity that before the judgment-seat of History a crown should be no protection to its wearer. There is no plea to the jurisdiction of history, if history be true to itself" (*History of the United Netherlands* [ed. 1875-76], vol. iii, pp. 505 f.). The last sentence reads awkwardly – one expects "*from* the jurisdiction…". Yet it is printed as I have quoted it in all the editions. Unless "to" is a slip for "from", Motley must have meant "no plea *in defence of a royal tyrant*".
4. See Life and Letters of Mandell Creighton, vol. i, pp. 368-378.
5. Published after his death by his widow in *The Quarterly Review,* vol. cciii, pp. 32-46 (July 1905).

hinder moral progress: he specified treachery and assassination as instances.

These closing avowals showed that Creighton had not been wholly unaffected by Acton's criticism. In his Hulsean Lectures on *Persecution and Tolerance* delivered at Cambridge in 1893-94, and published in 1895, he allowed himself to be much more severe. In persecuting, he maintained, the Christian Church forgot the rebuke directed by Christ against the intolerance of His disciples (Luke 9: 54-56); and her mistake was not intellectual – it was moral. She must be judged, not by her success, but by her fidelity or otherwise to her Master. Persecution arose from man's natural desire to have his own way, and from the State's wish for uniformity; but it could easily have been seen to be in open contradiction to the principles of Christianity.

Meanwhile Lord Acton, in his preface to L.A. Burd's edition of Machiavelli's *Il Principe* (1891), had criticized the constant habit of imagining statesmen to be exempt from all obligation to respect the moral law (especially such law as is admittedly binding on private individuals) and of reckoning success as their one sufficient title to our approval. When in 1895 he was appointed Regius Professor of Modern History at Cambridge, he took occasion, in his inaugural lecture, to denounce with unsparing severity the prevalent custom of finding all sorts of excuses for the dark deeds of the past, and pleaded on the contrary that we ought to maintain "the moral currency" in its purity: "if we lower our standard in History", he concluded, "we cannot uphold it in Church or State".[6]

In 1898 Dr. Creighton re-stated his position in an address on "Heroes", and summarized some of the arguments he had used in the earlier lecture on "Historical Ethics".[7] He finished with some rather stronger concessions to the demands of righteousness in judgment than he had previously made.

The veteran historian, Henry Charles Lea, in a presidential paper read to the American Historical Society in 1903,[8] discussed

---

6. *A Lecture on the Study of History* (ed. 1895), pp. 63-74, 135-142. This lecture was delivered in June 1895, was first published the same year, and is reprinted in Acton's *Lectures on Modern History* (1906), pp. 23-28, 340-342.
7. See Mandell Creighton, *Historical Lectures and Addresses* (1903), pp. 305 – 323.
8. Published in *The American Historical Review,* vol. ix, pp. 233-246 (Jan. 1904).

"Ethical Values in History" – interestingly enough, with special reference to Philip II. He started with a rejection of Acton's principle, on the ground that allowance must be made for the wide variation in men's views, from age to age and from race to race, as to what is righteous and what is wrong and punishable. It is not fair to judge an historical character on the strength of a moral code which he could not possibly have recognized. We must judge the individual by his conscientiousness only; and if, though conscientious, he acted badly, we must reserve our blame for the age in which he lived. Of Lea's specific application of this principle to Philip II we shall have to take note later. All that needs notice here is the general plea that, although Philip's actions were cruel and harmful, the blame for them must fall, not on him, but on the influences by which he had been moulded.

Miss Lily Dougall made a useful, if incidental, contribution to the discussion in the course of an essay she wrote for the composite work entitled *Concerning Prayer*.[9] She was not specifically dealing with historical characters (though she had occasion to refer to Dr. Creighton's Hulsean Lectures); she was discussing sin as such. Her main point was that sin, being any quality or deed of man which differs from God's ideal for him, is often present when men are doing what they suppose to be right; and it is present because they have not done their best to find out what *is* right. She disagreed therefore with Dr. Creighton's view that persecutors always knew that persecution is condemned by the spirit of the Gospel. She laid great stress on man's duty of ascertaining what really is God's Will, as being equally needful with the desire to do what he already believes that Will to be. On the propriety or otherwise of blaming others she hardly touched.

A frontal attack on the problem (rather on the lines adumbrated by H.C. Lea) was made by Mr. (now Professor) H. Butterfield, Fellow of Peterhouse, Cambridge, in his small book, *The Whig Interpretation of History*, published in 1931. He conceded to the historian the right of expressing his own personal preferences and antipathies, so long as he was aware that he was acting in a purely private capacity and that he was making

---

9. *Concerning Prayer* (London, 1916), pp. 140-166.

certain special assumptions for the purpose. Nay, more: he allowed that not only his intellect, but also his instinct and his sympathy, must be alive and awake. Nor must he forget that the characters of history were morally responsible. But he stoutly denied that, in his official capacity qua historian, he has any right to pronounce any particular act, institution, or person of bygone days to have been morally good or bad, right or wrong, sinful or righteous. His business is to be a witness, not a judge – to understand and explain, not to blame, excuse, or applaud – to forgive and reconcile, not to punish or avenge. Mankind cannot be divided into black and white, friends and enemies of progress; nor is it sufficient to admit that there have been good men on both sides of the great conflict. One must keep clear of the typical Whig fallacy, which – after abridging and oversimplifying the history of the past – insists on applying to it the standards of the present, traces a continuous line of freedom from Luther down through successive Protestant and Whig champions to the British constitution of to-day, and views Catholicism as alone responsible for conflict, cruelty, and reaction. As a matter of fact (Professor Butterfield urges), if Luther could have foreseen what liberty would become in our own day, he would certainly have combined with the Roman Church to suppress it. Catholicism was not solely responsible for the cruelty of the struggle; and freedom has developed, not from Whiggery alone, but from the conflict and co-operation between it and its opponent.

Professor Butterfield refers, towards the close of his book, to the very different use of history recommended by Lord Acton, and he condemns it as owing its origin, not to objective historical judgments, but to the Whig preferences of Lord Acton himself. To Acton's plea that it is better that our moral judgments in history should be too severe rather than too lenient, he replies that this reduces itself to saying "Better be unjust to dead men than give currency to loose ideas on questions of morals", and comes near to saying "Better be unhistorical than do anything that may lower the moral dignity of history".[10]

---

10. I have tried to give a fair summary of Professor Butterfield's position as a whole, without bothering to quote detailed references to this and that page of his short book. A very good instance of the application of his views may be seen in the rap over the knuckles administered anonymously in *The Times Literary Supplement,* January 16, 1937, p. 35, to Dr. Arnold J. Toynbee for

Something in the nature of a reply to Professor Butterfield was furnished in the Hulsean Lectures of Professor Herbert G. Wood, of Birmingham, entitled *Christianity and the Nature of History* (1934). After remarking that Acton's position had been anticipated by Sallust, Tacitus, and Froude, and Butterfield's by Thucydides, Hegel, and Bury, Dr. Wood declared his agreement with Mr. Butterfield on three points: (1) that greatness in history cannot be equated with moral goodness, and that the historian is primarily concerned with greatness; (2) that the distinction to be drawn is not simply one between black and white, saints and sinners; and (3) that the historian is probably not called upon to act as a judge, but as an expert witness. He adds, however, that the historian is still describable as "the arbiter of controversies", because his task is to give evidence on both sides. "The historian must not set out to show which party was in the right, but he should try to show how far each party was in the right". In conceding that the historian has to go to his work with instinct and sympathy awake, has to discover not only facts but significances, to give his expert witness correctly, to understand, reconcile, forgive, and so on, Professor Butterfield implicitly concedes that he must also pass moral judgments. It does not – as he seems to assume – follow from the frequency of indiscriminate and one-sided verdicts, that *all* our moral judgments on the past are purely relative; if they were, history could have no significance whatever – which is absurd. Even if we conclude that no "lesson" we can draw from history is ever more than probable, "yet the probability may be so clear and so strong that we neglect it at our peril". Finally, Dr. Wood denies that Lord Acton's theory of history was characteristically Whig, and observes that many of Mr. Butterfield's own particular judgments would probably have been endorsed by Lord Acton

---

bestowing blame on Mussolini in his *Survey of International Affairs, 1935*. "All this distribution of good and bad marks", says the reviewer, "produces some pungent writing. But it is surely beneath the dignity of serious history.... One cannot but respect the sincerity and depth of emotion which are evident in every line of these pages. But Dr. Toynbee writes as an angry man; and if it is true that *facit indignatio versum*, it certainly does not encourage clear thinking". Dr. Stanley Lane-Poole, in the preface to his volume on *Turkey* (1889), in the series entitled "The Story of the Nations", says: "While striving to escape the charge of prolixity, I have carefully avoided the sin of moralizing...."

himself.[11] Miss Hilda D. Oakeley, in her book, *History and the Self* (1934), does not directly attack our problem; but in the course of this "Study in... the Relations of History and Ethics" she throws out various observations which bear upon it. Her position generally is that of a "relativist", impressed with the scantiness of historical data, with the "invincible relativity of all our historic valuations and judgments,...", and with the impossibility of possessing direct knowledge of the particular nature and qualities of other selves. She believes, however, that pure relativism is transcended by the principle of freedom; and although here she has mainly in mind, not political freedom, but freedom of the will as opposed to determinism, this principle leads her to a profound regard for the personality of the human individual, both of the past and of the present, as an ultimate value of which history must take account. She does not work out the implications of this conclusion; but its relevance to the general problem of historical value-judgments is obvious.

A more recent consideration of the problem is that given by the veteran medievalist, Dr. G.G. Coulton, in his autobiography.[12] He contends, in the first place, that the true historical method is not something mysterious and esoteric, the exclusive perquisite of specialists, but a quest for probabilities under the guidance of common sense. He repudiates as pedantic and impracticable the attempt to write history without exercising or expressing moral judgments. One cannot understand without judging; and even those who claim that we can, act as judges themselves, not only in the selection and presentation of their material, but still more patently in their criticism of other historians. "Those who warn us off from judging Julius Caesar are most unsparing in their condemnation of Mommsen's conception of Caesar; yet, 'if I may think a German Professor wrong, why not a Roman General?'" True, we must avoid over-frequent, biased, and censorious judgments; but just as a judge, starting with complete impartiality, moves, in the course of

---

11. See H.G. Wood, *Christianity and the Nature of History* (Cambridge, 1934), pp. 111-142; cf. also pp. 23 f. and 144 ff. ("Christianity and Progress"), 181-183, 203. Cf. also G.G. Coulton, *The Inquisition* (London, 1929), p. 65 ("To ignore the question of human responsibility would make all history meaningless").

12. G.G. Coulton, *Fourscore Years* (Cambridge, 1943), pp. 317 f., 320-324.

fulfilling his duty, towards a fairly definite leaning in favour of one side or the other (in order to have some guidance to give the jury), so the historian must endeavour to reach a judicial decision regarding the facts lying behind his mass of evidence. "Why should not even the most scientific historian content himself with Goethe's confession of faith: 'I can promise to be sincere, but not to be impartial'?"

The latest contribution I have seen is in Mr. Desmond MacCarthy's review of Dr. Coulton's book in *The Sunday Times*, January 16, 1944. Agreeing largely with Dr. Coulton's main contentions, Mr. MacCarthy observes, by way of qualification, that "the Court of History is not necessarily ethical, though for Dr. Coulton it is,... History is also written from the point of view of development, whether of national power or of particular institutions or of economic changes. But here, too, the historian must continually pass judgments. He must judge which events or men were most important as causes of subsequent developments". In this he must beware of personal bias, and of twisting the facts. "The difficulty is... that the same cases are, so to speak, tried in different courts. And his [Dr. Coulton's] own faults as a controversialist are due to his shouting loud in the hope of being heard in a neighbouring court...."

This brief survey of a selection of recent opinions on the subject of moral judgments in history will suffice to show how fraught with pitfalls the subject is. Difference of opinion does not seem likely to arise regarding the injustice of any judgments based on insufficient acquaintance with the facts, on onesidedness in weighing the evidence, on unwillingness to allow for the circumstances of the time, or on a failure to understand the real motives of the agents concerned. Nor, on the other hand, need we in all probability hesitate to pass an adverse judgment in those rare cases in which the agent himself makes it clear to us that he knew he was doing wrong.[13] But what are we to do

---

13. The best example of this kind that occurs to me is Cicero's letter to the historian L. Lucceius (*Ad Fam*. V, xii, 1-3), in which he begged him to write a history of the Catilinarian conspiracy and, for the sake of friendship, to eulogize in it Cicero's own exploits even beyond what strict truth would justify ("Itaque te plane etiam atque etiam rogo, ut et ornes ea vehementius etiam

when we have no such confession to base a judgment on, but when we can claim to know reasonably well not only what a man did, but what were his motives and intentions in doing it? How far are we then in a position to praise or blame him personally? For motives and intentions include deeper elements; and the more conscientiously we try to analyse and assess these, the less competent shall we feel to pronounce a verdict of blame. Here surely we have the ground of our Saviour's emphatic injunction, "Judge not, that ye be not judged". In that sense, must we not leave the work of judging our fellow-men to the Knower of all hearts?[14]

But although we may not be in a position to blame the men, we *are* sometimes in a position to condemn their deeds. Who, for instance, can read Shakespeare's *King Lear* without passing judgment on the behaviour of Edmund, Regan, and Goneril – or *Othello* without contrasting Iago's treachery with the nobility of Desdemona? The same Teacher who forbade His hearers to judge others took it for granted that they were entitled, and indeed obliged, to distinguish right actions from wrong. The difference between these two operations may be a very subtle one for us to observe: but none the less we must needs observe it. The difficulty is well illustrated by the case of the very man who is the prime subject of this study. Philip II of Spain occasioned the violent deaths of at least several thousands of

---

quam fortasse sentis, et in eo leges historiæ neglegas... amorique nostro plusculum etiam, quam concedet veritas, largiare"). His editor, Mr. W.W. How (*Cicero: Select Letters,* vol. ii, p. 206), remarks that this request "violates modern standards of honour, though apparently Cicero saw nothing ignoble in it". But it is clear that Cicero did see something ignoble in it, otherwise he would not have referred to his unwillingness, on account of "pudor", to make his request verbally ("epistula enim non erubescit"); nor would he have written: "Neque tamen ignoro quam impuderiter faciam,... Sed tamen, qui semel verecundiæ finis transierit, eum bene. et naviter oportet esse impudentem...." He was perfectly well aware that it is an historian's first duty to be truthful. "So", rightly says Mr. How (p. 207), "his request to Lucceius is the more shameless". About opening letters not addressed to him, and writing letters in another man's name, Cicero apparendy did not feel the same scruples (How, p. 247).

14. So Samuel Johnson in his *Life* of John Dryden: "But inquiries into the heart are not for man; we must now leave him to his Judge" (p. 146 in the one-volume edition of 1881). It is largely because he sees this point so clearly that Professor Butterfield deprecates moral judgment: see *The Whig Interpretation,* etc., pp. 115 ("... what can the historian do about the secret recesses of the personality where a man's final moral responsibility lies?"), 119 ("because he [the historian] has the art of sifting sources and weighing evidence, this does not mean that he has the subtlety to decide the incidence of moral blame or praise").

innocent persons: yet he was unquestionably a most religious and conscientious man; and he declared on his deathbed that he had never willingly and knowingly wronged anyone.[15] His case illustrates the contrasted dangers to which all moral judgments passed on historical characters are exposed – firstly, the failure to give a man credit for goodness and sincerity of motive because his actions are morally repellent; and secondly, the failure to brand his actions as morally repellent, because his inner motives were presumably good and sincere.[16] The latter danger is just as grave as the former; and we must be on our guard against controversialists who try to block any pronouncement of an adverse sentence on deeds which stink in the nostrils of Heaven, because forsooth the doer thereof was acting honestly according to his lights.

It needs, moreover, to be added that we cannot rightly draw a sharp distinction here between the historian as judge and the ordinary man as judge, and say that, while the ordinary man is welcome to think and say what he likes about any historical character, yet *in his capacity as an historian* he must keep his mouth shut in regard to all value-judgments. I have always understood that the historian was a species or sub-species of the genus homo sapiens; and while, as Mr. Desmond MacCarthy urges, the interests of history are not exclusively ethical, yet ethics constitute a dominant and universal interest in human affairs; and I cannot see why the historian should be called upon to leave unused his ethical judgment any more than any other power he possesses for discerning the truth.

In this book, therefore, I shall not be concerned to condemn or censure either Philip II or any of his contemporaries. I shall, however, try to put before the reader certain of their deeds, and

---

15. Cf. S. Leathes in *The Cambridge Modern History,* vol. ii (1903), p. 80 (of Philip's father, Charles V): "… – the acts of a bigot perhaps, but a good man cannot do more than follow his conscience, and Charles was a conscientious Catholic." See below, pp. 70 ff.
16. The judge's task would become still more complicated if he had to take account of the subtleties of "moral theology" as a technical ecclesiastical study. Thus, Dr. K.E. Kirk (in *The Study of Theology* [London, 1939], pp. 369-374, 378-380) distinguishes between: (1) "action" (as either right or wrong); (2) "intention" (as either moral or immoral); (3) "motive" (as either virtuous or vicious); and (4) "temper" (as either conscientious or unconscientious). Either of the two alternatives in one class may be combined with either of the two alternatives in each of the other three classes. We thus get *sixteen* possible combinations; but only that which is unconscientious in "temper" is a proper object of blame!

the motives for them, in what I believe to be the true light, and invite him to form his own moral judgment on these deeds, as distinct from passing sentences of blame on the doers of them.[17]

The same principle that applies to our treatment of the characters of history applies also, as Dr. Coulton urges in the passage quoted above on page 8, to such criticisms as we may feel obliged to make of the ways in which some modern writers deal with historical events and persons. I shall have occasion to comment presently on the liability of conscious and subconscious motives to affect men who write controversially of past times. And though I may now and then express myself adversely on their views, and even speculate as to the motives contributing to the formation of those views, I wish it to be clearly understood that I do not call in question the good faith of any particular controversialist whose statements I may have occasion to criticize. It is not my business, because it is not within my power, to pass judgment on the sincerity of others. But it *is* within my power, and I conceive it to be my business, not only to see that my own motives are as free from distortion and bias as I can possibly make them, but also to know something about the objective character of the deeds of the past and something about the accuracy, or otherwise, of modern pronouncements about them, and to be able to offer some just judgments thereupon. It may save a good deal of misdirected criticism if both I and my readers endeavour to keep steadily in mind the limits which I understand to be thus set to my task.

Having vindicated to the best of my ability the right of the modern historian and student to express moral judgments on the doings of historical characters and of other historians, and having laid to heart the need for care, sympathy, and tolerance in the formation and expression of such judgments, I must now pass on

---

17. Professor Butterfield – a little inconsistently, I feel, with some of the things he says elsewhere – really concedes the legitimacy of doing this. "It may", he says, "be easy for the moralist of the twentieth century… to say perhaps that religious persecution would be wrong to-day, perhaps that it was wrong in all the ages. *It may be easy to judge the thing, to condemn the act,* but how shall the historian pass on to the condemnation of *people*…?" (*The Whig Interpretation*, etc., p. 118: italics mine). Cf. Coulton, *The Inquisition*, p. 77 ("Yet let us strive to strike an equal balance, and not to do the men injustice even when we condemn their action").

to observe some ways in which this right to judge is being exercised to-day.

One of the most unmistakable traits of the generation in which we live is its delight in rejecting or correcting the judgments passed by its predecessors. No doubt such judgments often need to be revised in the interests of truth: and indeed there could be no proper service rendered to truth itself, and no intellectual progress maintained, without freedom to modify, and even sometimes to reverse, the conclusions of the past.[18] At the same time, other impulses besides an unbiased love for truth find their satisfaction in the overthrow of long-accepted opinions: and psychology has taught us how woefully easy it is for us all to overlook the mixed character of our motives and the subconscious operation of unacknowledged desires. And when it becomes a question of value-judgments, as distinct from the mere reconstruction of facts, it is almost impossible to keep the claim which the objectively and inherently good has to our approval and admiration distinct from purely-subjective preferences. In any case, the opportunity of discrediting a widely-accepted view is itself a gratifying and exhilarating possession: and while such views do at times deserve to be discredited, precautions need to be taken against the possibility that, either in ourselves or in others or in both, ulterior motives lie – perhaps unrecognized – behind the refutation: for if they do, some weakness will necessarily inhere in the refutation itself.

What has just been said applies, of course, in some degree to all departments of human inquiry: but it applies with special force to the treatment of history. For there the task of estimating the characters and of morally judging the deeds of various persons enters in, as we have seen, almost as inevitably as the task of discovering what they did and why they did it. The likes and dislikes felt by the student or historian can hardly be excluded in the fulfilment of this task. Not only the extent of his knowledge, but his standards of judgment also, will naturally determine, not only what he thinks of this or that character, but also the distribution of his interest and the light in which he himself views characters and events, and desires others to view them. It will

---

18. Cf. the words of C.H. Firth, quoted by C.H. Williams in *The Modern Historian* X (London, 1938), pp. 48 f.

thus be seen what a happy hunting-ground history is bound to prove for those who are, perhaps more or less unconsciously, impelled by other considerations than a desire for the simple truth concerning facts and for a really-objective standard of value-judgments. Among such considerations the sheer love of dethroning the established view is sometimes apt to find a place. And even when we can be sure that the individual historian is personally free from it, or is at any rate able to prevent it from deflecting his judgment, there will usually be some among his readers who will be betrayed by a desire to prove their fellows and predecessors wrong into a hasty and uncritical acceptance of new opinions.

This tendency to put forward and to welcome revised versions in history frequently takes the form of an attempt, not only to "debunk" the idols, but to "whitewash" the villains, of the past.[19] Not but what there are cases in which such rehabilitations are long overdue. A reviewer of a recent book on the toad remarked that, after centuries of undeserved loathing, "bufo" was in these days at last coming into his own. Something analogous might be affirmed of certain historical characters. A century ago, the name of Oliver Cromwell would inevitably have suggested itself. Another instance of tardy justice being at last secured is that of Edward Seymour, Duke of Somerset, and Protector of England under Edward VI. But other and far more dubious reversals of fortune are now to be witnessed in plenty. When characters like Caligula, Nero, Chingis Khan, King John, King Richard III, the Borgia Pope Alexander VI, King Henry VIII, King James II, Judge Jeffreys, and Claverhouse, are found susceptible of whitewash, there must surely be few in history's portrait-gallery who cannot hope to receive some day or other the blessings of posterity in place of its hitherto customary frowns and curses.

Perhaps one of the most plausible reasons advanced in support of the abandonment of some long-current view is the plea that the historical works on the contents of which it was based are now antiquated. The attempt is made to rule them out-of-court by proclaiming them out-of-date. Such-and-such a writer, we are often told, had no conception of the "newer trends";

---

19. Cf. A. Weigall, *Nero* (London, 1933), p. 11, "… in this age of whitewash…"

the whole approach to the question has shifted since his day; and so on, and so forth. The suggestion that we ought to discount the evidence accumulated by former students of the original documents is one of those half-truths that can be made to do the same duty as a total inaccuracy. All histories written many years ago must necessarily *in some sense* be antiquated, owing to the discovery of at least some fresh material since they were written, and owing also to the exploration and trial of fresh points of view and fresh lines of interpretation. But well-written historical works are not out-of-date in the sense that their duly-supported statements have ceased to be true, or that we can afford to disregard them. The actual amount of freshly-discovered material relating to the sixteenth century, for example, is not so great as to call for much drastic revision of the story which the diligent investigators of the nineteenth century narrated.

While, as a matter of principle, we must always be ready to revise our views in the light of fresh evidence, it has to be borne in mind that what are commended to us as "the newer trends" are often simply the view-points which appeal to a particular author or school, or constitute a temporary fashion, but which possess no inherent right to supersede what went before.

To illustrate my meaning by what is perhaps an extreme example – the German Communist Karl Kautsky produced in 1908 a volume on early Christianity, arguing confidently that the interests of Jesus and His first followers were almost wholly economic, and that their movement was essentially a revolt on communistic lines against the tyranny of the wealthy classes and vested interests of their day. An English translation of the thirteenth German edition was published in 1925.[20] The whole idea is, of course, fantastic; but it appeals to the Marxist mind. Suppose now (which God forbid!) Marxism came to be the dominating force in English literature, any study of the life of Jesus or the character of the early Church which gave a prominent place to spiritual and ethical values as such would be discounted in the literary journals as "ignoring the newer trends".

---

20. K. Kautsky, *Foundations of Christianity: a Study in Christian Origins*. Its main thesis is summarized by H.G. Wood in *Christianity and the Nature of History* (pp. 41 – 53), and answered (pp. 53 – 77, 86).

This is, I admit, an extreme instance; but it will serve to illustrate the kind of danger against which we must be on our guard. The age in which we live has lost much of its predecessor's interest in religion, while economics have become a dominant concern in almost all quarters. Hence, naturally, the appearance of certain "newer trends", a certain "new historical method" – for ignorance of which so many of the classic productions of the last century are declared out-of-date. The critic does not need to be an atheist, or even a Marxist, in order to treat them in that way. He needs only to be personally not over-interested in religion, in order to declare that great historians like Macaulay, Motley, and Lecky, are out-of-date, not because their statements are demonstrably wrong, but because they wrote largely in terms of nineteenth-century Liberalism, and bestowed insufficient attention on economic issues and interests, out of regard for those on religion and morals.

Now let us frankly recognize that it is wise and right for us to have our attention drawn to the economic factor, certainly as a counterpoise to the dynastic and military affairs in which history has often been so disproportionately absorbed.[21] It still remains a question whether the obsession of the modern mind with economic problems may not induce a grave distortion of judgment, as we study the doings of men for whom, though they were not indifferent to economic considerations, other interests had far greater weight. Before I can accept the statement that some modern scholar has "exploded" or "demolished" this or that long-standing theory regarding the part played by religion in some phase of human history, I want to know how much the scholar in question is himself interested in religious issues. Just as Marxism gravely misinterprets history by making the economic factor the only one that really matters, so the modern "historical method" may lead us seriously astray by too-hastily assuming that the standards of importance widely accepted in

---

21. So R. Trevor Davies, *The Golden Century of Spain, 1501-1621* (London, 1937) p. v: the needed book on Spain "should deal with economic, social and cultural issues in preference to 'drum and trumpet' narrative of the nineteenth-century kind". Cf. Miss C.V. Wedgwood's carefully qualified words in *William the Silent. William of Nassau, Prince of Orange, 1533-1584* (London, 1944), p. 26.

this materialistic age were taken at the same valuation in the sixteenth century.[22]

Economics, as a factor supposedly superior to and more significant than religion, is not the only interest on behalf of which some reversals of traditional historical judgments have recently been advanced and welcomed. Another interest is Roman Catholicism: but for the discussion of this we shall need a new chapter.

---

22. Cf. A.W. Ward in *Camb. Mod. Hist.*, vol. iii (1904), p. 705 ("... governments and populations alike were in this age [the sixteenth century] more troubled by religious than by economic disturbances"); G. Unwin, quoted by C.H. Williams in *The Modern Historian*, pp. 109 – 113 (pleads for economic history as important, but rejects the "economic interpretation" as inadequate: economics have to be religiously and socially interpreted); G.N. Clark, quoted *ibid.*, p. 130 ("... new factors have to be taken into reckoning which are not rooted in economic life" – i.e., economics not the only key); A.J.D. Farrer in *Studies in History and Religion, Presented to Dr. H. Wheeler Robinson* (London, Lutterworth Press, 1942), p. 208 n. 2 ("I need hardly say that I reject the recently fashionable theory, that reformations are mainly an outcome of *economic* conditions, as one-sided, and blind to the spiritual side of man's nature and its supreme influence on his life").

Chapter Two

Catholic Revaluations in History

Willing as are non-religious economists and students of political history to avail themselves of the present-day fashion of discarding and reversing long-established judgments, their willingness and skill are far surpassed by those of the apologists of the Roman Catholic Church. For that institution has a very long leeway to make up in the matter of history's adverse judgments upon her. So effectively did her champions succeed by their ruthlessness in rousing to its very depths the moral disgust of the race, that Catholic propaganda, even to this day, finds itself seriously handicapped by the horror which words like "Jesuitical" and "Inquisition" still evoke among large masses of people. One of the hardest tasks facing the Catholic apologist is to clear his Church of the discredit involved in the longstanding charge of having shed innocent blood very abundantly.[1]

It is, therefore, only to be expected that propagandists of that particular school should welcome the whitewashing and debunking fashion of the day, and should seek to turn it to good account. The literary atmosphere of our time assures a ready hearing to any writer who, with any plausibility at all, can speak of the customary version of this or that historical incident or character as an out-of-date legend now abandoned by all serious students of the subject. Furthermore, the modern temper is distinctly hostile to theological animus in *any* direction: and if one can, by skilfully concealing one's own ex parte interest under a fair show of modern knowledge, give to the old-fashioned verdict the additional stigma of having been generated

---

1. To the Catholic, of course, the discredit resting on the Roman Church is due to Protestant one-sidedness. Thus, Professor Edmond Poullet, at the opening of the first of his two important articles, "De la répression de l'hérésie au XVIe siècle dans les Pays-Bas" (in *Revue Générale: Journal historique & littéraire*, Bruxelles, Paris, & Fribourg, tome XXVI, pp. 145-179 and 897-940 [August and December, 1877]), complains that so few defend themselves against historical prejudices, and observes, as one reason for this, that whereas the sixteenth century was religious, the nineteenth is irreligious. Here we have irreligion, to which in the last chapter I attributed the *overthrow* of certain customary Protestant beliefs acclaimed in the Catholic camp as the reason for their existence.

by Protestant prejudice, one can score quite heavily for the Catholic side.

Several different avenues are open to the diligent Roman Catholic apologists who wish to reverse the long-established judgments unfavourable to Rome's peculiar claims. One of them is exemplified by the systematic attempt made with much secrecy by the Westminster Catholic Federation, during the years 1923-27, to induce the publishers of the history text-books used in the public elementary schools of the London County Council to purge them of all expressions inconsistent with a pro-Roman version of British and European history. It was only by accident that full information regarding this extraordinary campaign became accessible to the public.[2] Usually the cards are played with greater skill. Representing as they do less than seven per cent of the population of Great Britain, and by their zeal and organization commanding an influence greatly in excess of what this proportion would appear to warrant, Roman Catholics are able to exert a very considerable influence through the press – an influence all the greater because its true origin is frequently and skilfully kept in the background. Holding posts of responsibility on the editorial staffs of many newspapers and journals, they are in an exceptionally favourable position for quietly excluding from the columns of the press most of what is distasteful to the authorities of their Church, while securing generous treatment for all literary contributions made on its behalf.

It is particularly interesting in this connexion to note the frequency with which opportunities for not over-blatant Romanist propaganda have been found in recent years in the pages of *The Times Literary Supplement*. I possess no positive inside information regarding the personnel of its editorial staff: but it seems reasonable to suppose that it makes use of a wide circle of expert reviewers who are not themselves actually included therein. As its reviews are regularly unsigned, and are always written with that air of authoritative impartiality proper to so important and national an organ of literary criticism, they

---

2. See the details set forth in my *Roman Catholicism and Freedom* (London, The Independent Press, 3rd ed., 1937), pp. 138, 147-149, 156 f.; also below, p. 23, II. 2.

naturally carry, with many readers, greater weight than do the signed reviews in less-widely circulated periodicals. A Catholic reviewer, or one sympathetic to Catholicism, has therefore a unique opportunity of firing a shot in the dark on behalf of the Church of Rome, if he is allowed or invited to review a book for this particular journal.

It would not be right to suggest one-sidedness in the contents of so valuable and highly respected a publication as *The Times Literary Supplement* without presenting some at least of the evidence on which the remark is based.

I specify first – for what they are worth – a number of suggestive headlines, not wishing to lay much stress on them, because one does not know how far they are the work of the *Supplement's* staff, how far that of the reviewers themselves. Their cumulative tendentiousness, however, is obvious.

"The Roman Catholic Minority. A dark corner of English History". April 4, 1936, p. 291.
"The Divorce of Catherine of Aragon. In defence of Pope Clement VII". June 20, 1936, p. 522.
"A Catholic in praise of Voltaire. Correctives to a legend". October 10, 1936, p. 808.
"Spain's Golden Age. The policy of Philip II". November 6, 1937, p. 814.
"King Philip II of Spain. A reconsidered estimate". February 19, 1938, p. 118.
"In defence of the Queen of Scots. An imaginative narrative". September 17, 1938, p. 590.
"Scourge of the Huguenots. The Family of Guise". January 28, 1939, p. 61.
"Hero of the Jacobites. John Graham of Claverhouse". May 27, 1939, p. 307.
"The Baroque Papacy" (in enormous letters). "Feats of the Counter-Reformation. Rome and the Genius of Bernini". April 27, 1940, p. 206.
"The Church in the Crisis. A Roman Catholic Programme". March 1, 1941, p. 98.
"Pope of Peace. Benedict XV". April 12, 1941, p. 180.
"Choice of the Christian. Cardinal Hinsley's Patriotism". June 14, 1941, p. 282.
"Churchman and Patriot. Cardinal Hinsley". March 4, 1944, p. 116.
"Truth in the Whole. A Roman Catholic Vision". March 18, 1944, p. 141.
"Cardinal Bourne. A patriotic prelate". April 8, 1944, p. 176.

In noticeable consistency with the tendency revealed by this group of headlines is the sympathetic and complimentary manner in which Catholic individuals and Catholic activities are frequently treated in the *Supplement*. Thus, the English Catholic minority "can hardly fail to rouse the interest and sympathy of English people of all persuasions" (April 4, 1936, p. 291). During the crisis in the French Church, "there stands out in bright relief the statesmanship of [Pope] Leo XIII" (May 30, 1936, p. 456). Under the headline "The Path to Invincibility", a Catholic study of *The Art of Suffering* (which reaches its climax in a touching description of the devotional fervour of Philip II on his deathbed) is given a sympathetic welcome (July 4, 1936, p. 522). A cardinal's speech in Conclave "reads as an example of perfect courtesy and charity" (December 12, 1936, p. 1024). "The troubles of the old Catholic families during a century" (1560-1660) "come as a surprise even to those who would say they were served right for the Marian persecutions" (December 12, 1936, p. 1027). The bibliography of *An Introduction to Medieval Europe, 300-1500,* is criticized because "on the ecclesiastical and intellectual side [it] unduly neglects the Catholic point of view" (June 25, 1938, p. 438). A Jesuit missionary who was martyred by the Red Indians is described, in the review of *The Travels and Sufferings of Father Jean de Brébeuf* as "one of the most heroic members of one of the most heroic bodies in the history of the world, the Jesuit mission to the Hurons,...": and the editor of his story is said to have "produced a splendid memorial to a saint and hero" (January 14, 1939, p. 20).

A review of the volumes of Ludwig von Pastor's *The History of the Popes,* dealing with the period 1621-1700, amid many compliments both to the author and to the Papacy, mentions "Urban VIII's College of Propaganda, which, served by heroic missionaries and sealing its work with the blood of innumerable martyrs, kept alive the faith in the midst of persecution in northern Europe,...." The Church's absurd persecution of Galileo is admitted to have been "a grave blunder"; but the criticism is qualified by the strange remark that "in the light of the relativity principle we can see that exclusive and absolute truth can be claimed neither for the geocentric nor for the heliocentric theory. Both are equally valid descriptions of the phenomena, and all that we can say for Copernicus and Galileo is that their description is much the more convenient". Moreover Galileo, in his treatment of Kepler, showed worse and less-excusable bigotry than the Inquisition showed in its treatment of him. "The judgment of the Inquisition upon him is not an act of the kind for which the Church has ever claimed infallibility". Finally, the gaudy baroque art of the period is enthusiastically defended against the charges usually levelled against it (April 27, 1940, pp. 206, 210).³

"The Roman Church, in fact, inspires", we are told, "some of the best of recent historical studies" (December 7, 1940, p. vi). Mr. Denis Gwynn, in his apologia for the line taken by the Vatican in European politics since 1914, is declared to have "preserved a broad and dispassionate outlook and produced an admirably lucid account of a large subject" (May 24, 1941, p. 248). The reviewer of Dr. William Paton's book, *The Church and the New Order,* patronizingly remarks that "at a time when the firmest statements of the function and meaning of the Church have usually been Catholic, it is reassuring to find a Protestantism which is at once virile and wise", etc., etc. (July 19, 1941, p. 344).

Of another defence of the attitude of the Papacy to international politics, by Professor Binchy, it is said: "Massive in its erudition, scrupulous in its impartiality, cogent in its reasoning, sound in its judgments, it is a model of contemporary history. He brings many advantages to his task. He is himself a Catholic, and – an important point – he lives in a Catholic country,…" The book, we learn, deals with the Pope's attitude to Italy's murderous attack on Abyssinia. "Those who charge the Vatican with pro-Fascist sympathies point to its conduct in the Ethiopian and Spanish wars. Professor Binchy retorts that only two fairly innocuous remarks by the Pope could be quoted from the period of hostilities; at the end of hostilities he allows that Pope Pius XI made one unfortunate reference to 'the triumphant joy of a great and good people', but he believes that this has been lived down".

---

3. Cf. the appreciative reviews of Dr. W. Weisbach's apologia, *Spanish Baroque Art,* in *The Times Literary Supplement,* May 31, 1941, p. 266, and of E.I. Watkin's *Catholic Art and Culture,* in the issue for October 24, 1942, p. 520.

Remarkable testimony, this, to the excellent qualities ascribed to the book higher up. The character of the apologetic almost reminds one of Sir Andrew Aguecheek's complaint against Sebastian for beating him: "Though I struck him first, yet it's no matter for that". I do not, by the by, see any allusion in the review to the fact that, shortly after the termination of the war, the Pope presented the Golden Rose to the Queen of Italy, and addressed her for the first time as "Empress of Ethiopia". As evidence for the Vatican's independence of the Fascist Government of Italy, Professor Binchy is said "to present a long record of friction between" them (October 25, 1941, p. 526). No mention, however, is made of the fact that many of these occasions of friction arose from the Vatican's disapproval of Mussolini's determination (prior to the Abyssinian war) to maintain the toleration he had promised to non-Catholic religious bodies in Italy. With the approach of the Abyssinian war, this toleration was more and more withdrawn.[4]

Great prominence was accorded in *The Times Literary Supplement* to certain volumes of the subtly but unmistakably pro-Roman work entitled *European Civilization: Its Origin and Development*, produced by various contributors, under the direction of Edward Eyre (Oxford, 1934-39). The late Mr. Edward Eyre was a wealthy and most ardent Roman Catholic propagandist.[5] The second volume was welcomed with a leading article under the headline "The Roman Achievement", ostensibly devoted to the work of pre-Christian Rome, but garnished with many delicate hints foreshadowing the greatness of the Medieval Church (September 19, 1935, pp. 569 f.). The reviewer summarizes the third volume in the headline "The Salving of Civilization. Rome's place in the Feudal Order", and offers

---

4. For the detailed evidence, see my *Roman Catholicism and Freedom,* 3rd ed., pp. 70-76, 191-195.

5. See two descriptive articles on this large work and its sponsor, under the title "A Pro-Roman Historical Survey", by J.W. Poynter in *The Freethinker*, vol. lxii, pp. 164, 179 (April 19 and 26, 1942). He states from personal knowledge that Mr. Eyre "financed and mainly controlled the efforts of that [Westminster Catholic] Federation to obtain, in the history books of the London County Council elementary schools, alterations of a nature which would have been decidedly favourable to the Roman Catholic view of the subject" (see above, p. 19). Dr. Coulton says that *European Civilization* was "published with the express object of modifying the unfavourable tone of post-Reformation historiography" (in *The Hibbert Journal,* vol. xlii, p. 229 [April 1944]).

a tenderly disguised apologia for papal authority (February 15, 1936, p. 125). The reviewer of the fourth volume, which deals with the Reformation, is frankly critical of the various contributors, with the exception of the one Protestant contributor (Professor F.M. Powicke) admitted to their ranks: but they are let down very lightly in the headline – "Christendom in Disruption. A Conflict of Evidence" (June 27, 1936, p. 540).

The new edition of the late Canon H. Rashdall's work on *The Universities of Europe in the Middle Ages* is given a front-page review in the *Supplement* under the headline "Medieval Universities. Children of the Papacy" (May 2, 1936, pp. 361 f.). In his text the reviewer does not claim much more for the Church than the privilege of having formally authorized the foundation of successive universities: but he advances this prerogative as justifying the startling expression used in his headline. After referring in broad terms to the custom of securing ecclesiastical sanction for university-work, he continues: "In a very real sense the medieval universities were the children of the Papacy; though, like our Government to-day, the Papal authority sought only very sparingly to intervene in the institutions it had blessed". But surely it is nothing less than a travesty of the facts to proclaim the medieval universities *generally* – and that in a large-type headline – to have been "Children of the Papacy", when in point of fact the papacy did not initiate more than one or two of them, but simply exercised the right, as the supreme religious authority, of formally sanctioning, when asked to do so, their foundation and maintenance.

Mr. Hilaire Belloc's defence of the exploded and improbable theory that Cromwell dishonestly contrived the escape of Charles I from Hampton Court to the Isle of Wight for the purpose of destroying him is described in the *Supplement* as "powerful pleading. There are other possible explanations, but none a tenth as plausible" (September 6, 1934, p. 595).[6]

It is only fair to recognize, alongside of these strokes on behalf of Romanism, the occurrence from time to time in the *Literary Supplement* of strictures on the Church and her representatives. As an example of this treatment, we may take the review of a

---

6. On the baselessness of this theory, see Isaac Foot's article in *The Contemporary Review,* vol. cxlvi, pp. 560-563 (November 1934).

strongly pro-Catholic work on *The House of Guise* by Mr. Henry Dwight Sedgwick (January 28, 1939, p. 61). The main contents are summarized in a disarmingly objective manner: "... the services of the Guises to the Catholic faith form the main theme of the book. He [the author] holds, indeed, that it was largely due to the Dukes of Guise... that France continued to walk 'in the sanctified path of Roman Catholic civilization'". Yet the author's bias is duly recognized. "At times this bias appears in rather odd forms, as when he says that 'the Duke of Alva... crushed the rebellion (in the Netherlands) with what seemed to the Protestants great cruelty'. He also passes somewhat lightly over the terrible executions following the conspiracy of Amboise, which provided, so astonishingly to our ideas, a spectacle for the Court". A few other flaws arising from the author's prejudices are noticed, of which the last is his feeling hurt "because the Guises are charged with – to use the Cardinal's own phrase – a 'holy dissimulation, a dissimulation full of piety'". The historical methods of Mr. Hilaire Belloc are refreshingly chastised in a review of a volume of his essays. "He is Clio's special pleader, and his interpretation of history is as rigid and doctrinaire as its opposite number, Marxism" (March 29, 1941, p. 154). Similarly severe is the criticism of Mr. Belloc's later book, *Elizabethan Commentary* (April 4, 1942, p. 178). Again, a long review of Mr. A.E.W. Mason's *Life of Francis Drake* quotes with frank sympathy the strong expressions in which the author speaks of Spanish and Catholic cruelty (October 11, 1941, pp. 506, 508). The reviewer of Father P. Hughes's study of *Rome and the Counter-Reformation in England* (April 18, 1942, p. 196) similarly aims at evenhandedness; and the treatment of Señor Ferrara's attempt to whitewash Pope Alexander VI (Rodrigo Borgia) is healthily critical (May 30, 1942, p. 268). The review of Mr. Otto Zoff's book on *The Huguenots* is sympathetic (April 24, 1943, p. 202). The notice of Archbishop Spellmann's addresses is on the whole adverse (July 17, 1943, p. 338).

Of special interest, on the other hand, is the way in which every nerve is often strained in order to reduce to a minimum, if it is impossible to remove it entirely, the obloquy traditionally resting on certain great representatives of the Roman Church.

This effort is most strikingly seen at work in the treatment accorded by reviewers in *The Times Literary Supplement* to two books dealing with Philip II of Spain, with which I shall be more especially concerned in the ensuing pages (see below, pp. 31 ff.). I therefore put aside for the present the extraordinary endeavour to rehabilitate this particular personage, and confine myself to noticing the analogous treatment meted out to certain others.

A welcome, for instance, is given to the attempt to explain psycho-analytically the cruelty with which the Inquisitor Torquemada treated the Jews in Spain: the book, we are told, "sheds a clearer and calmer light both on" Torquemada and the Inquisition "than many much more pretentious but more impassioned works. Mr. Hope [the author] sets out neither to condemn nor to justify the Inquisition, but rather to understand the man who was its driving force...." The Inquisition "tended to make the [Spanish] nation autonomous in religion.... As compared with more recent persecutions of the Jews, that of Torquemada and the Inquisition was to this extent more humane, that it attacked the religion and not the race...." (In practice, however, this distinction became largely a dead letter). "Nor were its methods, torture included, more cruel than those of the secular justice of the age..." (January 13, 1940, p. 16).[7]

Very characteristic is the review of Miss Alma Wittlin's biography of Isabella of Castille (June 27, 1936, p. 534). Once again come the helpful headlines – "Isabella the Catholic. Castille in the Great Age". The reviewer has nothing but praise for the glories of Spain during the heyday of the Inquisition, and will not listen to a word in her disparagement. The authoress, he observes, "is seriously misinformed" about the Inquisition: for Isabella, "the introduction of the Inquisition was only part of her general scheme of law and order". The authoress overstates, it seems, the numbers done to death by Torquemada; and the reviewer accuses her of inexactitude (through ignorance of the latest researches) regarding certain gruesome details connected with the public burnings. This type of criticism is extremely popular with apologists of a certain class. By

---

7. See below, p. 53 ff.

drawing attention to insignificant (if not imaginary) errors in detail, they write as if, once these errors are corrected, the innocence of the parties they are eulogizing is completely vindicated. But what of the numbers of persons whom Torquemada admittedly *did* burn? Does the reviewer deny, or want to forget, that many "heretics" *were* burnt in public at the virtual command of the Inquisition, that this was often done without their first being strangled, that the Church-leaders, the public, and sometimes the court, looked on at the hideous spectacle with full approval? Has he nothing to say about all *that,* as bearing on the credit of "Isabella the Catholic" and the glories of "Castille in the Great Age"?

I pass by the sympathetic review, in the *Supplement* (January 15, 1938, p. 40), of Joseph Gregor's *Das spanische Welt-theater,* with its warm appreciation of Spain's glorious achievements; and I come to the notice of Dr. Cecil Roth's work, *The Spanish Inquisition* (London, 1937), in the issue of January 22, 1938, p. 53. It closely resembles, in its one-sidedness, the review of Miss Wittlin's book on Isabella. The reviewer palliates the cruelty of the Inquisition (by comparison with the civil tribunals of the time); demurs to Dr. Roth's charge of native cruelty in the Spanish character; makes the utmost of every tiny concession modifying the horror of the picture; objects to strong phrases about its "unbridled ferocity", "wholesale burnings", and so on; warns the reader against the author's comparatively favourable view of Llorente's estimate of the numbers victimized by the Inquisition; and observes that "there are many signs that Dr. Roth's acquaintance with Spain is not intimate". I shall have occasion to remark later that the *numbers* slain and penalized by the Inquisition are not a vital matter in the determination of its moral quality (see below, pp. 51 f.). But it needs to be pointed out that Dr. Roth by no means committed himself to the accuracy of Llorente's figures. He admitted that they seemed "highly suspicious". What he did say was that the annual average which Llorente's total would imply did not appear to him to be out of the question (p. 123), and that his figure is actually exceeded by the estimate of "the intensely Catholic Amador de los Rios" (see his letter in *The Times Literary Supplement,* January 29, 1938, p. 75). For the rest, to try to create prejudice against Dr. Roth's whole book by saying – on the strength of two trifling slips – that his acquaintance with Spain is not intimate, is surely somewhat petty. His book, like its predecessor, *A History of the Marranos* (Philadelphia, 1932), is based on an exceptionally wide knowledge of the original sources: and to suggest that he writes without adequate mastery of his subject would be preposterous. His reviewer's parting shot is very interesting. After quoting Dr. Roth's allusion to Spain as illustrating the uselessness of a nation gaining the whole world if it loses its soul, he observes: "Yet it might well be argued that Spain lost her empire through her unwillingness to lose her soul". We may be thankful that he words this amazing suggestion in a qualified way. But we must needs ask whether an historical judgment could well be more unreasonable. To insinuate that religious toleration and the abandonment of one of the bloodiest and most merciless persecutions known to history would mean that Spain had thereby "lost her soul" reflects bias with a vengeance. Such a suggestion surely constitutes a far more serious disqualification for understanding the Spanish Inquisition than does partial ignorance about the climate of Spain or a trifling mistake regarding the birthplace of Cervantes.

The *Supplement* duly praises the great qualities of the Emperor Charles V. "He was the Roman Emperor, whose high task it was to defend the Church, to root out heresy and repel the infidel". Cruel persecutor of the Dutch Protestants though he was, he is praised without qualification as "a lover of justice".[8] Incessantly at war, and informing his soldiers that he loved peace no more than they did, he is here eulogized as "a man of peace" (December 2, 1939, p. 706). A eulogistic life of Hernán Cortes, the conqueror of Mexico, is favourably reviewed (April 11, 1942, p. 186), the ethical aspect of his cruelty and aggression being tacitly ignored by the reviewer.

Father James Brodrick has recently written a book on *The Origin of the Jesuits* (London, 1940), and – as might be expected – he gets a good press. "As interpreted by Father Brodrick, the spirit of the infant society is strangely reminiscent of that of Assisi; not only does it appear in the heroic simplicity of

---

8. See below, pp. 70-75.

St. Francis Xavier, whose missionary journeys are described in two moving chapters, but equally in St. Ignatius himself,…" (March 1, 1941, p. 104). I do not, however, find in this review any allusion to the fact that St. Francis Xavier petitioned in 1546 for the establishment of the Inquisition in India, and that this was effected in 1561. It is noted that "in the generation of St. Ignatius the Roman Church had to face the most deadly attack in its history,…" Moreover Father Brodrick, says the reviewer, "has portrayed with learning and charm a group of men of whom nearly all were admirable, many of outstanding ability, and some reached the heights of heroic virtue".

Mary, Queen of England, in the course of less than four years, caused to be burnt alive 225 men, 53 women (some of them pregnant and one blind), and one baby, born while its mother was actually in the flames. It was therefore not without reason that she became popularly known as "Bloody Mary".[9] None the less, she is a proper subject of rehabilitation. The books appear accordingly; and the *Supplement* does its best to recommend them. Thus we get, in the issue of August 10, 1933 (p. 536), an article headed "A Tragic Queen". Here we learn that Mary was "tragically misunderstood", and that her "long ill-fortune has followed her after death". "The smoke of the last years' pyres drifts across her memory. Three hundred died. 'In their prosperity they had excited disgust. In the flames they made'… the ruin of all that the passionate, sensitive woman who burned them had struggled with such courage to obtain". Another apologia for Mary is reviewed in the issue of October 10, 1935 (p. 628). The authoress of it, we are told, "sees in Mary Tudor not the 'Bloody Mary' of tradition, not the monster of cruelty pictured by Foxe and believed in by many generations of Englishmen, but an honest, kindly, loyal woman.… To redeem the reputation of the Queen is one of the objects of this book; and it will help to that end,… many readers will enjoy the book and learn the lesson.… The rise in the level of popular historical biography which has been a welcome feature of recent years is manifest in this

---

9. Cf. Dr. James Gairdner in *The Encyclopædia Britannica*, vol. xvii (1911), p. 814: "… unpleasantly remembered as 'the Bloody Mary' on account of the religious persecutions which prevailed during her reign,…"

book". At the close, the reviewer comments: "Nor are modern economic historians so convinced [as the authoress] that it was the Inquisition that ruined Spain". Yet a third work on Mary was reviewed on September 14, 1940 (p. 474). The article is headed "Mary Tudor: a sympathetic portrait". The authoress had, however, chosen as her sub-title, *The Life of Bloody Mary;* and the reviewer duly records his objection to it. Mary's "gallant spirit" receives due recognition from him: and "the hardening of her heart against the Protestants in the later years of her life" is, he suggests, to be explained by the remorse she felt over the forced acknowledgment of her bastardy. The authoress is complimented on her achievement.

The other Mary, "the Queen of Scots", has also called forth a crop of apologists. The welcome accorded to one of these may be seen in *The Times Literary Supplement* for September 17, 1938 (p. 590).

John Graham of Claverhouse, who identified himself with James II's Catholicizing policy,[10] and who persecuted the Scottish Covenanters so cruelly that he, too, like the Tudor Queen, was rewarded by posterity with the epithet "Bloody", is another who comes in for a share of the whitewash. A book eulogizing his admirable qualities, minimizing his atrocities, and strongly condemning his victims, is sympathetically if not altogether uncritically received (December 11, 1937, p. 938). Of another eulogistic biography of Claverhouse a reviewer says that its authors endeavour to "dissipate the charges brought against their hero in connexion with his activities against the Covenanters in the west. Although they write as manifest partisans and are entirely out of sympathy with his opponents, they succeed in making most of those charges appear to be without any real foundation". "Later historians [i.e. than Macaulay] have been able to do so much to clear the character of Claverhouse that it may fairly be accepted that he was 'Bonnie' rather than 'Bloody'" (May 27, 1939, p. 307).

John Dryden, the Poet Laureate, became a Roman Catholic on the accession of the Roman Catholic King James II in 1685. Was he sincere, or did he make the change in order to secure royal

---

10. See T.F. Henderson, in *The Dictionary of National Biography*, vol. viii (1921-22), P. 345.

favour? The case is argued at great length in a leading article filling two pages of the *Supplement* (April 17, 1937, pp. 281 f.). It is headed in enormous letters: "Dryden's Conversion. The struggle for faith". As might be expected, the poet comes out of the discussion with flying colours, and without a stain upon his reputation for either sincerity or intelligence, while his detractors (in primis, Macaulay, of course) are put to a notable shame.

I feel I must apologize to the reader for the length of this digression (pp. 19-31) describing the pro-Catholic trend visible in the columns of *The Times Literary Supplement* during at least the last ten or twelve years. Its length is necessitated by the fact that the evidence, in the nature of the case, is cumulative. I do not wish to suggest that *all* the arguments adduced, even in the pro-Catholic reviews, are of a question-begging or meretricious character. Valid pleas also are from time to time laid before the reader. The main purpose behind this assemblage of items of evidence is to illustrate the way in which advantage is often taken, in the Catholic interest, of the high status of the journal itself, the protection given by the anonymity and presumed impartiality and authority of its reviews, and the revolutionary fashion of our time, in order to commend to the general public somewhat ex-parte judgments on historical questions. More evidence to the same effect will incidentally come before us in the sequel.

I pass on now to deal with two works in which the pro-Catholic bias is as obvious as in any anonymous review, and which, furthermore, deal directly with the episodes I propose to discuss throughout this book. They were produced in 1937 and 1938 respectively. The former is *The Golden Century of Spain, 1501-1621*, written by the Rev. R. Trevor Davies, M.A., a history-tutor at Oxford, and published by Messrs. Macmillan and Co. The latter is *Philip II*, written by Dr. William Thomas Walsh, and published by Messrs. Sheed and Ward. Dr. Walsh is an American Catholic layman, who graduated at Yale University in 1913, and in 1933 was awarded the degree of Litt. D. by the (Jesuit) Fordham University. Since 1933 he has been professor of English at the Manhattanville College of the Sacred Heart, New York. Both volumes are of substantial size, and are beautifully produced, finely illustrated, and well documented: both are animated by a great admiration of Philip, an approval of the Spanish Inquisition, and a dislike of sixteenth-century Protestantism in general, and of the Protestants of the Netherlands and their great leader, William of Orange, in particular.

Taking Dr. Walsh's volume first, we note at the outset the unmistakable fact that the author is a very convinced Roman Catholic. That is obvious not only from the tone of eulogy in which he regularly speaks of Philip and the Roman Church, but also from his frequent allusions to non-Romanists as "enemies of Christ" or "of Christendom", as "Antichrist" or "anti-Christian".[11] On the point of scholarship, the book makes a mixed impression. The notes bear witness to extensive research and a wide acquaintance with the original authorities. On the other hand, the author falls into some very elementary errors. He gives, for instance, the name of the place to which Pope Paul III transferred the Council of Trent in 1546 as "Boulogne" (p. 79) instead of Bologna. The Jewish title "Ab-Beth-Din" (literally, "Father of the House of Judgment"), originally used in all probability of the High Priest, appears in his pages in the oddly erroneous forms "Abet Din" and even "Ab et Din" (pp. 240, 244). In quoting a French poem he presents the curious form "habìte" (p. 291). The Italian passive participle "eletto", used by the Spanish mutineers in the Netherlands to denote the captain they had chosen by

---

11. See W.T. Walsh, *Philip II*, pp. 216, 302, 394, 404, 408, 475, 527, 556, 567, 596 f., 601 f., 624, 626, 635, 639, 648, 702 f., 704, 706 f., 717. Occasionally, the anti-Romanist movement becomes "anti-religious" (p. 398: cf. p. 609). See also p. 302 (*odium Christi)*, 370 (the Council of Trent showed that the Church "could not be false to the teachings and example of Christ"), 702-704 (Philip's most creditable achievement his defeat of the "monstrous plot" to make Europe Protestant), 711 ("Millions of unborn Englishmen were condemned by Cecil to live and to die cut off from the mystical Body of Christ; worse still, cheated into believing it an evil thing, and setting up sham forms and sterile imitations of sacraments in its stead.... But the Faith they lost is still, thanks to Philip II, an unchanged reality to most of the Spanish people,..."), 714 (English Protestantism not Christian), 723 ("... Philip, who had spent so much of his life in conflict with God's enemies,...").

popular vote, he represents by the *active* English form "Elector" (p. 551). He does not, apparently, know the difference between the words "farthingale" and "fotherin-gay" (p. 629). His uncritical disregard of the difference between legend and historical evidence comes out in his acceptance of the statements that James, the son of Zebedee, preached and was buried in Spain (pp. 131 f.), and that a certain Eugenius was "first Archbishop of Toledo in Apostolic times" (p. 392); whereas the attestation of both stories is far too late to warrant belief – there being, for instance, no certain mention of St. James in connexion with Spain at all until the seventh century, no allusion to his burial there before the ninth, and the story of his having visited Spain being incompatible with our other early evidence, as even Catholic scholars now seem prepared to recognize.[12]

Dr. Walsh's naïve willingness to believe in the value and efficacy of relics (pp. 333, 392 f., 548, 627, 719) and in the occurrence of miracles in the sixteenth century (pp. 605, 627, 663, 713) one may perhaps regard as an implicate of his general position as a Catholic rather than as a sign of childish credulity. But his enthusiasm for the cause so dear to his heart occasionally robs him of his sense of humour. In King Philip's study on the eve of the Armada, he tells us (pp. 650 f.), "Every ship, every man, every biscuit and musket seemed to glow with life and purpose...."!

In view of our close concern with Dr. Walsh's book, the reader may be interested to see how it is treated in *The Times Literary Supplement*. The notice of it appears in the issue dated February 19, 1938, (p. 118). It is an almost unqualified eulogy of the book and of the man with whom it deals. Here are some of its phrases. "Certainly by contrast with the widespread opportunism and duplicity of his time Philip II's character stands out nobly" (this of the man whose mendacity and double-dealing in his diplomatic relations was constant and habitual). "This peaceful and affectionate man, as Dr. Walsh calls him, disliked violence, and, when it became necessary, used the suavest methods" (this of the man who did his best to keep France in a state of continual strife, and spilt in torrents the blood of the Protestants in the Netherlands). "The theme is vast and

---

12. See Duchesne in *Annales du Midi*, vol. xii (1900), pp. 145-179; A. Camerlynck in *The Catholic Encyclopedia*, vol. viii (1910), p. 280 b; and V. Ermoni in F. Vigouroux's *Dictionnaire de la Bible*, vol. iii (1903), col. 1083 f.

fascinating, and one may say at once that it has rarely been treated with so much understanding and sympathy..." "Dr. Walsh has the advantage of sharing" the king's medieval Catholic ideal. "Dr. Walsh is one of the few writers who have really understood Philip II.... He writes in no spirit of hero-worship"! "Dr. Walsh has been at infinite pains to produce this detailed and magnificent study of Philip II and his times. It is a work which will be read with keenest interest from the first page to the last".

It is, indeed, melancholy to reflect that this unstinted praise should be bestowed on a work suffused throughout with the narrowest and most censorious Catholic prejudice, in the columns of a literary journal enjoying a reputation for evenhandedness of judgment, and quick to rebuke any one-sidedness visible in the work of Protestant authors. This sad lapse is in part corrected by a more accurate estimate of Dr. Walsh's book in a shorter notice contained in a later issue of the *Literary Supplement* (March 26, 1938, p. 214). "Philip, 'the Spider of the Escurial'", it says, "is a fine subject for whitewash, the blackened surface is so large and black. It is well that a re-estimate of him should be attempted, but Dr. Walsh's portrait will not claim universal assent".

That this last-quoted cautious statement is well within the truth will be apparent from three reviews of Dr. Walsh's volume in reputable journals *other* than *The Times Literary Supplement.*

In *The Manchester Guardian* for April 5, 1938 (p. 7), its tone and style are said by Professor J.E. Neale to "give it the flavour of religious propaganda rather than dispassionate history... the book is often astonishingly lacking in judgment". Its speculations about Freemasonry are described as "fanciful" and as "nonsense". Dr. Walsh relies too confidently on Cabrera (the early Spanish biographer of Philip), and often shows an "uncritical judgment" in his choice of other authorities. In regard to English history, says Professor Neale, "I can only describe his errors of fact and interpretation as astounding". After specifying some examples, he goes on: "As for his treatment of Elizabethan history and its leading figures, it is a travesty of the truth punctuated with historical 'howlers'". "One's only concern", he concludes, "is that in this country at least it should not, by reason of its apparently learned documentation, pass for serious history".

The New Statesman and Nation for May 7, 1938 (pp. 790, 792) contained a review of Dr. Walsh's book by Mr. A.L. Rowse. He described the author's picture of Elizabeth as "a caricature which ruins all the English side of his biography". After enumerating several grave inaccuracies, Mr. Rowse observes: "There is a whole chapter of nonsense on 'Freemasonry in the Sixteenth Century'.... The Cecil myth, pernicious nonsense for which Mr. Belloc is more responsible than anybody alive, runs riot throughout the book:... What is worth protesting against is that Catholics allow themselves to be so fooled by these professional writers in the Belloc tradition who are engaged in rewriting the sixteenth century in the very teeth of the evidence and of common sense.... One must not expect any historical judgment in a book like this as to the larger issues of Philip's policy and career". The book displays "no conception of the blight that dragooned orthodoxy laid upon Spain's intellectual life, the almost total absence of an intellectual contribution to European civilisation".[13] "A lot of work... has gone into Mr. Walsh's 800 pages; but one may regard it as more or less wasted".

As a proof that Mr. Rowse does not write thus as a result of any bias he might have in favour of Protestantism, I would observe that he is as impatient with Protestant polemic as he is with Catholic. "A plague on both your houses", is his impolite expression. "The fact that stupid Protestants have made [Philip] out to be an ogre", he says, "is no reason for Mr. Walsh's polemicising about it". I shall discuss later in this book how far Philip's actions were ogre-like in quality: my purpose at the moment is to draw attention to the low estimate which one who is clearly no friend of Protestantism has formed of the historical value of Dr. Walsh's book, upon which the reviewer in *The Times Literary Supplement* felt himself entitled to lavish such unstinted praise.

A lengthier and more mildly worded critique of *Philip II* appeared in *The Church Quarterly Review*, vol. CXXVI, pp. 318-23

---

13. A friend acquainted with Spanish literature tells me he regards this last-quoted sentence as a serious over-statement.

(July-September, 1938), from the pen of Mr. G.V. Jourdan. Though we may sympathize with Philip's sufferings in his last illness, he says, "one cannot forget the crimes in which he was concerned… the reputation of this Spanish monarch is liable to remain permanently that of a gloomy religious persecutor, narrow in mind and cold in his cruelty, a harsh bigot,…" Mr. Jourdan specifies in detail a long series of Dr. Walsh's grave historical misrepresentations – in particular, his fancies regarding the Jewish influence behind Protestantism. "Mr. Walsh", he says, "no doubt did, in one passage, awaken to the fact that Jews have their uses, for he remarks that the first ten popes were Jews – a handsome admission, and all the more handsome because it is not supported by any competent authority". He deprecates Dr. Walsh's constant efforts to discredit the opponents of Romanism by unpleasant allusions to their personal appearance. He might well have asked why Queen Elizabeth's mouth was any more "apt for lies"[14] than that of the constant liar, Philip II. "In our opinion", concludes Mr. Jourdan, "Mr. Walsh, by having attempted too much, has marred what might well have been an excellent and useful biography".[15]

Mr. R. Trevor Davies's book, as befits the work of an Anglican scholar who is also a Fellow of the Royal Historical Society, is free from blemishes and errors of the kind that are plentifully bestrewn throughout Dr. Walsh's. He is a thorough master of the material, and writes throughout with an eye to the demands of scholarship. Yet he makes no secret of the place where his own sympathies lie. In his preface, indeed, he declares it to be his aim to "steer an even, though immensely difficult, course between the Scylla of Protestant, Liberal and Anti-clerical prepossessions and the Charybdis of Roman Catholic partisanship". It is just as well that we are told that this aim was "immensely difficult" of attainment: for nothing could be clearer than the author's failure to achieve it. Indeed, had it not been for the avowal in his preface,

---

14. Walsh, *Philip II*, p. 158.
15. B. Braunstein, reviewing another work by Dr. Walsh in *The Journal of Religion*, vol. xxii, pp. 105 ff. (January 1942), says: "We seriously question his ability as a historian", and mentions "these lapses from the objective truth of a historian".

no reader could have guessed that he had even so much as aimed at achieving it.

The book is written throughout from the point of view of Spanish and Roman Catholic interest. One searches it in vain for any definite expression of disapproval regarding the outrages committed either by Rome or by Spain, save in regard to Spain's treatment of the Moors (pp. 164, 243 f.), and the harmfulness of the Inquisition's censorship of Spanish literature (pp. 145-147). There occur on the contrary such sentences as these: "The suppression of Lutheranism was indispensable for the continuance of Charles's Empire" (p. 104); "The refusal of the Lutherans to attend the council [of Trent] freed Charles from all his obligations to them" (p. 106); "Cateau-Cambrésis… marks approximately the end of the hitherto triumphant and almost continuous advance of Continental Protestantism. Most of all, it marks the beginning of the period when the Spain of Philip II assumes the hegemony of the whole world" (p. 113); "… the tendency of the Council of State [in the Netherlands] to betray their sovereign…" (p. 183); "Mary Queen of Scots… as rightful Queen of England…" (p. 208); "the Spaniards, on their side, would not brook the humiliation of recognising the independence of rebel heretics" (p. 235); and so on. One of the chapters is headed, "The Protestant and Mohammedan perils" (p. 137); and the very title of the book looks like a handsome tribute to Philip, his father, and his son.

If this were all, one might at a pinch treat it as expressing simply the dramatic objectivity of an impartial historian, who naturally desires to exhibit the facts as they must have appeared to his leading characters and, like some dramatists, to keep his own opinions very much in the background. Mr. Davies, however, leads one to infer, without much room for doubt, that expressions such as those just quoted represent his own personal judgment as well as that of the Spanish monarchy and the Roman papacy. Not only does he everywhere put the most favourable construction possible on everything done by the representatives of those institutions; but he claims that the Spanish Inquisition "stood for social justice" and that its "value… as a royal instrument for strengthening the monarchy and unifying the country would be difficult to exaggerate" (pp. 12 f.; cf. pp. 161, 201); he calls William of Orange a "coarse and brutal materialist" (p. 156) and "that crafty prince" (p. 184 – though he never complains of Philip's habitual duplicity); he refuses to recognize any democratic ideals in "the Calvinist plutocracy of the English Great Rebellion" (p. 202); he writes of Philip: "Had he not interfered in French affairs France might well have become a Protestant power… He thus saved his many dominions that bordered on France from Protestant propaganda and intrigue. He decided… that Catholicism and not Protestantism should possess the preponderance in Europe for centuries to come" (p. 222); and he counts among the "achievements that mitigate the most adverse judgement of Philip's statesmanship". his "half-success of keeping France Catholic and of retaining the southern Netherlands" (p. 226). Not only do observations of this kind go beyond the ad hominem objectivity of dramatically written history, but those that are last quoted are surely surprising judgments to find coming from the pen of an ordained minister of the Church of England. It is in any case quite clear that the book reveals no sort or kind of "steering an even course" between the Protestant and Catholic extremes. Mr. Davies's strong dislike of Scylla has misled him into an unresisting surrender to the overpowering claims of Charybdis.

Now for *The Times Literary Supplement*'s account of the book (November 6, 1937, p. 814). As we have been led to expect, unstinted and even extravagant praise is bestowed both on it and on the country with which it deals. "A century of marvellous and original achievement in every field"; "we may well wonder at the greatness attained with means so inadequate"; "the mighty achievements in literature and art"; and so forth. Mr. Davies's view of the justice and humaneness of the Inquisition is swallowed whole. "The expulsion of the Moriscos in 1609, described by Lea as 'this despicable act of religious intolerance', is shown here in its true light". The claim made by the author in his preface to have tried to steer a middle course between pro-Catholic and pro-Protestant bias is quoted verbatim; and his success in doing so is applauded. "He has no prejudices to confirm", says the reviewer, "nor theories to prove. On every page we have evidence of a fair and open mind. This may disturb some of his readers.... But those who seek uncoloured truth are more likely to find it here than in more enthusiastic and glowing pages". Once more the customary, yet inaccurate, plea is advanced that now at last modern research has brought the real facts to light, and enabled us to correct the prejudiced misjudgments of the past. "To those who have not followed the results of modern research work, often hidden away in learned and obscure reviews, many of the conclusions here brilliantly presented may come as a surprise".

The reader will have to judge for himself, in the light of such relevant facts as are adduced in the following pages, how far this wholehearted praise is really merited. Pending this more leisurely investigation, let me here quote a warning sentence or two from D.L.K.'s review of Mr. Davies's book in *The Oxford Magazine* (June 2, 1938, pp. 714-16). His criticisms are the more significant in that the review is on the whole very appreciative. Mr. Davies's study of the Inquisition is judged to be "perhaps unduly favourable". "... justice is not always done to the opponents of Spain. The estimate of William the Silent, in particular, is marred by a curiously grudging tone, and some disinclination to recognise that hostility to Spain might be animated by a spirit as pure as that enlisted in its service". With reference to Mr. Davies's explanations of the economic decline of Spain, D.L.K. remarks: "But it may be suggested that it fails to include one which cannot properly be omitted, the wastage of national wealth in the maintenance of an over-endowed Church". The merits of this Church "may not always seem so clear to other eyes as to his own": for it appears "to have found coercion easier and more congenial than missionary effort, and the few exceptions to this rule seem only to confirm its general truth". Finally, D.L.K. is not so easily convinced as the reviewer in *The Times Literary Supplement* regarding our author's impartiality. "The reader may perhaps conjecture", he says gently, "from the tone of such references as Mr. Trevor Davies makes to other religious communions, that he has not always found it possible to steer the even though immensely difficult course to which he alludes in his preface". No, indeed.

I propose now to examine, in the light of all this recent Catholic apologetic, some phases of that gigantic struggle against Protestantism which Philip II and his father the Emperor Charles V waged for many years in the Low Countries. My main objective is to arrive at some just and tenable judgment regarding the ethical issues involved in the struggle itself and the ethical quality of the conduct of the main protagonists on either side. I shall busy myself with persons and events outside the history of the Netherlands, only in so far as they may serve to make the struggle that took place there more intelligible.

Chapter Three

The Character of the Inquisition

The first special topic which I select for examination is the character of the Spanish Inquisition and of the very similar institution long maintained by Charles and Philip in the Netherlands. Modern apologists for Catholicism are at pains to vindicate the Spanish Inquisition against the reproaches traditionally levelled against it. They view it in its proper setting as but one item in the total picture of Spanish life; and they are eager to bring out the comeliness of the whole. The slowness of Protestant governments to unlearn the persecuting habits which medieval Catholicism had taught mankind to take for granted, and certain differences as to what precisely the government of a country ought to suppress, afford opportunities for arguing that sixteenth-century Spain was a more tolerant country than England. Dr. Walsh, for instance, says: "Even the Inquisition might be called their Declaration of Independence against the domination of Jews and Moors" (p. 629); and he urges that the English censorship of books was far more severe than the Spanish (pp. 632 f.). Mr. Trevor Davies paradoxically describes Spain as a country "tolerant beyond all others yet the perfecter of the most efficient system of persecution in the world" (p. 3). "Though conservative and scholastic in its tendencies", Spanish university-life "was by no means unreceptive of new ideas" (p. 25). He adduces evidence of the prolific culture of the country, the high standard of its learning, the brilliance of its literature.[1] He mentions the humaneness shown to deported Moriscos (p. 170), to tramps (pp. 272 f.), and to the natives of Peru (p. 75).[2]

I would not deny that in all this eulogizing of Spain during her "Golden Century" there is a measure of truth. I would only remark in passing that a good deal of the gilt comes off the gingerbread when proper account is taken of one or two features in Spanish life which are not denied even by the apologists whom we

---

1. E.g., R.T. Davies, *Golden Century*, pp. 26, 289. Cf. *The Times Literary Supplement*, August 8, 1935, p. 494 (quoting Merriman).
2. This last-mentioned virtue is touched on also by S. Leathes in *Camb. Mod. Hist.*, vol. ii (1903), p. 101.

have just quoted. Thus, Mr. Trevor Davies admits that the treatment long meted out to the Moors in Spain was unwise and unjust (pp. 52-54, 164, 242-247). The cruelty exercised by the Spaniards on the American Indians was notorious.[3] Dr. Walsh rather grudgingly admits it: but his comment on it sheds an extraordinary light on the Catholic attitude to ethical claims. "It was not", he says, "that Spaniards were essentially any more humane than Englishmen; perhaps by nature they were less so. But Spanish Catholicism was Christian and English Protestantism was not. The real triumph was that of Christ, teaching His Gospel unto the ends of the world,..." (p. 714). Similarly striking is his bland remark about bull-fighting: he calls it "the bloody sport which Spaniards, true to their paradoxical history, loved only next to the religion of Christ" (p. 504).

Both of these authors allude to the serious financial chaos into which Spain fell in the course of this brilliant period.[4] They have not, indeed, overstated the magnitude of the trouble. Historians are unanimous about it. "The Spaniards could never be a great nation because they were never industrious."[5] In 1575 Philip was bankrupt, and in 1596 he again repudiated his debts. By the end of the century, says Mr. R.H. Tawney, "Spain, the southern Netherlands, including Antwerp, and a great part of France,... were ruined".[6] He describes Spain as possessed of "an incapacity for economic affairs which seemed almost inspired,..."[7] One is inclined to ask

---

3. The Spanish reputation is reflected in the writings (1719 and 1732 respectively) of Defoe (*Robinson Crusoe*, [ed. 1863], pp. 163 f., 203 ["... the Spaniards, whose cruelties in America had been spread over the whole country, and were remembered by all the nations [? natives] from father to son"], 228), and Daniel Neal (*The History of the Puritans* [ed. 1837], vol. i, p. 324), and is admitted by later writers (e.g., Froude, *Short Studies*, vol. i, pp. 462-72. E. Armstrong, *The Emperor Charles V* [ed. 1910], vol. ii, pp. 102-107).
4. See R.T. Davies, *Golden Century*, pp. 77 f., 256-260, 270-275, 280, 283, 289; Walsh, *Philip II*, pp. 270, 371, 545 f., 572-574.
5. S. Leathes in *Camb. Mod. Hist.*, vol. ii (1903), p. 100; cf. p. 101 ("... exertion, always distasteful to the Spaniards,..."); also E. Armstrong in *Camb. Mod. Hist.*, vol. iii (1904), p. 384.
6. R.H. Tawney, *Religion and the Rise of Capitalism* (Pelican edition, 1938), p. 82; cf. p. 77 ("... Spain, a corpse bound on the back of the most liberal and progressive community of the age, completed her own ruin by sacking" Antwerp [1576]).
7. R.H. Tawney, *op. cit.*, p. 78. Cf. Hallam, *View of the State of Europe during the Middle Ages* (ed. 1878), vol. iii, p. 418 ("... Spain, where improvement is always odious,...").

whether, after all, the term "the Golden Century" is not something of a misnomer.[8]

A further fact to be reckoned with is that the torpor which befell the intellectual life of Spain from the middle of the seventeenth century onwards is one of the almost unmistakable effects of the Inquisition. This judgment is one of the kind which, however plausible, it is difficult to demonstrate conclusively; hence apologists for Catholicism find it possible, without too patent absurdity, to deny it outright. A certain number of instances, for example, can be adduced in which the authorities displayed a surprising leniency in leaving men of letters unmolested; and these are contrasted with sundry manifestations of severity in other countries (including England). A contributor to *The Times Literary Supplement,* June 27, 1936 (p. 534), tries to get round the awkward objection by being superficially facetious. "Much has been written concerning Spain's decadence", he says, "her natural exhaustion after a Golden Age which lasted for two centuries; which is much like seeking abstruse reasons for the death of a man at the age of 150". But it stands to reason that no country could suffer so vigilant and powerful an organization as the Inquisition comprehensively and despotically to control the public and private life of its citizens for over three centuries, with the object of extinguishing every spark of religious dissent, without eventually atrophying their intellectual vigour, even if for a time it did not prevent an outburst of literary brilliance. Henry Charles Lea, after an exhaustive study of the available evidence, concludes that "the Inquisition paralyzed both the intellectual and the economic development of Spain".[9] Other historians have come to the same conclusions.[10]

---

8. On the terrible condition of Spain, economically, morally, and in other ways, at the time of Philip's death, see M.A.S. Hume, *Philip II. of Spain* (London, 1897), pp. 251 f.; also H.C. Lea in the *Amer. Hist. Review,* vol. ix, p. 245 (Jan. 1904).
9. H.C. Lea, *A History of the Inquisition of Spain* (New York and London), vol. iv (1907), pp. 528-531.
10. Cf. J.R. Green, *A Short History of the English People* (ed. 1881), p. 621 ("… enfeebled within by the persecution of the Inquisition, by the suppression of civil freedom, and by a ruinous financial oppression, Spain had not only ceased to threaten Europe…"); James Bryce in *The Atlantic Monthly,* vol. c, p. 146 (August 1907: "… the taking of Constantinople by the Turks, and the rise of the Inquisition in Spain, come pretty near to being unqualified calamities"); C. Roth, *The Spanish Inquisition* (1937), pp. 273 f. On the other hand, see the qualifications and warnings put forward by Professor Butterfield (*The Whig Interpretation,* etc., p. 74).

But it is not primarily about these things that I am now concerned to argue. I propose to concentrate on the ethical character of the attitude taken up towards religious freedom by the Spanish monarchs and by the Church to which they adhered. As I explained above (pp. 11 f.), I am not contending that these sixteenth-century persecutors were insincere men, that they were failing to act up to their lights, or that the persons they tormented and killed as "heretics" were in every respect wise, good, and tolerant men. But I do invite the reader to remember that persecution, objectively viewed, is morally harmful, that the evil of it is greatly accentuated when it is carried on with the ferocious cruelty customarily practised by the Spanish rulers and their agents, and that the victims, though often themselves intolerant, were less so than their persecutors, and were, by virtue of their very "heresy", at least on the way to curing themselves of the persecuting temper.

It is impossible to deny that Charles V and his son Philip II were two of the most zealous persecutors in Christian history;[11] and the question we have to face is this: What judgment ought we to pass on their persecuting? Granting that we are not in a position to pronounce their inner motives dishonest, what are we to say of the quality of their deeds?

Dr. Walsh makes it clear that he approves of the persecution practised by Philip. He justifies it, despite its apparent harshness and cruelty, as the needful judicial preventative of religious strife, which would otherwise have been introduced by "the enemies of Christendom".[12] He justifies it by the disparaging terms in which he regularly refers to all measures of toleration. Thus, L'Hôpital (the French Chancellor) "professed to be a Catholic. Yet one of his first acts (April, 1560) was to obtain through Catherine the Edict of Romorantin, which was the opening wedge for toleration of the new doctrines and which prevented the introduction of the Inquisition, a project of the Guises" (p. 282; cf. p. 674). "… his influence led to

---

11. I confess I do not understand Dr. Walsh's statement (p. III) about the Spain to which Philip returned in 1551, namely, that it was a country where "No man killed another for the cause of religion". I suppose he is referring to that particular moment. But how long was it to remain true? (cf. pp. 209 bott., 232 ff.).

12. Walsh, *Philip II*, pp. 235 f.: cf. p. 234 (people "came from villages for many miles around, not only to see *the enemies of God and man* punished, but to get a first glimpse of their new King". Italics mine).

the very violence Catherine sought to avoid, and delivered her into the hands of Coligny and the Calvinists..." (pp. 286 f.). The treaty of Amboise (March, 1563) he describes as "another humiliating surrender to the Huguenots", because it granted them an amnesty and freedom of worship (p. 294). He speaks of Catherine de' Medici and Charles IX throwing away the fruits of the Catholic victories "by the disgraceful peace of Longjumeau (March twenty-third, 1568)", by which a measure of toleration was conceded to the Huguenots (p. 463). He blithely justifies Philip for rejoicing and (as he imagines) laughing when he received news of the massacre of St. Bartholomew in 1572 (pp. 536 f.). He refers slightingly to Henry IV's Edict of Nantes (pp. 684 f., 705). He blames even his hero because he "set Protestantism above the world in England" (p. 484) – apparently an allusion to his having dissuaded Mary Tudor from persecuting the Protestants and from executing Elizabeth. Toleration in Austria is referred to as "compromise on religion" (pp. 485 f.), and Philip's general policy as "his sincere refusals to compromise on any teaching of Christ and the Church" (p. 487; cf. pp. 708, 724).[13] When he lay on his death-bed, "he had done his best against the enemies of God, and there was little they could do to him" (p. 717).[14]

Mr. Trevor Davies is at pains to convince us that the real motive behind the persecuting measures of the Spanish sovereigns was political rather than religious. "The suppression of Lutheranism was indispensable for the continuance of Charles's Empire.... Even if the Emperor had been himself Protestant in sympathies, he would none the less have been compelled to put down the Lutheran princes; for their Lutheranism was the stark negation of German unification under a central government".[15] He contends that the real motive of Philip's efforts to extirpate heresy was a dynastic zeal for the power

---

13. Yet on p. 90, when speaking of the expulsion of the Jews in 1492, he makes a curious concession regarding the futility of persecution. "Like all persecutions, it had proved of more benefit in the end to the victims than to the persecutors...."
14. The Catholic view of persecution is well illustrated by a sentence of decapitation and burning passed against a heretic at Venice in 1547. It was said to be "to the honour and glory of Jesus Christ" (W.E. Collins in *Camb. Mod. Hist.*, vol. ii [1903], p. 383).
15. R.T. Davies, *Golden Century*, p. 104. Cf. A.F. Pollard in *Camb. Mod. Hist.*, vol. ii (1903), pp. 144 f. (Charles's supreme motive was a desire to glorify the Hapsburg family).

of Spain. "Though he was by no means conscious of the fact, his policy was a completely secular one…" (p. 131) – a judgment which I regard as self-contradictory. "Philip's aims were those which almost any ambitious statesman, given his circumstances, would have adopted.… This postulated, especially, the destruction of all Protestant and Mohammedan movements within Spain…" (p. 135). It was the almost universal belief of the time "that more than one religion in one State would bring that State to destruction. There was abundant evidence in support of such an assumption;…"[16]

This thesis receives some support from the facts (1) that, on the advice of his father, Philip, as Mary Tudor's husband, dissuaded her on grounds of political expediency from persecuting the English Protestants; (2) that he saved Princess Elizabeth's life, and long supported her as Queen of England; (3) that he urged Pope Pius V to allow the Spanish Inquisition to condemn Carranza, Archbishop of Toledo, since otherwise the reputation of the Inquisition – the main support of his regal power – would be damaged; (4) that he is said to have offered in 1573 to establish the same measures of religious toleration in the Netherlands as prevailed in Germany, by reuniting them with the Empire, if the German princes would elect him Emperor; and (5) that, notwithstanding his general loyalty to the Papacy, he was frequently at issue with individual Popes, and that at times the tension was very serious.

But this apologetic, so far from rendering the persecution of so-called heretics any less odious, renders it only more so. It is at least some slight palliation of the evil of persecuting that it is done with a desire to safeguard the truths of religion. But to let the issue of religious toleration or its opposite turn on the question which of them was the more advantageous for the political power of oneself and one's dynasty is to deprive intolerance of even that meagre excuse. I am not forgetting here that under Queen Elizabeth Catholic priests were executed in England on

---

16. R.T. Davies, *Golden Century*, pp. 134 f.; cf. p. 278. See also E. Armstrong, *Charles V* (ed. 1910), vol. i, pp. 223, 250, 262, vol. ii, pp. 135 f., 266, 344; Butterfield, *The Whig Interpretation*, etc., pp. 39, 80-83; J.B. Black, *The Reign of Elizabeth* (Oxford, 1936), p. 87 ("… the rigid Spanish belief that the catholic religion was indispensable to the maintenance of civil obedience"); E.C. Ratcliff in *The Study of Theology* (1939), p. 459. ("From the point of view of the time, national unity and security undoubtedly demanded enforced conformity" – à propos of the England of Elizabeth).

what were at least largely political grounds: but this evil proceeding rested on something much broader than the desire to defend the personal or dynastic rights of a particular sovereign or royal house: it rested on the fear (warranted by what had happened under Elizabeth's predecessor) that the triumphs of the Catholic plots against her would result in the virtual enslavement of the entire nation.[17]

On the whole, however, I am disposed to think that Mr. Trevor Davies does Philip a little less than justice in declaring his motives as a persecutor to have been mainly political. His tenderness towards the English Protestants under Mary and his alleged offer of toleration in the Netherlands in 1573 were apparently in the nature of lapses or special concessions due to the particular political interests which happened to be then before him. Without imagining that the political and religious motives could in those days be kept entirely apart, I believe that Philip was largely actuated by purely religious considerations.[18]

As regards Charles, it is certain that, as a loyal Catholic, he regarded Protestantism with intense repugnance, altogether independently of the element of political danger believed to be inseparable from it. It has been claimed, however, that "he was no ferocious bigot".[19] The grounds alleged for this view are, first, that there was a lull in the activity of the Spanish Inquisition during the latter part of his reign;

---

17. "In the eyes of statesmen like Walsingham, for whom politics were, with much justification, a contest between Protestantism and Catholicism, light and darkness, Christ and Antichrist..." (F.M. Powicke, *The Reformation in England* [1941], p. 125).

18. This is the view put by the English poet George Chapman into the mouth of the French general Biron in his play, *The Tragedy of Charles Duke of Byron* (1608; Act IV, scene ii, lines 115-155), in the course of a general eulogy of Philip.

> "So he, with his divine philosophy,
> (Which I amy call his, since he chiefly us'd it)
> In Turkey, India, and through all the world,
> Expell'd profane idolatry, and from earth
> Rais'd temples to the Highest: whom with the Word
> He could not win, he justly put to sword...
> ...   'Twas religion,
> And her ful propagation that he sought; ..."

On the significance of this eulogy, see below, p. 146 n.

19. Armstrong, *Charles V* (ed. 1910), vol. ii, p. 344; cf. p. 70 ("until his latest years he was no fanatic"); also R.B. Merriman, *The Rise of the Spanish Empire in the Old World and in the New*, vol. iii (*The Emperor*, 1925), p. 129 ("Fanatic by nature he emphatically was not;...").

and secondly, that "in Germany his moderation excited the anger of Catholics". In regard to the inquisitional lull in Spain, such as it was, other factors than the suggested liberality of Charles would account for it; and it is interesting to note that he steadily supported the Inquisition in Spain, and that, when he heard that the country was permeated with heresy, he wrote in concern about it to his mother (the nominal queen) and his son (the Regent), and a new spell of persecuting activity ensued (1546). As for his moderation in Germany, it is surprising that Mr. Armstrong should adduce it as evidence that he was no bigot, for it is abundantly clear that his hands there were tied, because he was only Emperor and not territorial ruler,[20] and he had good reason to fear that, if he attempted persecution in Germany, he would encounter such strong opposition as to disrupt the Empire, and possibly to bring about his own dethronement. It has been said that the strongest motive behind his abdication was his unwillingness permanently to tolerate schism; and he certainly impressed on his son the duty of doing all he could to wipe heresy off the face of the earth.[21]

The instrument which both Charles and Philip normally used for the suppression of heresy, and incidentally for the maintenance of their own monarchical power, was the Inquisition. The Spanish Inquisition had certain features of its own, wherein it differed from the Inquisition practised in the Netherlands and elsewhere; but the points of difference are not such as to affect substantially any moral judgment which we may be led to pass on either.

The popular and historical memory of the doings of the Roman Church in the sixteenth century has invested the Inquisition, as it has invested the Society of Jesus, with the blackest disrepute. This general horror with which Protestants have become accustomed to think of the Inquisition is naturally apt to find expression in exaggerated or inaccurate statements regarding the details of its procedure. Wild assertions are often made regarding the number of its victims, the ruthlessness of its sentences, the publicity of its executions, and so on. Such

---

20. Armstrong, *Charles V* (ed. 1910), vol. ii, pp. 104, 109, 344.
21. Cf. Merriman, *The Emperor,* pp. 401 f.

exaggerations furnish Catholic and pro-Catholic writers with magnificent opportunities for exposing the falsity of the Protestant picture.[22] No doubt the general popular tendency to exaggerate something concerning which our feelings have been roused must be admitted and guarded against. We must be prepared to accept and welcome all that can be truthfully said regarding the institution under debate. But it would be a great mistake to suppose that the correction of popular exaggerations and inaccuracies relieves the Inquisition of all severe reproach on the ground of cruelty.

Some of the points advanced, while not without their historical interest, make very little difference to the general ethical character of the Inquisition, as Protestant tradition views it.

It is, for instance, technically incorrect to speak of heretics being burnt at an auto-de-fe. The auto-de-fe ("act of faith") concluded with the solemn pronouncement of sentence by the inquisitorial judges. The condemned persons were then formally "relaxed" (i.e., handed over) to the secular magistrates, whose business it was to execute the sentence.[23] Yet what material difference will this make to our ethical judgment when we remember that it was virtually, if not formally, at the direct bidding of the Church that the magistrates did the burning, that they rendered themselves liable to excommunication if they did not do it within a short specified time, and that they did it with all solemnity in the presence of ecclesiastics, nobles, and crowds of people, and with the full approval – if not actually under the eyes – of the king, his family, and his court?

One may well believe that not all the victims of the Inquisition were innocent men, and that there were cases in which it protected unpopular individuals, such as Jews, from mob violence.[24] There seems, moreover, reason to believe that the Spanish Inquisition was less severe in its treatment of those accused of witchcraft than were the Catholic tribunals elsewhere and even contemporary Protestant governments.[25] Yet he who warrantably urges this as

---

22. One may read a typical modern demurrer of this kind in *The Times Literary Supplement*, June 27, 1936, p. 534.
23. See R.T. Davies, *Golden Century*, p. 16; Walsh, *Philip II*, p. 233 ("... There were no horrors in an *auto*... There was nothing bloody about it....").
24. Walsh, *Philip II*, pp. 503, 670, 699, 702.
25. See W.F. Rea in *The Month*, vol. clxxvii, pp. 32-40, esp. 37 f. (Jan.-Feb. 1942).

"A Good Word for the Inquisition" has to admit that the Church did for long years encourage a most bitter persecution of witches, that "to the immense credit of Protestantism one of the first protests against the mass-murders came from its ranks, namely, in the work of Johann Weyer of Cleves, published in 1563", that between 1589 and 1600 five Catholic books were written against him, and that "in England there were far fewer executed than on the continent,…".[26]

Whether it be true or not that certain people maliciously spread the rumour that Philip intended to introduce the *Spanish* Inquisition into the Netherlands, and spread it in order to rouse increased opposition to his rule,[27] such was never actually his intention.[28] The erroneous nature of the rumour, however, matters very little, so far as our moral reactions to his proceedings are concerned. In fact, there seems some ground for pleading that the Spanish Inquisitors, though possibly more efficient, were somewhat less cruel than Inquisitors elsewhere. Philip himself asserted that the Inquisition established by Charles in the Netherlands was more pitiless than that in vogue in Spain.[29] How cruel the Inquisitors were in Spain, we shall see later. But the more the distinction just alluded to is pressed, the more barbarous must the cruelties inflicted in the

---

26. W.F. Rea, in *The Month* pp. 34-36. Karl Heussi summarizes the history of the matter thus: "In the earlier centuries the Church had rejected the illusion about witches along with the rest of popular superstition, but then-had entered into it and incorporated it into the ecclesiastical system of doctrine (first, Thomas Aquinas). In France the Inquisition had carried out numerous witch-trials as early as the thirteenth and fourteenth century. In Germany the Dominicans and Inquisitors of Cologne...., with the help of the Bull procured from Innocent VIII, '*Summis desiderantes affectibus*' (1484), first established the belief in and the prosecution of witches, and at the same time in their '*Malleus Maleficarum*' (Hammer of Witches) codified the illusion with all its grotesque details (1487 or 1488). The number of girls and women burnt as witches during the great witch-persecution 1400 – 1700 runs into hundreds of thousands. It was neither humanism nor the Reformation, but the Aufklärung, which was the first to set itself against this monstrous offspring of human craziness" (*Kompendium der Kirchengeschichte* [ed. 1909], p. 296: translation mine). We may note incidentally that the legal abolition of torture is also to be credited to the Aufklärung (Heussi, *Kompendium*, p. 467).
27. R.T. Davies, *Golden Century*, p. 159; Walsh, *Philip II*, pp. 339 f., 343, 347, 350, 404 Cf. E Poullet, "De la répression", etc., pp. 921, 926.
28. Walsh, *op. cit.*, pp. 338 ("… Protestant legend to the contrary notwithstanding, the Spanish Inquisition was never introduced into the country, at any time"), 347, 350. Cf. E. Poullet, *op. cit.* pp. 926-930.
29. Walsh, *op. cit.*, p. 347.

Netherlands appear, and the more violent will consequently be the moral loathing with which we shall recoil from it.

Efforts, again, have been made to assuage the horror with which the Spanish Inquisition has long come to be regarded by pleading that the numbers of persons actually burnt alive have been grossly exaggerated. Criticism has in particular been concentrated on the accuracy and even the veracity of Juan Antonio Llorente, who had access to the archives of the Inquisition, and in 1815-17 published a critical history of it. He stated that between 1480 and 1808 nearly 32,000 persons had been burnt by the Inquisition in Spain. There seems reason to believe that he was not over-exact in his methods; and it is customary with Catholic authors to make the most of his alleged habit of exaggeration.[30] The fact of the matter is that we must be content to do without precise statistics; and in regard to Llorente we may make his critics a present of the benefit of the doubt.[31] Henry Charles Lea enumerates the figures actually on record for the seven or eight chief towns (or provinces) in Spain for various specified periods, commencing with 1480 or soon afterwards.[32] Totalling the annual averages thus provided, we get about 130 burnings per annum – say 150 for the whole of Spain. This may possibly be near the true average for the first few decades of the history of the Inquisition, but it is certainly much in excess of it for the seventeenth and eighteenth centuries. However, as Lea says, "the material at hand as yet is evidently insufficient to justify even a guess at the ghastly total". Mr. Trevor Davies grants (p. 16) that "the number of baptized Jews and Mohammedans... who fell victims to the Inquisition during the first half-century of its existence... must have been enormous" (though, of course, not all of these were burnt). After the disorders in Aragon in 1591, the Inquisition wanted to send seventy-nine persons to the stake, but Philip reduced the number to six.[33]

The question of numbers is, furthermore, affected by the acknowledged fact that a condemned heretic, if he was penitent,

---

30. See S.F. Smith, S.J., in *The Month*, vol. lxxiv, pp. 382-386 (March 1892); Walsh, *Philip II*, p. 251 ("Sometimes the scandal-monger is an exposed cheat, like Llorente;..."): and cf. W.F. Rea in *The Month*, vol. clxxvii, p. 37 top (Jan.-Feb. 1942), and R.B. Merriman, *The Rise of the Spanish Empire*, etc. vol. iv (*Philip the Prudent*, 1934), pp. 78-83.
31. See, however, above, p. 27.
32. H.C. Lea, *Inquis of Spain*, vol. iv (1907), pp. 516-524.
33. R.T. Davies, *Golden Century*, p. 200.

was entitled to be strangled before his body was actually burnt; and we are assured that the great majority of those condemned to the stake escaped in that way the appalling torment of actual death by fire.[34] What the precise proportions were we shall never know: but allowance must be made for the facts (1) that a *relapsed* heretic was liable to be regarded as incapable of genuinely repenting a second time; (2) that some at least of the victims were nearly always burnt alive; and (3) that the strangling process was not always effective in extinguishing sensation, especially if the executioners had not been bribed. Sebastian Castellio of Switzerland refers to the bitter complaints which some theologians made when they saw a condemned heretic strangled, instead of being burnt alive in a slow fire.[35]

Interesting, however, as the question of numbers is, it is not of prime importance; for the main principle at stake lies elsewhere. Numbers are the measure of the efficiency of the Inquisition in finding heretics, not of the goodness or badness of its deeds.[36] Whatever the numbers may really have been, the question still faces us: What judgment must we pass – not on the characters and motives of the agents – but on their objective deeds? What judgment on the condition of the populace that sanctioned and applauded these deeds? What ought we to say about the public burning alive of even half a dozen persons each year, the public strangling and then burning of scores more, the imposition of severe penalties on an indefinite number of others, and the consignment of the condemned persons' children to infamy and destitution – all on the ground that they refused to submit their judgment in matters of religion to the dictation of a despotic Church and a despotic State?

It is often pleaded that persons arraigned before the Inquisition were given a fair trial, according to the contemporary ideas of what public justice required. No doubt some effort was made

---

34. W.E. Collins in *Camb. Mod. Hist.*, vol. ii (1903), pp. 396, 408; H.C. Lea, *Inquis. of Spain*, vol. iii (1907), pp. 192-195, vol. iv (1907), pp. 524 f.; R.T. Davies, *op. cit.*, pp. 14 f., 142 f.; Walsh, *Philip II*, p. 233 ("As a rule,…").
35. See W.E.H. Lecky, History of the Rise and Influence of the Spirit of Rationalism in Europe (ed. 1872), vol. ii, p. 34 n.
36. H.C. Lea, *Inquis of Spain*, vol. iii (1907), p. 33, vol. iv (1907), p. 525.

to safeguard the interests of the accused.[37] He was, for instance, allowed to name any personal enemies whom he might suspect as being liable to bring false accusations against him; and the evidence of any person so named was not used. On the other hand, he was not allowed to know who his accusers were.[38] As in Nazi Germany, so in Catholic Spain, children were encouraged to inform against their parents. Condemnation was usually accompanied by forfeiture of property (except in the case of children who had betrayed their parents); and the reputation and memory of the condemned were branded with perpetual disgrace.

The plea that the courts of the Inquisition were on the whole more humane and just than the secular courts of the time is, as we shall see, urged with special respect to their use of torture.[39] It is, in any case, a poor apologia for heartless cruelty that others are still more heartlessly cruel. But bad as all torture is, it is surely less excusable to torture a man because he is under suspicion of thinking for himself in matters of religion than to torture him in connexion, say, with a charge of wilful murder. When we take account of the *purposes* for which the Inquisition tortured and penalized men, its alleged comparative mildness is seen to fall very far short of a rehabilitation. But it is time we turned specifically to the subject of torture, on its own merits.

---

37. R.T. Davies, *Golden Century*, pp. 13 f. ("Popular tradition dies so hard that it is still necessary to point out that the Spanish Inquisition, judged by the standards of the times, was neither cruel nor unjust in its procedure and its penalties. In many ways it was more just and humane than almost any other tribunal in Europe...."); Walsh, *Philip II*, p. 356 ("... and everyone knew that the Inquisition was more impartial than the secular courts").
38. See the full study of the evidence on this point by Mr. Francis Darwin in *The Church Quarterly Review*, vol. cxxv, pp. 226-246 (Oct. 1937-Mar. 1938), and vol. cxxvi, pp. 19 – 43 (Apl.-Sept. 1938). Mr. Darwin also contributed a valuable essay on" The Organisation of the Holy Office" to the same *Review*, vol. cxxii, pp. 196-239 (Apl.-Sept. 1936). These articles have been separately reprinted. In the first-named of them, the author quotes two comments of H.C. Lea: "The suppression of the names of the witnesses was one of the crowning atrocities of Inquisitorial procedure". "It is impossible to resist the conclusion that the system of procedure was formed rather to secure conviction than to ascertain the truth. Guilt was *presumed* in the fact of arrest, and the business of the tribunal was to prove it". The reason of the suppression of the witnesses' names was, of course, the fact that otherwise no one would have dared to give evidence against an influential suspect.
39. H.C. Lea (*Inquis. of Spain*, vol. iii [1907], pp. 2 f., 18) says that the Spanish Inquisition was less cruel in the use of torture than either the secular courts or the Roman Inquisition.

Torture was a regular, if not an invariable, part of Inquisitional procedure.[40] It was applied, not as a punishment, but as a means of extorting evidence, whenever it was thought that an accused person might be falsely maintaining his innocence or otherwise concealing useful information (such as particulars regarding his heretical associates). The result was, of course, that not only those guilty of heresy, but many who were not guilty at all, were liable to be subjected to prolonged and excruciating pain before anything whatever had been proved against them.

Dr. Walsh leaves these unpleasant details regarding the Inquisition discreetly alone: but Mr. Trevor Davies makes a valiant attempt to palliate them. "Unlike almost all other tribunals in Europe at this time", he says, "the Inquisition was very sparing in its use of torture, and adopted methods of torture far more humane than was customary, especial care being taken to do the accused no permanent injury" (p. 14).

I have already alluded to the comparison drawn between the Spanish Inquisition and the other courts of Europe in favour of the former. There were, of course, regulations in force controlling and limiting the use of torture by the Inquisition.[41] How far it was really less severe than in other courts it is impossible without very extensive research to judge. Mr. Trevor Davies quotes no documentary authority for the assertions I have just quoted. Notwithstanding the important judgment of H.C. Lea on the matter, I am disposed to suspect that an exact investigation, supposing we were able to make it, would not go far towards exculpating the Spanish Inquisitors. At all events we should find no ground for reversing our impression that their proceedings were atrociously cruel. In view of such evidence as we have, I find it impossible to believe that tortured persons did not frequently receive permanent injury from the way they were treated, or to admit that the use of torture by the Spanish tribunals can be accurately described as "sparing".

There is, however, one particular direction in which we may profitably follow up this question of comparative severity a little further. Later in his book, Mr. Trevor Davies says something

---

40. H.C. Lea, *Inquis. of Spain*, vol. iii (1907), p. 1: "the habitual employment of torture by the Holy Office had been the most efficient factor in spreading its use throughout Christendom...".

41. H.C. Lea, *op. cit.*, vol iii (1907), pp. 3-11.

which possibly reveals part at least of the ground on which he is basing his assertion that the torture used by the Inquisition in Spain was comparatively light. He is dealing with the severe persecution of Roman Catholic priests in England in 1581, and he writes: "'The priests they succeed in capturing', wrote Mendoza[42] (August 12th, 1581), 'are treated with a variety of terrible tortures; amongst others is one torment which people in Spain imagine will be that which will be worked by Anti-Christ as the most dreadfully cruel of all'. Elizabeth was, *seemingly*, able to shock even the supporters of the Spanish Inquisition by her torture-chamber in the Tower".[43]

Now, it is unhappily true that torture was frequently used in England under Elizabeth and by her express orders. In Hallam's oft-quoted words – "the rack seldom stood idle in the Tower for all the latter part of Elizabeth's reign".[44] Moreover, a cruel wretch named Richard Topcliffe was explicitly allowed by the authorities to torture condemned priests at his discretion in the privacy of his own house; and he did so with diabolical ingenuity. Other forms of torture (besides the rack), which were sometimes employed, were the thumb-screw and – from 1591 onwards – the "manacles". These last-named were probably an instrument for compressing the whole body.[45] Mendoza reported that, when the rack failed to break the spirit of Edmund Campion, needles were run under the nails of his fingers and toes. It would be interesting to know if this was what Mendoza meant by the torture which Anti-Christ was expected to use. It has, however, been thought that he may have misunderstood the facts in some way.[46]

I am not concerned to palliate in any way the use in England of such abominations as the rack and the thumb-screw. I want only to try to test the accuracy of Mr. Trevor Davies's assertion that the Elizabethan government "seemingly" behaved worse than the Spanish Inquisition in the matter of torture. In this connexion

---

42. The Spanish Ambassador in London.
43. R.T. Davies, *Golden Century*, p. 212 (italics mine).
44. Hallam, *The Constitutional History of England* (ed. 1891), vol. i, p. 148. Cf. L.A. Parry, *The History of Torture in England* (London, 1934), pp. 36-41.
45. L.A. Parry, *op. cit.*, pp. 37 f., 49, 52.
46. Parry, *op cit.*, p. 49: "... This barbarity [i.e., the needles] is probably exaggerated; there is no record of this method having been used in England, and the Ambassador may have been thinking of the thumb-screws".

it is relevant to point out that the constant use of the rack in the Tower of London roused a great deal of public criticism in England, so much in fact that the Queen's ministers resorted to the discreditable expedient of entrusting Topcliffe with the task of torturing priests in private. Topcliffe's cruelties, in their turn, excited much popular indignation, even among Protestants: "and so loud and severe were the complaints to the privy council that Cecil, in order to mitigate the popular feeling, caused Topcliffe to be arrested and imprisoned upon pretence of having exceeded the powers given to him by the warrant; but the imprisonment was of short duration".[47] There is, I venture to say, not much evidence of similar protests being made in Spain, or in other Catholic countries for that matter, against the use of torture by the Inquisition.[48]

Except for the barbarities semi-officially perpetrated by Topcliffe, the methods of torture employed in England seem to have been limited to the rack (by far the most commonly used instrument), the thumb-screw, and (after 1591) the "manacles". Moreover, the Queen's spokesmen felt it was worth while to deny that torture was ever inflicted in connexion with charges solely relating to points of religious doctrine, or on persons not already virtually known to be guilty of treason.[49] It must always be borne in mind that no Catholic was executed in England until after Pope Pius V had issued his

---

47. Thompson Cooper in *Dict, of Nat. Biog.*, vol. xix (1921-2), p. 979 b. Other protests against the use of torture were made: see Neal, *Hist, of the Puritans* (ed. 1837), vol. i, p. 279; Hallam, *Const. Hist, of Eng.* (ed. 1891), vol. i, p. 148 n.
48. Cf. Walsh, *Philip II*, p. 234 ("The Inquisition was popular in Spain"). The Aragonese nobles opposed the Inquisition: but that was on account of their own claims to independence (R.T. Davies, *Golden Century*, p. 193; Walsh, *op. cit.*, p. 356; Armstrong, *Charles V* [ed. 1910], vol. i, p. 35, vol. ii, p. 69). There was always popular disappointment in Spain, when there were no victims to be burnt after an auto-de-fé (H.C. Lea, *Inquis. of Spain*, vol. iv [1907], pp. 525 f.). Dr. Walsh says that people flocked "to see the enemies of God and man punished,..." (*op. cit.*, p. 234). Per contra, see below, p. 58, about Luis Vives.
49. Hallam, *Const. Hist, of Eng.* (ed. 1891), vol. i, pp. 150 f.; Parry, *Hist, of Torture in Eng.*, pp. 37, 48. The latter quotes with approval (p. 50) the following words of J.A. Froude: "Protestant England, notwithstanding the cruelties to the Jesuits, was not below but above the average continental level. The torture-chambers of the Inquisition were yet more horrible than the cells of the Tower,..." Motley (*United Netherlands* [ed. 1875-76], vol. ii, pp. 276 f.) brings out the enormous difference between Elizabeth's persecution and that of Charles and Philip as regards numbers and excusability. Cf. my *Roman Catholicism and Freedom* (3rd ed.), pp. 45-47.

bull "Regnans in Excelsis" (February 1570), deposing Elizabeth as a heretic, absolving her subjects from their allegiance, and forbidding them, under threat of anathema, to obey her orders.

I wonder whether Mr. Trevor Davies's idea that the Elizabethan tortures were worse than the Spanish was derived in part from Mendoza's apparent allusion to the abominations practised by Topcliffe (which, as we have seen, were irregular and roused even Protestant denunciations). But it seems to me more likely that he has been misled by tacitly attributing to Mendoza an impartiality which, as a Catholic, he would be in the last degree unlikely to exercise.[50] For Catholics regularly stand aghast at any report of cruelties *practised on Catholics*. In such circumstances their moral feelings are given normal play; and they express themselves in the clearest and strongest terms about the wickedness of the severities inflicted. But when it is a case of equal or even greater severities being exercised by Catholics on heretics, schismatics, and apostates, it is an entirely different story. The normal rules of humane conduct simply do not apply. This severe treatment, it is urged, was not "persecution" at all; it was justifiable discipline. Its victims were not – as the Catholic sufferers were – innocent and heroic martyrs, but guilty transgressors undergoing richly deserved penalties. Doubtless the treatment they received was painful; but so is all punishment. I remember seeing a Roman Catholic acquaintance boil over with righteous indignation at the enormities of Cromwell, without seeming to realize the moral gravity of the far bloodier enormities of the Duke of Alva. Altogether different scales of value are applied, according to whether the sufferers were Catholics or Protestants. And if Mendoza, or any other Catholic, wrote in strong censorious terms of the tortures inflicted on priests in England under Elizabeth, that fact – to anyone familiar with the normal mentality of Catholic apologetic – would imply absolutely nothing in regard to the use of milder methods towards Protestants in Spain. I hope I am not here misunderstanding or misrepresenting the grounds of Mr. Trevor Davies's judgment. But his words quoted above (p. 55) give me the impression that his comparison between England and Spain, in favour of the latter, owes something to a failure to allow

---

50. It is worth noting that he had been on the staff of the Duke of Alva in the Netherlands!

sufficiently for the normal bias of any Catholic discoursing on Catholic sufferings.

We are not, however, without positive evidence regarding the extent and character of the tortures inflicted by the Spanish Inquisitors. The *Directorium Inquisitorum* of Eymericus, Inquisitor of Aragon about 1368, was printed at Barcelona in 1503 and passed through many editions. It contains a full account of the various methods of torture used. Simancas, a Spanish bishop, published in 1569 a work entitled *De Catholicis Institutionibus ad praecavendas et extirpandas Hcereses*. In this book he vehemently denounced the protests made in 1522 by the philosopher Luis Vives against the use of torture: "he defends the practice with great energy, on the authority of theologians; and he gives a very vivid description of different modes of torture the Inquisitors employed in their dealings with heretics.... Simancas notices that, in other countries, criminals were in his day tortured in public, but in Spain in secret...."[51] In 1583 Suarez de Paz published at Salamanca his *Praxis ecclesiastica et secularis*, in which he defended, on the analogy of the usage adopted in trials for treason, the legality of torturing anyone over fourteen years of age who was suspected of heresy, and of scourging those under fourteen.[52]

The scenes in the torture-chamber itself must have been horrible enough. The safeguards officially provided for the purpose of preventing excessive cruelty were frequently transgressed in practice.[53] For instance, the law allowed only one infliction of torture; but this restriction was easily and frequently evaded by talking about the suspension and resumption of the one spell.[54] Since wellnigh the whole surface of the body was liable to be subjected to agony, the victims, regardless of their sex, were customarily stripped stark naked, and then usually granted a diminutive covering round the loins.[55] Neither youth nor age was any protection. A girl of thirteen successfully resisted the torture, and was thereafter sentenced to a penance of a hundred lashes. An old man of seventy-six, and old women of seventy-eight, eighty,

---

51. Lecky, *Rationalism in Europe* (ed. 1872), vol. i, p. 331 n.; cf. p. 329 n. 1.
52. Lecky, *op. cit.*, pp. 328 f.n.
53. H.C. Lea, *Inquis. of Spain*, vol. iii (1907), pp. 8-10, vol. iv (1907), p. 533.
54. H.C. Lea, *op. cit.*, vol. iii (1907), pp. 18, 28 f.
55. H.C. Lea, *op. cit.*, pp. 6 f., 15-17, 24, 26 f.

ninety, and even ninety-six years of age, are recorded to have been tortured and/or burnt alive. Sentences of two hundred lashes were passed even on women.[56] Pregnancy gave no exemption, except that a woman with child was tortured in a sitting position, instead of being strapped down on planks.[57] The incidental accompaniments of the use of the most common forms of torture are said to have included the cutting-through of the skin and muscle to the bone by means of tight cords, the tearing-away of skin and flesh, the loss of fingers and toes, the dislocation and fracture of arms, and crippling for life.[58] The whole time during which the torture was going on, the secretary of the court stood by, recording every step of the process, every shriek of agony uttered by the sufferer, every question put to him, every word he spoke.[59] The great historian of the Spanish Inquisition prints in extenso, by way of a typical example, a translation of the original account of how the tribunal of Toledo in 1568 tortured a woman who, because she had refused to eat pork, was suspected of being secretly inclined to Judaism. Through two and a half pages of small print we read the sickening narrative of the proceedings. After being (despite her piteous protests) stripped of her clothing, she was tortured by means of cords fastened tightly round her arms and stretched to breaking-point, the only reply vouchsafed to her frantic appeals for mercy, her declarations of innocence, her confessions of guilt, and her entreaties for death, being the reiterated demand of her tormentors, "Tell the truth".[60] Such were the normal proceedings of an institution which Mr. Trevor Davies says (p. 13) "stood for social justice" in what he describes as "the golden century" of the foremost Catholic power in Europe.[61]

In the Horniman Museum at Forest Hill in south-east London

---

56. Cf. C. Roth, *Marranos*, pp. 142 f., *Span. Inquis.*, pp. 126 f., 197, 203, 306.
57. H.C. Lea, *Inquis. of Spain*, vol. iii (1907), pp. 13-15.
58. H.C. Lea, *op. cit.*, pp. 18-23, 29.
59. H.C. Lea, *op. cit.*, p. 18: "... nor would it be easy to conceive anything more fitted to excite the deepest compassion than these coldblooded, matter of fact reports".
60. H.C. Lea, *op. cit.*, vol. iii (1907), pp. 23-26.
61. Was it perchance because he had seen this extraordinary claim that the late Dr. John Oman (who died in May 1939) wrote, in his posthumously published work, *Honest Religion* (1941): "Nor are those who know something of the spirit of toleration ever likely to admit that toleration was merely of man's slackness and not of God's mind; and *the defence of the Inquisition as*

there stands a steel torture-chair. It comes from Cuenca, a city about midway between Madrid and Valencia. A photograph of this horrible instrument is before me as I write; and the recollection of having frequently gazed on it during my boyhood lives with me still. It includes a movable seat, with rack and pinion, manacles for hands and feet, a skeleton-helmet with screws to put pressure on the top of the head, to pierce the ears, and to torture the nose and chin, a gag for the mouth with rack-action for forcing the mouth open and dragging forward the tongue, screw-forceps for extracting toe-nails, single and double thumb-screws, and various other padlocks, buckles, chains, keys, turnscrews, etc. Along with it was found a steel whip, having eight thongs each of which ends in a blade. On the mouth-gag are engraved the words "Santo Oficio Caballero" ("the noble 'Holy Office'", to wit, the Inquisition), and the date – 1676. It would be interesting to hear what our modern apologists for the Inquisition, who are so anxious to rectify the unappreciative "popular tradition" of Protestants about it, would have to say regarding this instrument. Were they to observe that its date is long posterior to the times of Philip II, I should be constrained to ask them whether the methods of torture employed in Spain in 1676 were likely to have been more severe than they had been a century earlier, when the struggle between the Roman Church and heresy was being waged at fever heat.[62]

So much, then, for Spain. But when all allowance has been made for the particular usages of that country, the picture of the cruelties inflicted there by the Inquisition will serve well enough as a broadly accurate characterization of the cruelties of the Inquisition and of Spanish administration elsewhere. As a sample of the views held outside Spain, we may mention the work of Prospero Farinacci, Procurator to Pope Paul V (1605-1621), entitled *Praxis et Theorica Criminalis*. He died in 1618: his work was regarded as authoritative, and was several times republished. His discussion of torture occupies over 250 closely printed folio-pages with double columns. "The length at which the subject is treated is one of the best proofs

---

an eminently just tribunal shocks them as a denial of what they are most assured is Christian" (p. 14: italics mine)?

62. Daniel Neal wrote in 1732: "There is at this time a bloody inquisition in Spain" (*Hist. of the Puritans* [ed. 1837], vol. i, p. xliii).

of the science to which it had been reduced.... An immense variety of tortures is mentioned, and the list tended to grow, for, as Farinaccius says, judges continually invented new modes of torture to please themselves."[63] We have the unimpeachable evidence of Philip himself that the Inquisition in the Netherlands was "plus impitoyable" than that of Spain. In the Netherlands in the time of Alva, a man sentenced to be burnt alive would often be prevented from speaking by having his tongue screwed tight between two irons, and the tip of it burnt with a red-hot iron, so that it swelled up, and could not be drawn back.[64] The practice of burying women-heretics alive is another indication of the degree of cruelty which marked the Spanish kings' attempt to suppress religious freedom among their subjects in the Low Countries. The law of 1535 imposing this dreadful penalty had fallen into desuetude, when in 1597 it was called again into operation at the demand of the Jesuits. An unoffending woman-servant of forty, Anna van den Hove, who read her Bible and held Protestant views, was in that year brought to Brussels, and called upon by the authorities to renounce her errors. On steadfastly refusing, she was led out of the city, and solemnly buried alive.[65]

"What strikes us most", wrote Lecky in 1865, "in considering the mediaeval tortures, is not so much their diabolical barbarity, which it is indeed impossible to exaggerate, as the extraordinary variety, and what may be termed the artistic skill, they displayed. They represent a condition of thought in which men had pondered long and carefully on all the forms of suffering, had compared and combined the different kinds of torture, till they had become the most consummate masters of their art, had expended on the subject all the resources of the utmost ingenuity, and had pursued it with the ardour of a passion. The system was matured under the mediaeval habit of thought, it was adopted by the Inquisitors, and it received its

---

63. James Williams in *Encyc. Brit.*, vol. xxvii (1911), p. 77.
64. T.M. Lindsay, *A History of the Reformation*, vol. ii (1908), p. 25 n.
65. Motley, *United Netherlands* (ed. 1875-76), vol. iii, pp. 418 f. ("... Of all the religious murders done in that hideous sixteenth century in the Netherlands, the burial of the Antwerp servant-maid was the last and the worst. The worst, because it was a cynical and deliberate attempt to revive the demon whose thirst for blood had been at last allayed, and who had sunk into repose. And it was a spasmodic revival only, for, in the provinces at least, that demon had finished his work"), vol iv, p. 498.

finishing touches from their ingenuity".[66] Later he refers to "the old stern Inquisitor, so unflinching in his asceticism, so heroic in his enterprises,[67] so remorseless in his persecution – ... the men who multiplied and elaborated the most hideous tortures, who wrote long cold treatises on their application,..."[68] Their victims, he says, perished by a death "which was carefully selected as among the most poignant that man can suffer. They were usually burnt alive. They were burnt alive not unfrequently by a slow fire. They were burnt alive after their constancy had been tried by the most excruciating agonies that minds fertile in torture could devise".[69]

I know it is the fashion nowadays to snigger at Lecky as "out-of-date". But Lecky had a very full first-hand acquaintance with medieval literature; and I am not aware that any of his statements has ever been proved to be inaccurate.[70] Moreover, it is perhaps worth while reminding the reader that a duly-attested historical statement is rendered neither untrue nor negligible by the fact that it was made seventy or eighty years ago.

After thus calling attention to the most glaring horrors committed by the Inquisition, we seem to be facing something of an anti-climax in referring to its value as a money-making organization. This aspect of its activity is not, I think, alluded to either by Mr. R.T. Davies or by Dr. Walsh. Heresy was made to pay for its own suppression. As has already been mentioned, it was the normal practice to confiscate the whole property of the condemned heretic. "The filthy odor of gain pervades all the active period of the Inquisition".[71]

I conclude this part of my subject by asking the reader to say candidly whether or not it was for the good of mankind and for the advancement of the religion of Jesus Christ that such an institution should be resisted and ultimately abolished. Let him

---

66. Lecky, *Rationalism in Europe* (ed. 1872), vol. i, pp. 328 f.
67. On the courage of the Inquisitors, cf. R.T. Davies, *Golden Century*, p. 197.
68. Lecky, *Rationalism in Europe* (ed. 1872), vol. i, p. 345.
69. Lecky, *op. cit.*, vol. ii, pp. 33 f.
70. See, however, below, p. 79, n. 1, for the one exception known to me – a natural error of judgment on Lecky's part.
71. H.C. Lea, *Inquis. of Spain*, vol. iv (1907), pp. 527 f.

bear in mind by all means that virtually the whole of Europe took for granted the legitimacy of torture as a part of judicial procedure, that rules had been laid down against excessive severity in the use of it and in penalization generally, that Protestant writers have exaggerated the severities of the Spanish Inquisition and the numbers of its victims, that it was not as cruel as the Roman Inquisition, that the Inquisitors were actuated by the noblest motives and were personally virtuous in many ways, and so on. Yet the question remains: What is to be our resultant judgment on the ethical character of the Inquisitional practice in Spain and the Netherlands? Is a national uprising which aimed at bringing it in the latter country to as speedy an end as possible deserving of our censure, or of our warm admiration and gratitude?

Chapter Four

The Spanish Monarchy and the Netherlands

The main issue at stake in the long war waged between the Netherlanders and the monarchs of Spain (1567-1609) was the right of an irresponsible autocracy to survive as a system of government, especially when exercised over a foreign people and maintained by sanctions of savage cruelty. The rulers against whom the Netherlanders were in revolt believed themselves entitled to dictate at their own will not only what their subjects were to do, but what they were to believe and how they were to worship. They regarded their dominions as their personal property, and assumed the right to bequeath or otherwise dispose of them according to their personal wishes, regardless of the desires of the human beings inhabiting these dominions.[1]

It goes, however, without saying, and should be borne in mind in the perusal of these paragraphs, that, while the Spanish and other monarchical governments were at this period broadly speaking autocratic, there were in almost all territories local usages and traditions which claimed to put certain limits to the arbitrary decisions of the sovereign. For practical reasons, both Philip II and his father often paid respect to these: but they were really an incongruity in the monarchical system of government as monarchs of the day conceived it, and hence were not infrequently disregarded and overridden.

Doubtless it may be truthfully pleaded that this autocratic theory of government was very widely taken for granted in the sixteenth century, even by the governed, and that this was necessarily the case at a time when, while public affairs had to be regulated somehow, there was as yet no machinery, or at least no sufficient machinery, for regulating them otherwise than by the dictates of an anointed sovereign. It needs to be borne in mind by us moderns, to whom the deference shown to medieval monarchs often seems extreme and absurd, that such deference was the only equivalent then generally possible for that very

---

1. Charles V regarded government as "founded on the principle of making all other men merely instruments for carrying out the ends of one" (M.A.S. Hume, *Philip II* p. 26).

needful sense of loyalty to the public interest which we to-day are able to express in other and more suitable and direct forms. In the case of the Netherlands, it has further to be borne in mind that the King of Spain could provide a far more centralized and unified administration than could the ramshackle political system of the Lowland states themselves, and that this centralization was in many ways a blessing to the country.

We shall consider presently how far these pleas on behalf of autocracy constitute a real justification for the attempt of the Spanish monarchs to exercise a despotic sway over the Netherlands. But admitting for the moment that the attempt sprang from the conscientious convictions of the despots themselves, and was in the main in harmony with the ideas generally held at the time, we are still faced with the question whether – in the light of the situations to which it gave rise – the theory of government from which the attempt sprang ought or ought not to have been challenged, discredited, and replaced by one better fitted to meet the demands of the case. Our experience of the recrudescence of autocracy in the form of modern European dictatorships is a confirmation, if any be needed, of the only possible answer to this question. The existing system was fraught with evil, and needed to be abolished.[2]

That being so, it is a matter of comparatively subordinate importance to examine with precision the exact legal relation in which this congeries of highly-civilized but loosely-connected principalities, which we designate collectively as "the Netherlands", stood to the crown of Spain. Yet it is not without interest to note the main features of the situation.

From the end of the fourteenth century onwards, these territories were, as the result of a marriage-alliance, included in the dominions of the Dukes of Burgundy, When in 1477 Charles the Bold of Burgundy fell at the battle of Nancy fighting against the Swiss, he left an only daughter, Mary, who received the sovereignty of the Netherlands (now become the main portion of the Burgundian territory) on condition of conceding to her subjects

---

2. Cf. Henry Ireton's words, reported by A.S.P. Woodhouse, *Puritanism and Liberty* (1938), p. 93: "... to say we should prefer the King's rights before a general good, was as unworthy and as unchristian an injury as was ever done by any to men that were in society with them,..."

certain extensive privileges. Shortly afterwards she married Maximilian of Austria, son of the Emperor; in 1479 she bore him a son Philip, and in 1482 she died. After a period of disorder and conflict, during which Maximilian claimed the right to interfere in the affairs of the country as regent for his young son, he was himself elected Emperor (1494), and thereupon handed over the rights of government to Philip. Two years later Philip married Juana, who soon became the heiress of her parents Ferdinand and Isabella, the sovereigns of Spain. Philip's son Charles, the future King of Spain and Emperor, was born at Ghent in 1500. A few years afterwards Juana's reason began to give way; and when her husband Philip died in 1506, and the boy Charles succeeded him as Duke of Brabant and Count of Holland, she became completely deranged, and so remained until her death in 1555. Such was the hereditary title of Charles V and later of his son Philip II to be the supreme rulers of the Netherlands.

The cities and provinces constituting this patrimony had secured a considerable measure of local liberty and various privileges by bargaining with their rulers: and the latter, though promising to respect these rights, naturally tended from time to time to infringe them. Thus Philip, Charles's father, managed virtually to release himself from the necessity of complying with the charter, which he had renewed, known as "the Great Privilege". Charles himself normally respected the privileges of the States: but this still left him in possession of a great deal of autocratic power which he did not hesitate to use. In various ways he acquired the sovereignty of several Dutch provinces (Friesland, Utrecht, Groningen, Gelderland, etc.) which had not previously been included in his inheritance; and thus he gradually consolidated (by 1543) his rule over virtually the whole of the country, with the exception of Liége).

Charles had become Emperor in 1519; and during the early part of his reign, the Low Countries (which were under his direct government in a way that the German states never were) were regarded by many as an integral part of the Empire, though they did not acknowledge the Emperor's right to tax them for imperial purposes. Had Charles been able to secure the succession of his own son as Emperor, he would probably have been content to incorporate them permanently in the Empire. As, however, he was unable to achieve this, he pursued the policy of virtually separating them from the Empire, and ultimately attaching them to the crown of Spain. He thus kept together the territories he himself knew best, and gained a geographical advantage over France. As early as 1530 he declared, in spite of the complaints of the imperial Diet, that the Low Countries were exempt from all imperial jurisdiction. In 1543 he transferred them in effect to Spain. But their status was not legally settled until the Diet of Augsburg, 1547-49. It was then laid down that they were not to be subject to the laws of the Empire, but were to be entitled to its protection and obliged to contribute to its revenues: moreover, they were to be kept together in the matter of succession. This arrangement, however, meant virtual separation from the Empire, since the stipulations about contribution and protection soon became a dead letter. In 1568-69, when Alva's atrocities were at their height, the Emperor did indeed presume to protest to Philip II in favour of peace: but his plea was emphatically rejected. The question of reincorporating the Netherlands into the Empire was discussed by William of Orange with the States in 1575; but nothing came of it. No practical help against Spain was ever forthcoming from any of the Protestant states of Germany: and a feeble claim made in 1608 by the Emperor Rudolf to have a hand in the peace-negotiations with Spain was firmly resisted by the Dutch themselves.

The Emperor Charles was genuinely and proudly devoted to his hereditary and acquired dominions in the Low Countries; and they were, on the whole, loyal to him. He had endeavoured, even at the cost of an occasional clash with local privileges or municipal regulations, to weld the States into a compact and nationally-minded unity, prosperous and peaceful, under a tolerably centralized system of administration.

Whatever the precise reason or reasons may have been, the doctrines of the Protestant Reformation (which is usually reckoned to have begun in 1517) found early and widespread (though, of course, far from unanimous) acceptance in the Low Countries, especially perhaps in the provinces to the north.[3] The generally advanced state of culture, the tradition of local liberty, the influence and reputation of the great humanist Erasmus of Rotterdam, and other conditions, may have contributed to the force of the Protestant appeal. Mr. Trevor Davies and Dr. Walsh, being concerned to make out as good a case for Spain as possible, speak of the Dutch tendency to Protestantism as if it were itself an offence. Here, for instance, is Mr. Trevor Davies, failing to make any sufficient distinction between the views of his main historical characters and his own: "The Netherlander was everything the Spaniard was not. The Spaniard was not – and despised – everything the Netherlander was: a trader, a drunkard, a glutton, reputedly indifferent to religion, and, worst of all, essentially a civilian.... Heresy – as might have been anticipated from their geographical position and their pursuits – had come early to the Netherlands.... For the Netherlanders, though Catholics, had little of the Spanish abhorrence of heresy. Their Catholicism was of the humanist reforming sort of which Erasmus had been the typical representative. They were keenly alive to the abuses of the Church and looked forward to a reformation from within. They recognized that the aims which influenced the heretics were not altogether unlike their own...."[4] For Dr. Walsh, all opponents of Roman Catholicism are ipso facto "enemies of Christ".[5] Doubtless to the papal curia also, to the Spanish monarchs, and to most loyal Romanists of the time, *all* Protestants seemed guilty of presumptuous insolence and impious blasphemy: and for rulers who took it for granted that only one form of belief and only one method of Church-government were tolerable in any state, the presence of a growing number of dissenters must have been a source of considerable apprehension. But can modern historians, even if convinced

---

3. See P.J. Blok, *History of the People of the Netherlands* (Eng. trans.), vol. ii (1899), pp. 312-315. Dr. Geyl, on the other hand, denies that Protestantism was inherently stronger in the north than in the south, and attributes its ultimate predominance in the north simply to the geographical conditions which determined the outcome of the military struggle (*Revolt*, etc. pp. 16, 64 f., 84, 112-114, 120, 258). His general tendency, however, is somewhat to minimize the force of the religious element: and while other factors doubtless contributed towards shaping the final result, the religious condition itself must have had much to do with the military outcome.
4. R.T. Davies, *Golden Century*, pp. 153 f.; and see above, pp. 36-39.
5. For evidence, see above, p. 32.

Romanists themselves, be allowed without protest to endorse this ancient and discredited censure, and to deny to the men of the sixteenth century the right to serve God in their own way?

Before reviewing the measures taken by Charles to deal with heresy in the Netherlands, let us take a glance at his general character. It would be very wrong to deny or forget that it included a number of admirable qualities. Notwithstanding his gross gluttony, he was free from the habit of drunkenness. Of his two known illegitimate children, one was born before his marriage and the other after his wife's death. He was devoted to his wife; and he impressed on his son Philip the evils of marital infidelity. He was a devout and conscientious Catholic, not only punctilious in the observances of his religion, but responsive to its spiritual and ethical demands. If we set aside his treatment of the Moors and the Protestants, and his ambitions as a Hapsburg, we may fairly regard him as a conscientious, just, and humane ruler. It is doubtful, however, whether we can ascribe to him – as he claimed – a love for peace; for although he was entitled to urge that war was often forced upon him against his will by his faithless enemy Francis I of France, as also occasionally by the pope, it does not follow that, had it not been for them, he would have remained at peace. It is known that he took a personal pleasure in campaigning (see above, p. 28): and it was his life-long desire to be free from entanglements with France and the Lutherans, in order to be able to fight the infidel Turks. As it was, the expense of his constant wars proved to be, apart from heresy, the one great cause of tension between himself and his subjects in the Netherlands. As a populous and prosperous country, it was expected to furnish a very considerable proportion of the money he needed – even of what was needed for purposes for which the inhabitants were in no way responsible. So heavy in consequence was the taxation that resentment was often roused and the risk of revolt incurred. The city of Ghent did, in fact, refuse payment and rebelled; but this resistance collapsed when Charles occupied the city in force in 1540, and Ghent was punished by the execution of nine ringleaders, by the payment of a heavy fine, and by the loss of all her privileges. At his abdication in 1555, Charles left the public treasury burdened with debt.

Reference has been made above (pp. 47 f.) to Charles's personal attitude to heresy. What of the policy he applied to the treatment of it in the Netherlands? He began (1520) by ordering all Lutheran books to be burnt, under threat of confiscation and other arbitrary punishment. A second edict of the same tenor was promulgated the next year; and under it the papal legate Aleander carried out several literary holocausts. Feeling, however, that these measures were not sufficiently drastic, Aleander expressed the wish that the Emperor would burn half-a-dozen Lutherans, and confiscate their property. In pursuance of this stronger policy, Charles secured from Pope Adrian VI (his own old tutor) approval for the appointment of two Inquisitors for the provinces (1522-23). Under them obstinate heretics were to be burnt alive, and penitent heretics beheaded.[6]

In July 1523 two Augustinian monks of Antwerp – the proto-martyrs of the Reformation – were burnt alive for heresy at Brussels. Three fresh Inquisitors were, on Charles's application, appointed by Pope Clement VII (1524-25). Imperial proclamations forbade, under heavy penalties, all secret meetings for Bible-reading, preaching, or religious discussion (1525-26). Professor Poullet mentions, among his instances, the payment of an executioner "d'avoir miz à la torture violente", and subsequently beheaded, a man named Lamph Motton, who was accused "d'avoir soustenu des propositions et querelles contraires à la sainte Église" (1526).[7] Anabaptists were felt to be even more dangerous than Lutherans, and were more cruelly treated: three of them were slowly roasted to death at The Hague in 1527. In 1529 the death-penalty was threatened for omission to hand over Lutheran books in one's possession. Next year ten Anabaptists were beheaded at The Hague on a single occasion by the Emperor's order, and their heads exposed on poles at Amsterdam. In December printers of unlicensed books were threatened with public whipping or branding or the loss of an eye or hand – at the discretion of the judge. Previous edicts

---

6. E. Poullet, ("De la répression", etc., pp. 175-179, 897 f.) describes the precise circumstances in which these Inquisitors were appointed. It should be noted that the machinery of Charles's persecution in the Netherlands was more secular than ecclesiastical, and depended more on instigation from headquarters than on local enthusiasm. The local authorities were often unwilling to carry out the sentences passed on heretics, and indeed refrained from doing so.
7. E. Poullet, *op. cit.*, p. 907; cf. p. 161 top.

were from time to time renewed in a completer form, and reinforced by the threat of still severer penalties. In 1532 three Anabaptists were roasted alive at Haarlem, and the wife of one of them drowned. An edict forbade Anabaptists to be harboured, and offered money-rewards for the betrayal of them; and a little later a single opportunity of repentance was allowed to them.

This lavish use of scourging, imprisoning, racking, roasting, and drowning failed to check the growth of Anabaptism. In a number of towns around and near the Zuider Zee a majority of the inhabitants took it up. Several efforts to escape from the country, or to seize and hold a town were checkmated, and bloodily punished (1534-35). Occasionally armed resistance was offered, as can hardly be wondered at; and hysterical extravagances now and then appeared. Provoked by these disturbances, and doubtless also by the wild excesses of the Anabaptist rebels in Münster (who were finally overthrown in June, 1535), the Emperor issued a more severe decree: re-baptizers of others were to be burnt; re-baptized persons and harbourers of Anabaptists were to be decapitated; women guilty of these offences were "only to be buried alive".

In 1537 Pope Paul III appointed two fresh Inquisitors with wide powers. In 1544 and 1546 severer penalties were announced for offences against the government's control of printing. About the same time, the powers of the Inquisitors were enlarged: they were authorized to act in complete independence of the bishops, and the instructions issued to them by Charles put them entirely under the control of his own administration.[8] There were indeed a few provinces into which the Inquisition was not introduced: but in them the same work was entrusted to the episcopal and secular courts.[9] A "placard" or edict which Charles issued in April 1550, superseding previous edicts against heresy which were not considered sufficiently thorough, and annulling any privileges which might hamper the Inquisitors, provoked such strong protests that it had to be modified. Another was therefore issued in September, not mentioning the Inquisitors under that name, and making some local concessions as regards foreign heretics, but still threatening with death (by methods similar to

---

8. E. Poullet, "De la répression", etc., pp. 899-904.
9. E. Poullet, *op. cit.*, pp. 913 f.

those mentioned above) persons guilty of heretical beliefs or actions: the judges, moreover, were strictly forbidden to mitigate the prescribed penalties. In 1553 Charles's Regent sent Inquisitors to the northern provinces with special instructions to extirpate Anabaptism. In January 1555 Charles modified the legal penalties in the case of persons judged worthy of indulgence. It is also probable that there was some slackening in the persecution of Lutherans towards the end of his reign. It was about this time that Protestant leadership in the Netherlands was passing from Lutheran to Calvinistic hands.

How many persons were roasted or burnt, beheaded, hung, buried alive, drowned, branded, scourged, mutilated, exiled, and imprisoned in the course of Charles's administration of about forty years, it is, of course, impossible to say. Many of them were devout, law-abiding Lutherans and Calvinists; and even of the more extreme Anabaptists only a small proportion had allowed the government's cruelty to goad them into acts of rebellion. It is known that Charles's edicts were only partially enforced. William of Orange estimated that, up to 1566, 50,000 persons had been either put to death or driven into exile under the government's orders. On that basis, we might perhaps estimate 30,000 for Charles's reign.[10] Seeing that the Regent Mary, in a letter written to her brother Charles in 1533, expressed the opinion that, while error should be extinguished with severity, care should be taken that the provinces should not be depopulated,[11] such a figure cannot be considered a gross overestimate.[12]

---

10. T.M. Lindsay (*History of the Reformation*, vol. ii, p. 239) quotes an estimate of 30,000 for Charles's reign; but this refers only to those put to death.
11. Motley, *The Rise of the Dutch Republic: a History* (ed. 1874), p. 43. Cf. Armstrong, *Charles V* (ed. 1910), vol. ii, pp. 346 f. ("Mary was neither a bigot nor a coward, and had much reason for the severe view which she took of the situation").
12. Cf. K. Heussi, *Kompendium*, etc. (ed. 1909), p. 368 ("Die Zahl der unter Karl in den Niederlanden Hingerichteten betrug mehrere Tausend; meist waren es Taufgesinnte"). P.J. Blok gives a far lower estimate, and thinks that the numbers of those *actually put to death* did not exceed 1,000, though "thousands and thousands were persecuted and punished" in other ways (*Netherlands*, vol. ii, pp. 317 f.; cf. pp. 320, 324 f.). E. Armstrong says that "the number of victims has been grossly exaggerated" (*Charles V* [ed. 1910], vol. ii, p. 345); but he gives no particulars or figures. P. Geyl (*Revolt*, etc., p. 40) observes that local unwillingness resulted in the persecuting edicts being far less thoroughly carried out than the government wished, and that the government refrained from exerting too much pressure, because of its need of

This was the persecution which Mr. Stanley Leathes describes as "in effect not especially severe".[13] Yet even the Catholic Professor Edmond Poullet says: "Ce système était sans contredit anti-juridique et cruel".[14] Mr. Armstrong admits that the placards were "increasingly severe", and speaks of "the extreme ferocity of the legislation against" the Anabaptists,[15] although this does not prevent him from describing Charles's rule in the Netherlands as "the brightest feature of his troubled reign",[16] and generally defending his policy. Mr. Trevor Davies, while crediting Charles with a "superb power of managing men and affairs" (p. 36), concedes that heresy was "fiercely persecuted by Charles V in a series of Placards... of the most stringent kind" (p. 153): but whether he intends these terms to convey an expression of disapproval is more than doubtful.

Despite his recognition of the cruelty of Charles's system, M. Poullet is at great pains to excuse it in the light of various historical facts which he adduces. I am not disposed to challenge the accuracy of his statements of fact, nor do I wish to pass a sentence of personal condemnation on Charles or his representatives. I deny only that the facts adduced in their defence constitute any justification of their persecuting acts *as acts*. These must stand condemned, whatever may have to be said of the good intentions of the agents. It may well be the case that the medieval Catholic system uniting Church and State had long been in possession of the field, and that certain benefits had followed from it:[17] that is no proof that it was not high time that

---

    money. The frequent repetition of the edicts points in the same direction. It does not, however, follow that numerous executions did not take place.
13. In *Camb. Mod. Hist.*, vol. ii (1903), p. 103.
14. E. Poullet, "De la répression", etc., p. 171: cf. pp. 914 f. ("Considéré dans ses détails, il respirait toute la dureté des mœurs de l'époque. Les placards étaient d'une sévérité draconienne et d'une économie essentiellement vicieuse…"). Cf. also Pirenne, *Belgique*, vol. iii (1912), pp. 310, 345 ("C'est lui [Charles V] et lui seul qui a donné au conflit religieux le caractère d'une persécution sanguinaire et créé, pour la répression de l'hérésie, la législation la plus impitoyable que l'Europe ait jamais connue. S'il n'a pu l'imposer à l'Allemagne, il l'a organisée à sa guise dans [the Low Countries], et durant tout son règne, il ne cessera, comme pris de vertige, d'en augmenter sans cesse la cruauté et l'absurdité"); Geyl, *Revolt*, etc., pp. 35, 54-56, 59.
15. Armstrong, *Charles V* (ed. 1910), vol. ii, p. 345: cf. pp. 122, 344, 348, vol. i, p. 320.
16. Armstrong, *op. cit.*, vol. ii, p. 348.
17. E. Poullet, *op. cit.*, pp. 146-155. On p. 914 he frankly rests his justification of Charles's persecution on the fact that his government was "en possession de

the system should be changed. Doubtless the repressive measures taken by Charles and Philip were constitutionally quite legal:[18] one can only reply that the law needed revision. In punishing heresy the sovereigns, we are reminded, were only keeping their oaths to uphold the Catholic faith and to defend the Church:[19] but if this is to be regarded as carrying with it an obligation to persecute, we must reply with Shakespeare's Earl of Salisbury:

> "It is great sin to swear unto a sin,
> But greater sin to keep a sinful oath.
> Who can be bound by any solemn vow
> To do a murderous deed, to rob a man,…
> To force a spotless virgin's chastity,
> To reave the orphan of his patrimony,
> To wring the widow from her custom'd right,
> And have no other reason for this wrong
> But that he was bound by a solemn oath?"

Many contemporary Netherlanders agreed with the persecution:[20] yes, but they ought not to have agreed. The punishments inflicted on heretics, though they seem so cruel to us, were simply those customary in that day in dealing with crimes of a non-religious kind:[21] then all one can say is that, if that were the case, they were barbarous, "Scythian" customs, which it was a Christian duty to resist and defy.

Mr. Armstrong's apologia takes the form of an insistence on the real danger of political revolt – a danger inherent, he says, in the very principles of the Anabaptists, and clearly manifested in the horrors which they committed at Münster, and which they would have committed at Amsterdam if their effort to gain control of it in 1535 had succeeded.[22] In reply to this, it may be observed:

(1) that the argument does not affect at all Charles's severe

---

la *vérité*", that the Catholic society involved was "toute imprégnée de la vérité", and that what Charles was repressing was "*l'erreur*"

18. E. Poullet, "De la répression", etc., pp. 145 f., 159, 163, 168, 898 f. He describes the precise legal position, especially as between the respective provinces of the Church and of the State, on pp. 163, 167, 169 f., 171, 173-175, 899 f., 904 ff., 909-911.
19. E. Poullet, *op. cit.*, pp. 151 f.
20. E. Poullet, *op. cit.*, pp. 152, 163. Geyl points out (*Revolt*, etc., p. 45) that the nobles were inclined to side with the court which enriched them, rather than with the middle class.
21. E. Poullet, *op. cit.*, pp. 168, 170 f., 172: cf. De Cauzons, quoted by Coulton, *The Inquisition*, pp. 62 f.
22. Armstrong, *Charles V* (ed. 1910), vol. i, p. 320 ("The extreme ferocity of the legislation against the sect would have provoked reprisals, even if violence

persecution of Lutherans and Calvinists, by whom no political uprising was threatened;

(2) that the dangerous rebelliousness and other excesses of the Anabaptists were by no means features of their usual programme: on the contrary, their strict Biblicism normally inclined them to a rather extreme form of pacifism. It was only when they had been goaded into desperation by several years of atrociously cruel persecution, that any danger of hysterical excess and armed resistance was seen.[23]

In moving on to the story of the persecution under Philip II, I propose to confine myself as far as possible to the matters relevant to my main theme, though it will not be either profitable or even possible to avoid all reference to other features in the history of the reign. With the persecution itself and the reaction to it in the early years of Philip's rule, there were bound up a number of other issues, which, however, it must suffice to mention only quite briefly. Philip, to begin with, was – unlike his father – personally unpopular in the Netherlands. He could not speak Dutch; and from the autumn of 1559 onwards he never visited the country. He was thus felt to be a complete foreigner.[24] The fact that he kept Spanish troops in the country was resented. His scheme for increasing the number of bishoprics (feared rightly as an instrument for the better repression of heresy, and wrongly as a possible prelude to the introduction of the Spanish Inquisition) was resented. The ascendancy of his most trusted servant, Cardinal Granvelle, in the Regent's Council, was resented. All these factors went to swell the volume of opposition to the policy of the placards, though in many ways independent of it.

On being presented in 1549 to the States-General, as prospective Duke of Brabant and Count of Holland, Philip had solemnly sworn to observe and respect all the traditional charters and

---

were not a necessary consequence of its original programme"), pp. 321 f., vol. ii, pp. 136, 344, 346 f.

23. So T.M. Lindsay, *Reformation*, vol. ii., p. 237, middle (where a "not" has been accidentally omitted). Mr. Armstrong himself admits this (see quotation in last note), though he does not seem to feel that it calls for any criticism of Charles on the ground of cruelty. Cf. also Pirenne, *Belgique*, vol. iii (1912), pp. 115-117, 332, 355-360, esp. 358; Geyl, *Revolt*, etc., p. 58.

24. Dr. Walsh (*Philip II*, p. 341) attributes his unpopularity partly to the fact that "it became known that he would be a loyal Catholic", and that a deliberate propaganda had consequently been working against him. Cf. Armstrong, *Charles V* (ed. 1910), vol. ii, pp. 219 f., 351.

liberties of his subjects. On his father's abdication in 1555, he "again solemnly swore to maintain in each province all ancient rights, privileges, and customs, without infringing the same or suffering them to be infringed".[25] But he had also promised to protect the Holy Church and to maintain the placards. In little over a month he issued instructions to the Inquisitors, confirming the edict of September 1550, and enjoining the strict execution of its requirements. He was indeed only continuing his father's policy: but the recent termination of the struggle in Germany with the Peace of Augsburg made men elsewhere less ready to take persecution as a matter of course. Some modification of severity was sanctioned in April 1556; and the resumption of war with France in 1557 inaugurated a lull in the attack on heresy, and a consequent absence of public opposition to the government. The conclusion of peace, however, in 1559 changed the situation. William of Orange, when staying in France as a hostage for the execution of the terms of the treaty, learned directly from the French King Henry II of a secret understanding between himself and the King of Spain to extirpate heresy in their respective dominions by fire and sword.[26] Resolved in consequence to drive the Spaniards out of the Netherlands, William succeeded on his return in persuading the States-General to make the withdrawal of the Spanish troops a condition of complying with Philip's demand for money. Before leaving the country a little later (August 1559), Philip gave the Regent (his illegitimate half-sister Margaret, Duchess of Parma) strict secret instructions to have the edicts against heretics carried out in all their rigour.[27] Persecution recommenced with a vengeance; and while the local

---

25. G. Edmundson in *Camb. Mod. Hist.*, vol. iii (1904), p. 183. Cf. Ruth Putnam, *William the Silent, Prince of Orange: the moderate man of the sixteenth century* (ed. 1898), vol. i, p. 77 n. ("... It was distinctly understood that the inhabitants promised obedience only on condition of their privileges being respected"), and *William the Silent, Prince of Orange, 1533-84, and the Revolt of the Netherlands* (in series "Heroes of the Nations": 1911), pp. 406 f.; P.J. Blok, *Netherlands*, vol. iii (1900), pp. 149 f.

26. Philip's "idea, as he had already told Catherine, was to have the heads of the principal Huguenot leaders all cut off at the same time; and if she had followed his advice in 1559,... such splended men as Duke Francis of Guise would still be walking the world... 'they resolved to give the heads of the Huguenots a Sicilian vesper'" (Walsh, *Philip II*, p. 382). See below, pp. 187 f.

27. While waiting for a favourable wind, Philip learned that some heretics imprisoned at Middelburg had been examined with insufficient stringency:

authorities and several of the nobility were unwilling to co-operate in executing its sentences, the Inquisition (led by the notorious and brutal Peter Titelmann) pushed on steadily its merciless and bloody work.

The story of how the situation steadily worsened between 1559 and 1566 (when rebellion was on the point of breaking out) is one of absorbing interest; but the detailed narrative need not detain us here. The main features can be briefly mentioned: the growing numerical strength of Protestantism, the growing resentment against the severities of the Inquisition and against the newly-instituted bishoprics associated therewith, the growing embarrassment of the Regent, her repeated appeals to Philip, her unwilling but enforced leniency pending his replies, the appeals and deputations of noblemen both to her and to the King, the latter's evasive obstinacy, the development of organized opposition on the part of the lower nobility, the more cautious but equally indignant ill-will of the higher. A few particular events call for specific mention. In March 1564, the unpopular foreigner, Cardinal Granvelle (Philip's somewhat unwilling tool) left the country. In August the same year, Philip commanded Margaret to publish and enforce the Decrees of the recently-concluded Council of Trent. He repeated this order in October 1565 (after Egmont's unsuccessful mission to Madrid), when he finally decided to adhere resolutely to his policy of repression.[28] He instructed the Regent to make no concessions to heresy. "As to the Inquisition", he wrote, "my will is that it be enforced by the Inquisitors as of old, and as is required by all law, human and divine. This lies very near my heart, and I require

---

he thereupon wrote to the authorities insisting that the men should be tortured (C.V. Wedgwood, *William the Silent*, p. 38).

28. I pass by as unconfirmed the once widely-accepted view that, when they met at Bayonne in June/July 1565, Catherine de' Medici, her daughter Elizabeth (or Isabella), Queen of Spain, and the Duke of Alva concerted measures for the instantaneous extinction of heresy throughout the French and Spanish dominions by means of massacre. The best modern authorities disbelieve the allegation; and certainly Catherine de' Medici, notwithstanding what she did in 1572, would not be very likely to agree to a wholesale massacre of Huguenots in 1565, or to any step likely to increase Spanish power in the Netherlands. At the same time, heresy was regarded in France as well as in Spain as a danger and a reproach; and since the two powers were at this moment on friendly terms, it is not improbable that joint steps against heresy were considered. Perhaps the truth is that Spain suggested massacre and that France hedged. See M. Hume in *Camb. Mod. Hist.*, vol. iii (1904), p. 489, and in *Philip II*, p. 125; Merriman, *Philip the Prudent*, pp. 262-264; J.B. Black, *Elizabeth*, p. 128 n.; Walsh, *Philip II*, pp. 535 f. (Cabrera, believed it); J.E. Neale, *Age of Catherine de Medici* (1943), pp. 68 f., 80 f. (sceptical).

you to carry out my orders. Let all prisoners be put to death, and suffer them no longer to escape through the neglect, weakness, and bad faith of the judges. If any are too timid to execute the edicts, I will replace them by men who have more heart and zeal".[29] The publication of the king's decision heated the popular resentment to boiling point;[30] and the proceedings of the Inquisition encountered ever greater wrath and opposition. So threatening were the signs of national discontent that Margaret made yet another desperate attempt to induce Philip to retract; and in the summer of 1566 he expressed his willingness to change the mode of punishment, so long as some equally efficacious mode were substituted: he shrank, he said, from the effusion of blood, and announced his intention of shortly visiting the country in person.

Everything goes to show that he had no real intention of abating his severity: nevertheless, the lull in the persecution and the issue by Margaret of an edict of so-called "Moderation" served greatly to encourage the Protestant interest. Refugees returned from abroad; and enormous crowds gathered to hear free public preaching, at first in country-parts, and then in towns and cities. The Regent's edict of July 3, 1566, against these meetings remained a dead letter.

In response to a deputation, and in reply to another alarming report from Margaret, Philip wrote to her again in August 1566, consenting to abolish the Inquisition, and promising a large measure of toleration and pardon, so far as this was consistent with the maintenance of Catholicism. But his contemporary letters to his ambassador in Rome and a formal declaration made by himself before a notary and the Duke of Alva clearly show

---

29. Quoted by Lord *Acton, Lectures on Modern History* (1906), p. 144. M. Poullet ("De la répression", etc., pp. 922-926) gives fuller details of these negotiations. Walsh relates (*Philip II*, p. 397; cf. p. 401 top) that Philip told Egmont "that he would make no compromise with any imitation or perversion of *Christianity*. The Catholic Church was the one Church of Christ... and Philip earnestly told Egmont that he would rather die than betray it; Indeed, he would rather lose a hundred thousand lives, if he had them, than tolerate any compromise that sought by indirect methods *to eliminate Christ* from his kingdoms" (italics mine). Egmont had carried back with him to Brussels a letter refusing concessions, but allowing Margaret to consult with bishops and theologians as to the best methods of procedure. Their proposals, suggesting certain very minor modifications in the severity of the treatment of heretics, were submitted by the Regent to Philip, who rejected them in the letter quoted in the text. A Venetian report quoted by Von Ranke, *History of the Popes* (Eng. tr. 1847-51), vol. i, p. 405, to the effect that 36,000 persons were killed in the seven or more years preceding 1562, is an evident exaggeration.
30. Cf. Geyl, *Revolt*, etc., pp. 75, 78, 83 f., 86-89.

that he was doing this as a mere blind, until he should feel himself strong enough to crush heresy by sheer force, as he had now determined to do. Wild outbreaks of iconoclasm on the part of the mob, which led to the destruction of innumerable works of art in the cathedrals and churches throughout the country (August 14 to 22), helped to precipitate the crisis, as well as to cause some reaction in the government's favour. The Regent, however, still found herself compelled to dissemble, and issued an edict of qualified toleration on August 23. In a few places the government suppressed disorder with bloodshed – a Calvinist force was cut to pieces outside Antwerp in March 1567, and in April Valenciennes had to surrender, and a savage vengeance was inflicted by the execution of many hundreds of its inhabitants.

But still darker days were imminent. In January 1567 Philip had commissioned the Duke of Alva to proceed with an army to the Netherlands, and to crush sedition and heresy by force. Alva crossed the border in August, and for over six years did his best to serve his master's cause. His proceedings were of such a character as to call for detailed discussion in a separate chapter of this treatise. Suffice it to say here that they exhibited with special clarity the hideous cruelty of the Spanish policy.[31]

Having already agreed with Alva that he was to inflict sentence of death on Count Egmont for having lent some little support to the protests against Margaret's government, Philip – a fortnight before Alva left Madrid – wrote Egmont a flattering letter, expressing gratification at his loyalty. Remonstrances were addressed to Philip

---

31. It is at this point that reference must he made to the statement emanating from the Dutch historian Bor (early in the seventeenth century) to the effect that on February 16, 1568, the Holy Office of the Inquisition in Spain solemnly sentenced all the inhabitants of the Netherlands (with a few specified exceptions) to death for treason and heresy, and that ten days later Philip confirmed the sentence, and ordered it to be put into execution. Bor purports to give the text of this decree. The allegation was repeated by certain subsequent Dutch historians, was accepted on their authority by Motley (*Dutch Republic* [ed. 1874], p. 364 b: cf. *United Netherlands* [ed. 1875-76], vol. i, p. 289, vol. iii, p. 506), and is believingly quoted by Lecky (*Rationalism in Europe* [ed. 1872], vol. ii, p. 33, n. 2) – and in 1928 by myself (*Catholicism and Christianity: a Vindication of Progressive Protestantism* [1928], p. 569). M. Poullet, however, without impeaching the bona fides of Bor, confidently pronounces the statement apocryphal ("De la répression", etc., pp. 935 f.). While its *spirit* shows some kinship with that of Alva, in whose governorship of the Netherlands it is placed, one must admit that it would have been legally quite inconsistent with inquisitorial procedure. The best modern authorities omit it as fabricated propaganda; and I accept their verdict.

by the Emperor, firstly, with a view to saving the lives of Egmont and Hoorn, and later, protesting against the cruelties of Alva:[32] but in both cases without effect. The Baron of Montigny, the brother of the Count of Hoorn, had gone to Spain in June 1566 to plead with Philip for some relaxation on the king's part in deference to the needs and rights of the Netherlands. He was courteously listened to, but was prevented, despite his repeated requests, from returning. In August 1567, shortly after Alva's arrival in the Netherlands, Montigny was imprisoned at Segovia. The news of his brother's execution in June 1568 was secretly conveyed to him. In March 1570 he was sentenced to death by Alva at Brussels, after a long-drawn-out trial in his absence. By Philip's contrivance, he was removed to Simancas, and secretly strangled in his prison there in October, and a lying pretence put up that he had died of fever. His poor mother had besought Philip's new bride, Anne of Austria, on her journey through Brussels, to intercede for Montigny's life; and Anne promised to do so. But she reached Spain too late to be of any use. Philip had got wind of her promise, and arranged for Montigny to be murdered before she arrived. Neither Mr. Trevor Davies nor Dr. Walsh apparently sees anything to criticize in this dark deed. The former simply says (p. 161) that Montigny was "secretly executed". The latter, who gives the facts in some detail (pp. 453-456), clearly regards Montigny as guilty of treason, and remarks that Philip "did not consider publicity a requisite of trial or execution": he apparently sees nothing wrong in the needless public lie.

We can pass rapidly over Philip's treatment of the Netherlands during the remaining years of his reign. The arrival of Alva's successor Requesens late in 1573 inaugurated a series of efforts to induce William of Orange to abandon his resistance; but as he insisted on religious freedom, on the restoration of ancient liberties, and on the withdrawal of all Spaniards, the struggle continued. Orders were repeatedly sent to Requesens from Madrid to get William and his brother Louis murdered. In June 1574 a general pardon was offered by Philip's authority to his rebellious subjects, on condition of their returning to the bosom of the Church. The following year there were peace-negotiations at Breda,

---

32. Mr. Trevor Davies (*Golden Century*, p. 162) discounts these protests on the ground that the Emperor was "a crypto-Protestant and a man of exceptional humanity"!

Philip going so far as to allow an interval of time for non-Catholics to sell their property and leave the country. Requesens died in March 1576; and Don John (Philip's illegitimate brother) succeeded him, with instructions to do his best for the conservation of the true religion. On the eve of his arrival, the whole of the Netherland-states concluded an agreement, known as "The Pacification of Ghent", whereby all bound themselves to unite to drive the Spanish soldiery from the land. William of Orange was recognized as governor of Holland and Zealand, the settlement of the religious question was left over to be dealt with by the States-General after the war, and meanwhile all the placards against heretics were suspended. In February 1577, large concessions were granted by Don John in "The Perpetual Edict"; and these received the subsequent approval of the king. Convinced of the insincerity of the government's intentions, William of Orange did his best to prevent the agreement being accepted. By dint, however, of playing on the Catholic susceptibilities of the southern states and cities, and of exploiting his personal charm, Don John managed to detach several of them from their recent compact with Holland and Zealand. In January 1578, with the help of young Alexander Farnese, son of the late regent Margaret, he succeeded in completely defeating the army of the States at Gemblours. A period of disunion and confusion followed. Philip continued to insist on the maintenance of the royal supremacy and of the Catholic religion as upheld by his father; and such of the States as still supported Holland and Zealand continued intransigent.

Don John died in October 1578, after vainly appealing to Philip for help and instructions. He was succeeded by Alexander Farnese, Prince (and later Duke) of Parma. A general and politician of consummate ability, and utterly loyal to Philip, Farnese succeeded by force, threats, and bribery in eventually regaining the whole of the southern States for Spain. These provinces were still for the most part strongly Catholic, and thus very lukewarm towards William of Orange's constant plea for reciprocal toleration for Catholics and Protestants alike – especially as the Calvinists in their midst had begun to act very violently. Hence they preferred, or were induced to prefer, the Spanish yoke to the toleration of heresy in their midst. In

January 1579, a number of the southern States united themselves in "the League of Arras" for the defence of Catholicism under the control of Farnese. Protestant inhabitants resident in them were allowed two years in which to become Catholics or decamp. The League of Arras was answered the same month by the formation of "the Union of Utrecht" on the part of the main Protestant provinces of the north.

Among the chief military events was the storming of Maestricht by the Spanish troops in June 1579, in which the bulk of the population were ruthlessly massacred – the women, who had co-operated in the defence, being slaughtered with particular barbarity. In this case, Philip himself deprecated the severity used.[33] In 1581, Holland, Zealand, Utrecht, Gelderland, and even Flanders and Brabant, solemnly abjured their allegiance to Philip on account of his tyranny and misrule: William of Orange provisionally accepted the title of Count of Holland and Zealand; and two years later it was decided to make it hereditary.

After Philip had in 1584, succeeded in compassing the assassination of William of Orange (a deed for which the canons of 's Hertogenbosch performed a solemn Te Deum of thanksgiving[34]), the strife dragged on. Farnese managed eventually to detach the whole of Brabant and Flanders from their alliance with Holland. He captured Antwerp in 1585, and Sluys in 1587. Philip thought he had been too lenient in his treatment of the heretics in Antwerp: they had been allowed *four* years in which either to conform or depart. The rising military power of William of Orange's son Maurice turned the tide of success; and when Farnese died in 1592, though his successor was under orders to continue the campaign, and moreover to hang all prisoners taken, the northern Netherlanders soon saw their territory free from the presence of Spanish garrisons. The Spaniards were, however, in complete control of the southern provinces; and although the fiercer forms of persecution had died down (largely owing of course to the Protestant minorities

---

33. Walsh, *Philip II*, pp. 616, 618, 620.
34. On the rejoicings of Granvelle, Farnese, and other Catholics over the murder of William, see R. Putnam, *William the Silent*, etc. (ed. 1898), vol. ii, pp. 415 f., *William the Silent*, etc. (1911), pp. 471 f.

having emigrated), there was a horrible exhibition of it in 1597 when, on the demand of the Jesuits, the humble woman-servant Anna van den Hove was buried alive at Brussels (see above, p. 61). Maurice's victories, however, continued; and when Philip II died in 1598, though the struggle was still raging and the southern provinces were firmly under Spanish control, the independence of the north was virtually secure.[35]

Such in brief outline is the story of the treatment of the Netherlands by Philip II. We have yet to take account of the exceptionally sanguinary proceedings of the Duke of Alva, sent into the country by Philip, and acting under his instructions and on the whole with his approval. But even without adding in Alva's enormities – if Philip's administration does not fully deserve to be described as a bloody tyranny, I know no administration in history to which such terms could be justly applied – nay, I cannot see how we can continue to use English words intelligibly.[36]

Its keynote was the steady and persistent denial by the king of one of the elemental rights of man as a moral and spiritual being – the right, namely, of believing in and worshipping God according to the dictates of his own conscience, and not at the authoritative bidding of a third party. Philip might at one stage promise to allow such rights to Protestantism in the Netherlands as were allowed in Germany: but that was only a temporary aberration. At another stage he might grant Protestants an interval in which to leave the country; and so on. But these grudging concessions were not toleration in any real sense: moreover, Philip was so given to temporizing and lying that even these favours were by no means reliable offers. He never really meant to concede to his subjects what Orange never ceased to demand – liberty to believe and worship as they felt they ought, and to preach the Gospel as they understood it. "Let them well understand", said Philip in 1590, "that since others, who live in error, hold

---

35. Cf. Geyl, *Revolt*, etc., p. 236: "... they had escaped from the stifling embrace of the foreign monarchy with its bureaucratic and aristocratic régime".
36. The fact that Philip desired to give his subjects in the Netherlands a unified or centralized administration does not, to my mind, constitute a justification of his measures. The question as to whether or not we can agree with Dr. Walsh (*Philip II*, p. 707) that it is unhistorical to speak of Philip's "failure" in the Netherlands is purely a question of terms.

the opinion that vassals are to conform to the religion of their master, it is insufferable that it should be proposed to me that my vassals should have a different religion from mine – and that too being the true religion, proved by so many testimonies and miracles, while all others are deception".[37] If it be urged, as assuredly it will be by some, that virtually all parties in those days regarded only one form of public worship as consistent with public order, I reply that that fact does not disprove the tyrannical character of the government.

So much for the tyranny: now for the bloodiness. After summarizing the history as we have done, we hardly need to adduce further proof on this point. How came it to be even plausible for William of Orange to estimate that, from Charles's first placards down to 1566 (i.e., *before* the war and the rule of Alva began) 50,000 persons had been killed or exiled for heresy in the Low Countries? From the Regent's warning to Charles in 1533 against depopulating the provinces (see above, p. 72), what conclusion does the reader think he ought to draw as to the mortality under Charles's equally conscientious son? Add to that the deeds done on Philip's behalf by Alva – the latter's reported boast that, besides those slain in and after battle, he had had 18,000 persons executed?[38] "At one time, in his despair, Philip had resolved either to drown or burn all Holland".[39] If these facts do not justify us in calling Philip's rule in the Netherlands "bloody", again I can see no purpose to be served by the use of language. It is true that Philip deprecated the massacre of the women-defenders of Maestricht, and that there was some lull in the burning and hanging after Alva's departure in 1573. But what does that amount to, when set against the rest of the evidence?[40]

---

37. Quoted by Motley, *United Netherlands* (ed. 1875-76), vol. iii, p. 35. Cf. the similar words written by Philip in 1585 and quoted by Walsh (*Philip II*, p. 623), to the effect that he had waged a long war in Flanders "until at last I should reduce them to the obedience of the Holy Catholic Roman Church, and to my obedience, as I trust in God I shall do, it being His cause".
38. This number, however, must not be too confidently pressed as factually true. See below, pp. 96 f., n. 2.
39. M. Hume in *Camb. Mod. Hist.*, vol. iii (1904), p. 498. Cf. his *Philip II*, p. 169.
40. There seems to me therefore an element of perversity in Dr. Mandell Creighton's suggestion (published in *The Quarterly Review*, vol. cciii, p. 45 [July 1905]), that the reason why the Spanish attempt to recover the Netherlands is regarded as an outrage against the cause of liberty is because it was unsuccessful.

Not only was Philip's rule over the Netherlands tyrannical and bloody; it was also perfidious. It involved the repeated violation of the oath, which he had twice taken, to observe faithfully the ancient charters which guaranteed to the various provinces within his Flemish and Dutch territories certain local liberties and privileges.[41]

The Catholic scholar, M. Poullet, has the candour to admit that the stringent regulations Philip issued in October 1565 were needlessly and blamably severe.[42] Not so Dr. Walsh. He is fairly frank in describing the revolting facts; he mentions (p. 347) that Philip himself knew that the Inquisition at work in the Netherlands was "more pitiless" than the Spanish; he hints that Philip regretted that he had alienated the inhabitants of the Netherlands, and says he profited by this experience in dealing with Portugal (pp. 604, 607 f.). But he sees nothing to apologize for. Philip was dealing with the enemies of Christ, and it was not therefore an occasion for pity. The cause of Catholicism in Europe was at stake; and the Netherlands were in some sense the strategic centre of the struggle (pp. 703 f., 708, 724). We shall note later his admiration for the Duke of Alva. But of the years before that hero's arrival on the scene, Dr. Walsh says: "At no time, during the eight years after his return to Spain, could Philip's policy in the Low Countries be called tyrannical. He made one concession after another.... He went to great pains to avoid any undue interference with the lives and privileges of his subjects. As regards religion, he insisted that the Catholic Faith must not be destroyed. What else could a man say of a truth he believed to be divinely ordained?" (p. 352;

---

41. Cf. T.M. Lindsay, *Reformation*, vol. ii, pp. 245 f.; Merriman, *The Emperor*, p. 396; J.B. Black, *Elizabeth*, p. 87 ("... their insistence upon old liberties, charters, and immunities, dating back to Burgundian times, ran counter to the royal conception of monarchical authority;..."): also Motley, *United Netherlands* (ed. 1875-76), vol. iii, pp. 462 f. ("As if the most Catholic and most absolute monarch that ever breathed could be tied down by the cobwebs of constitutional or treaty stipulations;..."). See above, pp. 64 n. 1, 75 f., and below, pp. 128, 189.

42. E. Poullet, "De la répression", etc., p. 926: "Ces résolutions royales étaient profondément regrettables et inexécutables dans l'occurrence. Elles étaient regrettables, non parce qu'une résolution contraire eût désarmé le mouvement révolutionnaire qui se préparait, mais parce qu'en soi l'acceptation des idées de la junte eût consacré un progrès réel dans lé sens de l'humanité et de la saine justice distributive, sans que le gouvernement eût l'air de plier devant l'assaut de l'hérésie et favorisât son élan par un semblant de recul". Even Catholic supporters of the government did not believe that it was possible any longer to maintain "les placards anciens dont il était impossible de nier la rigueur excessive".

cf. p. 341). We have seen what Philip regarded as necessary to the non-destruction of Catholicism, and also what his "concessions" really amounted to. As for the Anabaptists, according to Dr. Walsh they deserved all they got. Philip tolerated them only so long as he lacked force to suppress them. "It is unhistorical to pretend that he was a tyrant in any sense in which a man of the sixteenth century (with no heretical axe to grind) would have understood the word" (p. 354). There is no doubt that Philip honestly regarded Catholicism as divinely true, and that he shared the widespread view of the time that a ruler had the right to dictate the religious beliefs and practices of his subjects. But if this is all there is to be said, then we must insist that nothing has been said which calls for any modification of our judgment that his rule was a bloody tyranny.

Although the title of this book does not commit us to pursuing our subject beyond the year 1598, when Philip II died, it may be worth while to take a glance at the next two reigns, as their events will in some small way help to elucidate those that occurred during the preceding period.

Philip III, the son of Philip II and Anne, daughter of the Emperor Maximilian II, was like his father personally devout; but, being disinclined towards politics, he left the whole administration of public affairs to the Duke of Lerma, and gave himself up to the occupations of court-life, the pleasures of the table, and the exercises of religion. Under Lerma, the government was carried on much as before – there was the same mischievous intriguing in the affairs of foreign countries, and the same gross financial inequalities and mismanagement (general poverty alongside enormously wealthy ecclesiastics, officials, and courtiers). A new feature was supplied by the grasping venality of Lerma himself, who – along with his subordinates – had to be heavily bribed for the performance of every service required of them, who shamelessly sold the numerous appointments in his gift, and by such means accumulated a vast fortune. He controlled the public affairs with despotic power, in the face of widespread popular discontent. In 1609-10 the Spanish government expelled from the country the whole Moorish population (variously estimated by competent investigators at 150,000 and 500,000).

It was an act of unspeakable folly, injustice, and cruelty – supposed to be necessitated by the danger of revolt which the previous oppressive treatment meted out to the race had rendered possible. Lerma is said to have received 250,000 ducats from the confiscated Moorish property.

Nevertheless, the "Golden Century" of Spain does not terminate till 1621: and Mr. Trevor Davies is accordingly at some pains to show that the reign of Philip III does not altogether belie the flattering title. In regard to the Moors, he admits that the oppression which had made them a danger was wrong: but he observes (p. 253) that this "was not the especial fault of Lerma or Philip III"; and he holds that, in view of the situation which had in point of fact developed, "Lerma took the best possible course". He is quite frank (p. 233) about the government's financial misdeeds: nevertheless he pleads mitigating considerations: "... it should be remembered that everywhere at this time those who served the king were justified by the custom of the day in looking for large rewards. Also, splendid spectacles, games, and stage plays were the fashion of the day among great nobles and kings all over Europe. But for the serious economic decline of the country during his period of power Lerma would probably have escaped with a much milder judgement from posterity" (p. 233). In accepting 250,000 ducats from the property of the ejected Moors, says Mr. Trevor Davies (p. 253), "Lerma was merely following the usual corrupt practice of the age, in which few royal ministers – from Thomas Cromwell to Mazarin – failed to enrich themselves during their period of office". There are clearly more senses than one in which a period of history can be described as "golden".

Under Philip II's final instructions, his territories in the Low Countries were to be erected into an independent principality under the rule of his nephew the Archduke Albert and his wife Isabel (Philip's eldest daughter). The southern provinces welcomed these two "Archdukes"; and as the northern provinces were still in revolt, not only over the issue of religious liberty,, but also over the freedom of their flourishing foreign trade, overtures of peace were made. Since, however, the Archdukes were firmly opposed to any concession being made on either of these issues, the war went on. Maurice defeated the Archduke at

Nieuport, and captured Sluys: the Spaniards, after a terrific siege, took Ostend. A Spanish fleet was destroyed by the Dutch off Gibraltar: and the Spanish admiral's papers were found to contain secret instructions signed by the King, and enjoining the ruthless persecution of the Netherland Protestants and any other opponents. As it became increasingly clear that the United Provinces could not be reduced by the diminishing power of Spain, peace-feelers and negotiations were tried again. These were long rendered fruitless by the obstinate insistence of the Spanish government on the restoration of Catholicism, or at least freedom for Catholic public worship, and on the abandonment of the Dutch foreign trade, and by its fraudulently disguised intention to reassert Spain's sovereignty over the northern provinces. At last, in 1609, a truce for twelve years was actually agreed upon. The United Provinces were recognized as free states, over which the Archdukes made no pretentions to any authority: the Provinces gave no undertaking to tolerate public Catholic worship; and they secured from Philip III in a secret treaty a promise that their foreign trade should not be impeded.

A period of comparative quiescence in the religious struggle now ensued. But in the Netherlands the truce was not destined to eventuate in a permanent peace. In 1618 the Thirty Years' War broke out: in 1619 the imperial throne was mounted by the strongly Catholic Ferdinand II: in 1621 Philip IV, the new King of Spain, instigated thereto by the Pope, renewed the war against the Dutch. The contest was finally concluded by the Peace of Munster in 1648, when the severance of the United Provinces from the Spanish Netherlands was recognized as permanent. It was this same Philip IV whose ambassador was requested by Oliver Cromwell in 1654 to secure for British seamen and traders visiting Spanish ports liberty of religious worship there, and was met by the reply that such a request was equivalent to asking for the king's two eyes.[43]

Before we leave the discussion of the treatment meted out to the Netherlands by the Spanish monarchy, we must take note of one or

---

43. Carlyle, *Letters and Speeches* (ed. Lomas), vol. ii, pp. 514 f.; John Buchan, *Cromwell*, p. 445 (cf. p. 493: "… the intolerant Catholicism which embarrassed English traders in every port of her [Spain's] empire").

two of its other attendant features. The peculiar character and behaviour of the Spanish soldiery calls for special comment. Of their military prowess and efficiency there could be no doubt. The Spanish infantry had the reputation of being the most formidable in Europe. There were moreover occasions on which their most warlike commanders could show personal kindness and courtesy in a striking fashion. But their military glory did not relieve them of their share of the dislike with which in the Low Countries Spaniards generally were regarded. On the contrary, all the more on account of their invincibility and ruthlessness, they were hated everywhere except in Spain itself. They had committed atrocious barbarities at the sack of Tunis in 1535. Nowhere were they more detested than in the Netherlands.[44] We may recall that, at the commencement of Philip's reign, the demand for the removal of the Spanish troops from the country was vigorously pressed, and at length became so insistent that it had to be conceded. With the arrival of Alva in 1567, the provinces were once again subjected to the tender mercies of these gallant warriors. They doubtless took their part in the mass-executions which now became the order of the day – as at Valenciennes in January 1568, at Mons from December 1572 to August 1573, at Haarlem in July 1573, and at numerous other places. After defeating Louis of Nassau at Jemmingen in 1568, Alva devastated the country as far as Groningen; and the next year he quartered a regiment of Spanish soldiers at Utrecht because of that city's refusal to pay his exorbitant tax. In the course of the war, the following towns were captured and sacked, and the garrisons and inhabitants wholly or in large numbers massacred or executed: Mechlin, Zutphen, and Naarden in 1572, Haarlem in 1573, Oudewater and Bommenede in 1575, Maestricht (where the Spanish soldiers fought behind the bodies of Dutch women) and Antwerp in 1576, Maestricht again in 1579 (see above, p. 82), Neusz in 1586, Lagny and Corbeil in 1590, Dourlens in 1595, and the forts outside Ostend in 1603.

One of the most terrible of these murderous stormings was the sack of Antwerp in November 1576. It was committed entirely without provocation, by mixed bodies of troops in the

---

44. Cf. Geyl, *Revolt*, etc., p. 70.

Spanish service who were mutinying and thirsting for loot, because they had not received their wages. Such little opposition as could be offered was speedily overcome; and the prosperous city became for three days a scene of the most diabolical pillage, rape, and slaughter.[45] The deed was not done by order of the Spanish government or with its approval – for the troops were in a state of mutiny: but it serves none the less to illustrate the quality of the soldiers with whom the Netherland rebels had to cope.

Even when the Spanish troops had lost their loyalty to Philip, they did not lose their devotion as Catholic Christians. It was their regular custom, before going into action, to kneel in prayer before banners depicting the crucified Saviour of mankind and His mother Mary, and to pray to them for victory. The name of St. James, their patron saint, was their normal war-cry.[46] It would never occur to them to doubt whether the cause for which or the sanguinary method in which they intended to fight were congruous with the spirit of the Prince of Peace or were such as God could approve. So blinded by this Catholic habit were they to the moral demands of their Christian faith, that their customary devotions were performed when they

---

45. Dr. Walsh says (*Philip II*, p. 560): "One of the most striking facts about the Spanish Fury at Antwerp on November fourth, 1576, was that it seems to have been caused chiefly by Germans, a great many of whom were Protestants". This strikes me as a singularly lame attempt to shield the Spanish army from obloquy. The fact is that, when the city had been once broken into, certain of the German and Walloon troops who had been sent to defend it abandoned the defence and joined in the pillage. Whether they were to any extent nominal Protestants or not is quite uncertain: and in any case, as Dr. Walsh's own narrative (pp. 551, 559, 561 f.) makes clean the bulk of the assailants were Spaniards. He uses the strange phrase: "They... *succeeded* in butchering thousands and driving seven thousand others to death in flames or water.... Thus" he adds, "was the sacking of the fine old churches in Antwerp in 1566 avenged" (p. 562: italics mine).

   Mr. Trevor Davies (*Golden Century*, p. 183) attempts no palliation, but confines himself to briefly recording the incident. He calls it a "bloody day".

   Miss Wedgwood quotes an eye-witness as having written of the sackers: "... they slew great numbers of young children... and as great respect they had to the church and churchyard as the butcher hath to his shambles..." (*William the Silent*, p. 166).

46. Dr. Walsh has many allusions to this phase of Catholic religiosity (*Philip II*, pp. 494, 515 f., 520-522, 525, 529, 561 f., 657). One quotation must suffice. Speaking of the battle of Lepanto (1571), he says: "Hoarse shouts of victory burst from the Christians on the *Real*, as they brushed the disheartened Turks into the sea and hoisted the banner of Christ Crucified to the enemy masthead. There was not a single hole in this flag, though the spars and masts were riddled,..." (p. 522). But Dr. Walsh does recognize (p. 531) that force was limited to the *negative* task of defending the church from destruction.

were on the point of launching a murderous assault on an unoffending city like Antwerp for the sole purpose of gorging themselves with its plunder.[47]

The soldiers of Farnese barbarously mutilated the persons – not soldiers only, but men, women, and children – on board the vessels which brought provisions into Antwerp during the siege of 1584-85 and which they "succeeded" in capturing.

In the autumn of 1598 and the following winter – i.e., at about the time when Philip on his death-bed was declaring that never in his whole life had he wittingly wronged a single human being – a Spanish army, under the command of Francesco de Mendoza, admiral of Aragon, was inflicting on the unoffending inhabitants of the neutral states of Münster, Cleves, and Berg, the most appalling cruelties. He "converted those peaceful provinces into a hell. No outrage which even a Spanish army could inflict was spared the miserable inhabitants. Cities and villages were sacked and burned, the whole country was placed under the law of blackmail. The places of worship, mainly Protestant, were all converted at a blow of the sword into Catholic churches. Men were hanged, butchered, tossed in sport from the tops of steeples, burnt, and buried alive. Women of every rank were subjected by thousands to outrage too foul and too cruel for any but fiends and Spanish soldiers to imagine".[48]

In the campaign between Maurice of Nassau and the Spanish Archduke in 1600, it was the Archduke's firm intention to put all his prisoners to death except Maurice himself and his brother. He butchered the garrisons of forts to which he had granted favourable terms of surrender. He laid it down that there was no military law at sea, and that all persons on board captured enemy merchant-vessels, including even sick and wounded soldiers, should be hanged. In the execution of these barbarous orders, drowning and burning were also practised.

But we must give even fiends their due. It is only fair to these disciplined brigands who brought misery and death wherever they went, to mention the fact that, thanks to the financial incompetence of their royal master, and despite the piteous and

---

47. Dr. Walsh notes this fact; and – so far from feeling upset – he seems quite pleased about it. He calls the Spanish soldiers "those furious crusaders who could mingle religion with war only as those whose ancestors had fought for a thousand years against the Moslems could do" (*Philip II*, p. 562).
48. Motley, *United Netherlands* (ed. 1875-76), vol. iii, p. 548: cf. p. 549, and vol. iv, p. 13.

urgent appeals of their general, the Spanish troops under Farnese were kept chronically short of pay. King Philip, who always had plenty of money for furnishing his palaces, maintaining plots and intrigues in foreign countries, and generously subsidizing the Guises, somehow found himself too poor to pay regular wages to those who bore the heat and burden of the day for him in the Netherlands. The consequence was that they were often in a condition bordering on destitution and mutiny: thus they were not only exposed to disciplinary penalties, but had at least a colourable excuse for discarding control and fending for themselves.

One last fact calls for notice before we close this chapter. It is the dreadful desolation which beset all the territories recovered by the Spaniards in the course of the struggle, and the starvation and misery to which the inhabitants of every class were reduced. "Thousands of [Belgium's] inhabitants, and those the most enterprising and intelligent, fled from the Inquisition, and made their homes in the Dutch republic or in England. All commerce and industry was at a standstill; grass grew in the streets of Bruges and Ghent; and the trade of Antwerp was transferred to Amsterdam".[49] In these respects, as well as in their ecclesiastical complexion, the Catholic provinces formed a striking contrast to the well-governed, diligent, and prosperous regions which refused allegiance to Spain, in so far as they could be protected from the blighting presence of the Spanish armies. It was not until after the truce of 1609 that the Archdukes were able to effect some material restoration of prosperity in their exclusively Catholic domains.

---

49. G. Edmundson in *Encyc. Brit.*, vol. iii (1910), p. 673 b: cf. Pirenne, *Belgique*, vol. iv (1911), pp. 407 ff.

Chapter Five

The Duke of Alva in the Netherlands

The proceedings of the Duke of Alva during the six years (1567-73) he was exercising supreme authority in the Netherlands as Philip's representative do not display or illustrate any principle of government essentially or ethically different from what we have already observed as the policy normally favoured and pursued by the king (unless we are to reckon Alva's "Council of Troubles"[1] as constituting an exception). But being more thorough and extreme than the severities exercised by his predecessors and successors, these proceedings of his reveal with a specially unmistakable clarity the truly diabolical character of that policy. It is for this reason that they deserve to be treated in a separate chapter.

At the time when he entered on his sanguinary task of reducing the Netherlands to submission, the Duke of Alva was already an experienced general and diplomatist of sixty years of age. He had rendered distinguished service under Charles V; but the Emperor came to suspect his ambition. He warned Philip to beware of getting too much under Alva's influence or letting Alva tempt him with women, and urged him to employ the Duke predominantly in foreign affairs and in war.[2] Alva's feelings towards the Protestants and those who sought to shield them from persecution may be inferred from his reply to Philip, when the latter asked him in 1563 for his advice in regard to a letter of protest sent to the king by Orange, Egmont, and Hoorn. "Every time", said Alva, "that I see the missives of these three Senors, they fill me with rage, so that, unless I exerted the utmost control over myself, my opinions would appear to your Majesty those of one frenzied". He therefore counselled severe chastisement; but as it was impossible to get the three noblemen beheaded at once, the king had better dissemble for a time, and divide their forces by gaining over Egmont.[3]

---

1. See below, pp. 95 f.
2. Armstrong, *Charles V* (ed. 1910), vol. ii, pp. 81, 174 f.
3. G. Edmundson in *Camb. Mod. Hist.*, vol. iii (1904), p. 195: cf. Walsh, *Philip II*, p. 359. For the possibility that Alva proposed a massacre of the Protestants to Catherine de' Medici at Bayonne in 1565, see above, p. 77, n. 1.

Philip's decision to send Alva to the Netherlands with an army, for the purpose of forcibly subduing and chastising heresy and opposition, was taken at least as early as December 1566: but, as we know from his correspondence (see above, pp. 78 f.), he had before that date decided to crush resistance as soon as he was able, and his concessions in the matter of persecution were, as he confidentially admitted at the time, pure temporizations. The violent outburst of iconoclasm in the Low Countries in August 1566 undoubtedly confirmed the king's decision to employ armed force, and hastened the execution of it. The method Alva was to pursue was clearly settled beforehand: it embraced the execution of the leading nobles who had pressed for a milder regime, and the lavish use of the death-penalty for heretics and malcontents of the rank and file. Vengeance was to be freely meted out, not only against those who were unsound in the faith, but also against all persons – Catholic or Protestant, clerical or lay – who had pressed for the retention and observance of local and time-honoured liberties.[4] Both Philip and Alva were anxious to have it believed that their prime object was not the suppression of heresy, but the suppression of political rebellion. There was an element of accuracy in this plea; but it was at best a half-truth, for the destruction of liberty was intended to be but the prelude to the destruction of heresy. On leaving Spain, Alva informed the papal nuncio that it was needful to give this political colour to his measures, in order to keep Germany and England quiet.[5]

Alva left Spain for Italy in April 1567, and assembled there a well-equipped army of over 10,000 men. With these he left Italy for the north in June; and in August he reached the frontier of the Netherlands, with his numbers swollen by the accession of some German mercenaries. The army was accompanied by a

---
4. Geyl, *Revolt*, etc., p. 100.
5. See the evidence quoted by M. Poullet, "De la répression", etc., (pp. 934 f.): "… Au moment de son départ d'Espagne, le duc d'Albe expliqua franchement au nonce du Pape que, selon lui, il convenait de conduire les affaires des Pays-Bas 'de façon qu'il ne paraisse pas que l'entreprise soit faite dans l'intérêt de la religion et contre les hérétiques, et qu'on puisse dire qu'elle a pour but la cause de l'Etat et est dirigée contre les rebelles; c'est le moyen (ajoutait-il) d'empêcher les Allemands, les Anglais et d'autres de remuer sous prétexte de défendre leur foi'". On p. 919, Poullet states that the heretical movement became more and more political, and that political offenders used to declare themselves heretics in order to transform themselves into martyrs.

troop of 2,000 Italian courtesans, officially recognized by the general, and properly organized in battalions and companies.

It is no part of my task to narrate in full the story of Alva's six years in the unhappy country to which Philip II had sent him. It will suffice to summarize briefly, the relevant aspects of it. Put roughly, his policy was ruthless butchery both in peace and war, thinly disguised in peace-time by a veneer of judicial form.

One of his earliest measures was to arrest Counts Egmont and Hoorn (see above, pp. 79 f). In November they were questioned in their prisons; in January 1568 they were furnished with written accusations, which they had to answer at once without legal or other assistance; in May the case against them was declared closed; and early in June they were publicly beheaded in Brussels. Their deaths had been decided upon before Alva entered the country (as had also the early execution of William of Orange); their arrests were carried out only after their suspicions had been allayed by a lavish show of hospitality and kindness on Alva's part; the process against them was the merest travesty of justice; and their execution caused for a time a paralysis of terror, and for ever after an undying hatred. The way in which Count Hoorn's brother, the Baron of Montigny, was secretly done to death in Spain by the joint agency of Alva and Philip has already been recounted.

Alva had hardly been in the Netherlands a month before he set up at Brussels a special tribunal to exercise under his presidency exclusive jurisdiction on such persons as should be reported to it on suspicion or charge of heresy or disaffection. The official title of this court was "the Council of Troubles" or "Tumults": but it soon acquired and permanently kept the popular name of "The Council of Blood". Its existence and constitution depended on the despotic will of Alva himself: it was otherwise destitute of any fragment of legality, and it violently overrode the long-standing privileges of the country. We are not concerned with the personnel of this body: but it is worth mentioning that, of the whole court of twelve, only two members had the privilege of voting, and they were both Spaniards;[6] and all decisions were subject to Alva's irresponsible assent or veto.

---

6. One of these, Juan Vargas, was grossly cruel, and keenly enjoyed administering torture (C.V. Wedgwood, *William the Silent*, p. 100).

It is hardly possible to exaggerate the tyranny and cruelty with which this body did its work. The slightest action or omission to act, which was likely to have displeased the king of Spain, or to have embarrassed his representatives, was construed by the court as high treason; and the penalty for it was immediate death. The country was scoured by Alva's agents to collect the names of and evidence against any persons (women and children as well as men) who might be proceeded against: cartloads of information poured in, and very large numbers of accused persons were arraigned. Wealth added to the victim's danger, since severe confiscations accompanied the death-sentences, and the Duke had promised his royal master a handsome income from this source. Numbers of Catholics, as well as Protestants, fled from the country, though Alva's measures of prevention made escape increasingly difficult.

The evidence thus accumulated was examined in the most summary fashion. So intense was the thirst for blood that the Council soon had recourse to the method of condemning the accused in batches, instead of singly. Within the first three months of its existence, it had condemned 1,800 persons to death. The records speak of forty-six inhabitants of Mechlin, eighty-four inhabitants of Valenciennes, and groups of thirty-five and ninety-five persons from different places being condemned together on four different occasions. At Shrovetide, as Alva wrote callously to Philip, he ordered the execution of 1,500 persons who had been seized in their beds. Immediately after Easter, another 800 were killed at one time. The executions took place all over the country, sometimes by hanging, sometimes by decapitation, sometimes by fire. Towards the end of the period they were accompanied by atrocious torture (see above, p. 61). Year after year the terrible work went on: the whole land was bathed in human blood.[7] On leaving the country in December 1573, Alva was said to have boasted that, not counting men slain in battle and executed after victory, he had had 18,000 persons put to death in the Netherlands.[8]

---

7. Cf. Geyl, *Revolt* etc., p. 104: "Never was nation subjected to a reign of terror with more calculated deliberation or more systematic persistence".
8. This statement rests on the authority of a number of early Dutch historians (Meteren, Grotius, etc.), and can be traced back as far as the year 1582, when it appears in the instructions given by the States-General to their ambassadors to the imperial Diet. The figure appears, however, as 8,000 two years earlier, in the

In February 1568 William of Orange's eldest son Philip William, Count of Buren, then a boy of thirteen studying at the University of Louvain, was inveigled by Alva into agreeing to be sent to Spain to be educated there as a Catholic. It is not easy to understand how he came to be left by his father (who had quitted the country in the previous April) thus exposed to the power of the enemy.[9] In May William's brother Louis won a victory at Heiliger-Lee in the north over the army sent thither by Alva. Alva's wrathful response was to have eighteen prisoners of distinction executed together at Brussels, to order the sentences already passed against Egmont and Hoorn to be carried out a few days later, and to take the field himself against Louis of Nassau. After defeating him at Jemmingen in the far north, he made his way back to Utrecht, subjecting the country en route as far as Groningen to the cruellest and most atrocious devastation. At Utrecht he was joined by his illegitimate son, Don Frederic of Toledo, with large reinforcements. Here, too, he ordered the execution of a rich old Catholic lady of eighty-four, because her son-in-law had eighteen months earlier given a heretic hospitality in her house: needless to say, her estates were confiscated. In October William of Orange invaded Brabant. When Alva approached him, William sent him a herald to suggest that all prisoners who might be taken should be exchanged instead of executed. The unfortunate envoy was seized on dismounting from his horse, and instantly hanged. The campaign was a failure from William's point of view; for Alva declined to engage in battle, and William found it impossible to keep his army together: no town would receive him, for all dreaded

---

State's negotiations with the Duke of Anjou, and as 6,000 in a Spanish official document of 1574, not quoting Alva, but reporting adversely upon him. See the discussions in M. Gachard, *Études et Notices historiques concernant l'Histoire des Pays-Bas* (Brussels, 1890), vol. ii, pp. 366-368, and Pirenne, *Belgique*, vol. iv (1911), p. 10, n 3. Cf. P.J. Blok, *Netherlands*, vol. iii(1900), p. 75, and R.B. Merriman, *Philip the Prudent*, p. 282. The moderns incline to the lower figure; and they may be right, for the liability to exaggerate must be admitted. On the other hand, if, as seems likely, the alternation of 8,000 and 18,000 is due to a clerical slip, the higher figure is as likely to be correct as the lower.

9. Miss Putnam's first suggestion (*William the Silent*, etc., [ed. 1898], vol. i, pp. 270, 288) was that Philip William's presence might prevent his father's estates being confiscated: later (*William the Silent*, etc., [1911], pp. 192, 194), she added that it may also have been intended to conciliate Alva. F. Harrison (*William the Silent* [1897], p. 85) adds that he may have tried thus to avert the reputation of being a refugee. Miss Wedgwood (*William the Silent*, p. 96) says: "… to allay suspicion he had deliberately left a hostage in the Netherlands".

Alva's vengeance. In November he withdrew into France, and later on into Germany, while the Duke betook himself to triumphal rejoicings in Brussels. He had a colossal statue of himself in classical costume, with a boastful inscription, erected at Antwerp. Having now overcome those whom he called "a people of butter" – and that, as he somewhat inaccurately claimed, "without violence" – he felt free to resume his earlier idea of subjugating the French Huguenots, and doubtless thereafter the Protestant realm of England.

Meanwhile the dreadful work of persecution went on. At the end of 1568 or in the course of 1569 Alva reintroduced the Inquisition. When so many lives were being destroyed, it seems disproportionate to chronicle single incidents; but one, occurring early in 1569 is worthy of mention. An Anabaptist prisoner who had escaped was pursued by an officer across the ice. He gained safety; but the officer fell through the broken ice into the water, crying for help. The heretic returned, and at great peril to himself rescued his pursuer. The latter was most unwilling to proceed further against the man who had thus saved his life, but was compelled by the local burgomaster to rearrest the fugitive. A few months later the recaptured prisoner was slowly burnt to death.

It is to the credit of Philip, Pope Pius V, and others, that they wished Alva's sanguinary severities to be slowed up, now that the military position seemed secure. In February 1569 Pius urged on Philip that an amnesty be published; and he sent the necessary documents authorizing it, in order to avoid delay in the procedure. Philip, however, did not forward the needful instructions to Alva until November, and Alva did not proclaim the amnesty till July 1570. Even then, needless to say, full repentance and submission to Catholicism was an essential condition of reaping any benefit from it.[10]

The flames of war were rekindled in 1572. The capture of Brill in the April of that year by the Dutch privateers, authorized and commissioned by William of Orange, inaugurated a period of better success for the rebels. One town after another in Holland and Zealand declared for him; and in May his brother

---

10. Cf. Blok, *Netherlands*, vol. iii (1900), pp. 51, 59; L. von Pastor, *The History of the Popes* (Eng. trans.), vol. xviii (1929), pp. 101, 103.

Louis took Mons. The patriot forces were, however, still worsted in the field. Orange himself suffered defeat near Mons, and was compelled to disband his army beyond the Rhine, and to make his way with only a few followers to Holland. During his retreat his life was in danger from a would-be assassin, who had been promised a large reward by the Duke of Alva in the event of success.

The great massacre of the French Huguenots, which took place in August, deprived Orange of all hope of help from France. Louis was compelled to surrender at Mons. Alva granted the garrison favourable terms, and allowed Louis, who was ill with fever, to depart in peace. But at the close of the year and thenceforward till the following August, there took place at Mons, under the superintendence of Noircarmes, a terrible series of executions, by hanging, decapitation and fire. Then followed a number of sieges, mostly conducted by Alva's son, Don Frederic. Those of Alkmaar and Leyden (the latter concluded after Alva had left the country) were unsuccessful: but at Mechlin, Zutphen, Naarden, and Haarlem the Spaniards were victorious; and the fall of each was followed by wholesale massacre. Mechlin – despite the clergy's appeal for pity – was handed over for three days to the Spanish soldiery, who raped, tortured, pillaged, and murdered at their will (October 1572). At Zutphen Don Frederic was ordered by his father to burn down every house and slay every man in the city – a command almost literally obeyed. The burghers were tied two-and-two, and flung by hundreds into the river. Women were indiscriminately outraged. The little town of Naarden on the Zuyder Zee, having refused to surrender when summoned to do so, soon found its strength unequal to its defence, and admitted the Spaniards on promise that the lives and property of the citizens should be respected (November 1572). Once within the city, the enemy massacred almost the whole population, amid circumstances of the foulest outrage; and the city itself was razed to the ground. In July 1573 Haarlem surrendered after a long siege on promise of lenient treatment: all the surviving Dutch soldiers were butchered, and several hundreds of the citizens likewise: many were tied together and thrown into the lake, as at Zutphen. Executions went on incessantly for several days, until 2,300 persons had been slain. The rest of the population was spared, on payment of a large fine. During the subsequent siege of Alkmaar, which proved unsuccessful, the Duke of Alva expressed his indignation at the ingratitude with which his clemency at Haarlem had hitherto been requited by the Dutch citizens he had commanded to surrender. He asked Philip to allow him to burn to the ground every town that resisted. In sending his son to attack Alkmaar, he ordered him to slay every living creature within its walls.

What the Church-historian Duchesne says of the Orientals, namely, that they "are accustomed to being massacred", must have become increasingly true of the Netherlanders during Alva's régime. Brabant and Flanders had been scourged back beneath the Hispano-Roman yoke; and the northern provinces had suffered terrible afflictions. Yet Alva's policy of terror failed to secure the results he had hoped for; and in December 1573 he left the country, his hands reeking and dripping with innocent blood. He advised his successor to burn down every city in the Netherlands, except such as could be permanently garrisoned with Spanish troops. As year after year had passed by, the detestation felt for him had steadily grown; and it developed at length into a wild and passionate hatred. When at last he departed, he carried with him the curses of the people he had decimated; and for long years afterwards his name was never mentioned without a shudder. He had not even earned the satisfaction of receiving the approval and appreciation of his royal master.

Let us now see how this monstrous purveyor of homicide is treated by the modern pro-Catholic historians.

Mr. Trevor Davies is cautiously just to the facts. "Alva", he says (when discussing Philip's first counsellors), "stood for stern and active measures against all disorder and a 'mailed fist' policy in which tact and temporising had no part. He was the only grandee who ever enjoyed a considerable measure of Philip's confidence" (p. 123). He briefly describes the steps taken by Alva during the early years of his governorship in the Netherlands, and adds: "… the Council of Tumults sent so many others to the scaffold that few have hesitated to describe it as the Council of

Blood. The total number who suffered cannot be discovered, as the archives containing the criminal processes were burnt a few years later. There is little doubt, however, that those executed are to be reckoned in thousands" (p. 161).

Then follow Mr. Davies's attempts at palliation. "The effect of these executions upon public opinion is difficult to gauge" (p. 162). If he means public opinion in the Netherlands, one would have thought that the frantic resistance put up by the northern provinces and the hatred with which the Duke was regarded did not leave much room for doubt as to the effect of his actions on public opinion.

"For it should be remembered", he goes on, "that the court, numbering usually nine or ten judges in all, consisted of natives of the Netherlands of high character and great reputation such as Berlaimont, Noircames and Viglius – with the addition of only three Spaniards". He does not, however, mention that it was only the Spanish members who had the privilege of voting, and that all decisions were subject to the presidential veto or assent of Alva himself. As for the alleged "high character and great reputation" of some of the Netherland-members, the fact that a certain number of Catholic public men in the country sympathized and co-operated with Alva's tyranny is only what one might have expected, having regard to the normal Catholic estimate, customary in those times, of the merits of heretics. Moreover, a man's character and reputation must depend on his deeds; and the undisputed deeds of the Council of Blood brand the good name of those who participated therein with an indelible stain. Reader, look at the record.

> "If thou wouldst,
> There shouldst thou find one heinous article,...
> Mark'd with a blot, damn'd in the book of heaven".

"Also", proceeds Mr. Trevor Davies (p. 162), "the penalty of high treason everywhere was death in one of its most horrible forms;..." I have before this (see above, p. 74) protested against the contention that cruel deeds may be condoned by an historian on the ground that they were legal or customary. And when the definition of high treason is extended so as to include protesting against the new bishoprics, the Inquisition, or the placards, failing to resist public preaching, or asserting that the king had not the right to override the liberties of the provinces or that the Council of Troubles was bound to observe any laws or charters – even the paltry excuse that the customary punishment of treason everywhere at that time was a cruel death, completely loses whatever force it might otherwise have possessed.

"… and rebellion was almost invariably followed by wholesale slaughter of defeated rebels. British history, for example, provides plentiful records of equally terrible wholesale executions, in the Ireland of Elizabeth, or in Scotland after the failure of the '45. These things did not apparently disgust contemporary public opinion;…" *(ibid.)*. But it is a poor defence of cruelty in one country to adduce other instances of it in other countries. That cruelty was practised in Ireland under Elizabeth and in Scotland in 1746 is true; but it is quite irrelevant to our judgment of the deeds of the Duke of Alva. In the first place, the circumstances were in neither case really parallel. The execution of the surrendered Spanish garrison at Smerwick in 1580 and the murderous raids made on disaffected areas inhabited by the Irish natives, however cruel we may rightly judge them to be, constitute no real analogy to the merciless proceedings of the Council of Blood; and even the Smerwick-execution was totally different from the indiscriminate outraging and butchery of civilians in the Dutch towns captured by the Spaniards. As regards 1746, when the rebel Highlanders were brutally slain after Cumberland's victory at Culloden, it must be borne in mind that in the previous year they had invaded England and got as far as Derby; and not unnaturally the sense of relief at the overthrow of such dangerous enemies blunted the public conscience for a time to the cruelty shown towards them after they were defeated. But the national sense of decency was not long in asserting itself; and the Duke of Cumberland was nicknamed "The Butcher" as early as four months after his victory.[11]

"and there is little evidence to show that Alva's executions caused much discontent" *(ibid.)*. How then are we to account for the detestation which he roused, and the desperate struggle which was waged against him and against the cause he stood for

---

11. Cf. E.M. Lloyd in *Dict, of Nat. Biog.*, vol. xxi (1921-22), p. 342 b.

by the whole of the northern provinces – not only while he was personally in office, but for long years afterwards?

"It is true that the Emperor remonstrated with the Government, but he was a crypto-Protestant and a man of exceptional humanity" (*ibid.*). But what does that prove except that the government to which he sent his protest was lacking in humanity, and that it was Protestantism to which Europe and mankind had to look for the needed improvement in the matter of humane feelings?

"Elizabeth of England, on the other hand, saw nothing excessive in the executions – she had just quenched in blood the rebellion of the northern Earls – and congratulated Philip on his victory over the rebels" (*ibid.*). Once again, the analogy is quite unconvincing. The northern earls were in revolt, in the interests of a Scottish queen, not against a foreign Power, but against their own home-government. Eight hundred persons only suffered death in the suppression of their movement. Elizabeth was no model of clemency, and in any case was always disposed, out of regard for royal authority, to disapprove strongly of rebels of all kinds, whatever their case. The fact that at the moment (1569) she desired to keep on good terms with Philip would amply suffice, in these circumstances, to explain her comparative indifference to the sufferings of the Dutch. Moreover, she was keeping up all the time communications with both William of Orange and the Huguenots.[12] Under other political conditions, her indignation at Catholic cruelty found overt and unambiguous expression – as in the case of the French Huguenots.[13]

Mr. Trevor Davies next adduces (pp. 162 f.) the fact that in 1568 neither Louis of Nassau nor William of Orange, on invading the Netherlands, received any considerable support from the local population, and as a result were both completely defeated, and had to withdraw. But this does not prove that Alva and his

---

12. Blok, *Netherlands*, vol. iii (1900), p. 49. The English translator, however, in writing "Elizabeth…, who *had* coquetted with the Huguenots and the prince, *now* began to evince a friendliness for Spain,…" somewhat obscures Blok's meaning. His original Dutch and the German translation both make it clear that Elizabeth's relations with all three parties were contemporaneous. Cf. Merriman, *Philip the Prudent*, pp. 290, 315.
13. Her subjects, in any case, knew where they stood. "England was burning with indignation at Alba's *régime* of blood in the Netherlands" (M.A.S. Hume, *Philip II*, p. 126).

executions were not unpopular: it proves only – what we can well believe – that the country was cowed by the terror of his vengeance, and that he was a more skilful general and in command of better troops than his two opponents. Mr. Davies's inference is disproved by the fierce resistance which was afterwards, under more favourable circumstances, put up against the Duke's forces.

Finally (p. 163): "What really caused widespread discontent was not so much the Council of Tumults as the taxation that followed.... Alva propounded to the States-General in March 1569 his scheme for raising a large sum of money.... After much remonstrance from the States-General Alva postponed his scheme in return for grants of the old-fashioned kind. It was not till the spring of 1572 that the new system was enforced. Then, at last, the Netherlanders were ready to rebel...."[14] Now in order rightly to assess the real character of Alva's rule, and its effect on public opinion in the Netherlands, there is no necessity to overlook the strong commercial interest of the inhabitants, or to doubt that the peculiarly oppressive form of his schemes of taxation was a powerful adjunct to the motives animating the revolt against him. In particular, it must have made Catholics much more inclined than before to join forces with the Protestants who were up in arms on the religious issue.[15] Nor can it be denied that the general revolt did commence in earnest in 1572. But it is extremely doubtful whether that commencement was occasioned by Alva's taxation. Several other factors may well have operated, and doubtless did operate, to produce it: for instance, hope may have been raised nearer to the pitch of adventure by the Dutch privateers' capture of Brill on April 1, 1572; also, the malcontents may well have felt goaded to take a fresh plunge by the dreadful massacre of the French Huguenots in August. Furthermore, in June of the same year the worst of Alva's tax-measures were authoritatively suspended in view of the opposition they had aroused. So that the outburst of revolt could hardly have been due to those

---

14. Cf. Merrimen, *Philip the Prudent*, p. 301: "The primary cause of it [the revolt]... was economic, though it was to need the additional impetus of Calvinism to give it victory in the Northeast."
15. Cf. R. Putnam, *William the Silent*, etc. (ed. 1898), vol. i, p. 535, Vol. ii, p. 2; M.A.S. Hume, *Philip II*, pp. 148-150; Geyl, *Revolt*, etc., pp. 110, 112, 127.

measures being enforced. But in any case, what sort of a reading of human nature is this, which believes that a freedom-loving people would feel no strong objection when their fellow-citizens were ordered off to execution by a foreign-controlled court, in tens, scores, fifties, and even hundreds at a time, but would fly to arms in wild rebellion as soon as their pockets were touched by the imposition of an unwonted and oppressive tax?[16]

Let us now see what Dr. Walsh makes of Alva. Integral to his version of the facts is his assumption that all divergence from Roman Catholicism was an act of enmity against Christ and God and deserving of severe punishment. Thus – "Things had come to such a criminal pass now that it was necessary to blot out the prevalent false teachings with the blood of the guilty, and not to spare the ringleaders, even if they gave themselves up, without great evidence on their part of repentance and submission and willingness to do whatever it might please His Majesty to command them;…" (p. 414). Dr. Walsh quotes with approval the words of Cabrera, Philip's Spanish and Catholic biographer: "For even if people complained justly, and made an uproar with some reasonable cause, their insolence must be chastised, that they might not become accustomed by riotous ways to proceed to injustice. It was too late for the remedy of ordinary laws and ministers. And so there must be named men of extraordinary powers, grave and energetic…" *(ibid.)*. Alva, continues Dr. Walsh (pp. 420 f.), "had never made any great secret of what he would do to the enemies of his King if he had the chance: he would cut off the heads of the leaders, he had said repeatedly, and scare the rest into obedience. Nor was such a mind as his, accustomed to seeing things as either black or white, very likely to make fine distinctions. He had his orders. He meant to carry them out. A memorandum drawn up for him before he left Spain shows what they were: The chief offenders to be punished; those recognizing their errors and wishing to live as good Catholics to be pardoned; the authority of the placards of Charles V and of the Inquisition of the Netherlands (not of Spain) to be re-established;…" When in 1572 Philip

---

16. Miss Wedgwood points out (*William the Silent*, pp. 123, 132, 137) that the revolt cost the rebels in voluntary taxation far more than Alva's taxes would have done.

was anxious to conciliate the Netherlands as soon as possible, that his hands might be free to deal with the Turks, "Alba wrote him that this idea was a temptation of the devil. In his view, the menace to Christendom from the Protestants was far more serious than that from Islam...." (p. 542).

Dr. Walsh's narrative of the actual facts regarding Alva's proceedings in the Netherlands suffers from his constant effort to minimize and excuse the Duke's severity. Thus, speaking of the Council of Troubles, he says: "The number of persons executed by orders of this tribunal during the few years of its jurisdiction has been variously estimated, from Cabrera's 1,700 to the highly exaggerated Protestant total of 8,000",[17] and he goes on to note that every execution "gave splendid inflammatory material to the anti-Catholic propaganda organization,..." (pp. 421 f.). He refers briefly to the arrest and execution of Egmont and Hoorn (pp. 445, 469), without a word of disapproval regarding the settlement of the sentence before the arrest, the treachery used in effecting the arrest, and the harshness of the judicial procedure that ensued upon it. He observes (p. 422) that Egmont and Hoorn were executed by order of Philip himself, to whom Alva applied for instructions. Of Alva's reaction to Louis of Nassau's victory at Heiliger-Lee in May 1568, he says (p. 469): "In his indignation he decided that, if the rebels wanted blood, they should have it. First taking the precaution of building a strong castle at Antwerp, and having a statue of himself set up in the public square that all might know who their master was, he resolved on the earliest possible judicial execution of Egmont and Hornes; this execution took place in June". He summarizes in full, with evident approval, the indignant replies which both Philip and Alva gave to the Emperor's plea on behalf of Egmont and Hoorn, and on behalf of the inhabitants of the Netherlands generally, for whom he had ventured to ask a truce (pp. 468, 470-474). The replies took the form of an appeal to the admitted necessity of suppressing rebellion; and Philip's answer adduced the additional necessity of compelling his subjects to submit to the Roman Catholic Church.

Dr. Walsh justifies Alva's butchery of the fugitives after his victory over Louis of Nassau at Jemmingen (July 1568), as a

---

17. On this figure, see above, pp. 96 f., n. 2.

reprisal for corresponding butchery on the other side (p. 470). He refers to Philip's autograph letter of thanks to the general "who had carried out the Duke's orders to behead all the rebels he could capture at Roramund" (*ibid.*), but not to Alva's brutal devastation of the country in the course of his return to Groningen (see above, p. 97).

Here is his version of the series of butcheries in the towns captured in 1572 – 73: "Alba's troops sacked Mechlin so thoroughly that even the Catholic burghers, hardly recovered from maltreatment by the Calvinists, complained bitterly to King Philip of the pillaging and cruelty of his troops. At Zutphen he caused all the armed men to be slain. He was so irritated by the defiance of Harlem, and the atrocities against Catholics there, that he sent his son, Don Fadrique, to attack it, with orders not to leave alive a single one of the Walloons, French or English; but to spare, however, the citizens. Unfortunately, the Spanish in the heat of victory went beyond their instructions. The Duke punished those guilty of outrages, most of them mutineers, and gave very lenient terms to the defeated burghers. Nevertheless, his expedition had taken on an appearance of ruthlessness to which no complete answer was possible" (pp. 539 f.). The Duke's "account of the taking of Naerden in Holland is characteristic. It was only a nest of Anabaptists, he wrote, who had refused to surrender; hence he had told Don Fadrique to put all the men to the sword, and he was pleased to be able to tell the King that not one of them escaped. Doubtless God had permitted this. Only men whom God had blinded would have attempted to defend such a place. The Duke rejoiced that he was able to make an example of so evil and heretical a population".[18]

Our author, of course, makes the most of the Duke of Alva's soldierly virtues. Alva generously praised the gallantry of the defenders of Haarlem – of one Dutch gunner in particular – for his own losses were heavy (p. 540), though we must set alongside this generosity the brutal severity with which the conquered city was treated. The stern discipline maintained in

---

18. Walsh, *Philip II*, p. 541 – an example, apparently, of those "salty and matter-of-fact letters" of Alva's, of which Dr. Walsh speaks appreciatively in the immediate sequel.

Alva's army is appreciatively mentioned (pp. 199, 604). Dr. Walsh says that his "men knew from experience that the violation of a woman would be followed at once by a hanging": but he does not refer to the official band of 2,000 Italian prostitutes (see above, p. 95); nor does he seem to take any account of the innumerable outrages committed on women in the various cities taken by his troops or in the districts devastated after the victory of Jemmingen – though it is true that for these latter misdeeds some of the soldiers who had behaved worst were hanged.

On the whole, Dr. Walsh regards Alva as a grand old man. "The heroic history of Spain seemed sometimes to live and speak in him" (p. 413). "A gallant figure was the old Duke with his long, white beard falling over his steel breastplate, and his garments of white and azure" (p. 603).

And what of his cruelty? "Useless bloodshed he abhorred", writes Dr. Walsh (p. 63). "War to him was a fascinating intellectual exercise, in which the pleasure consisted in seeing how quickly and how safely one could accomplish a certain task for the glory of God and one's King; meanwhile killing as many of the enemy as need be, and losing as few of one's own troops as possible. Stern though he was, he was just". The odious reputation of his Council of Blood "was bewildering to Alba, and troubled him much later on. He was not a cruel or bloody man. In all his wars he was noted for shedding only such blood as might be necessary to attain his objective. If the court be judged by the standards of the time, it compares very favorably in methods (less favorably, perhaps, in numbers, but only slightly so) with the tribunals which condemned so many English Catholics to far more brutal deaths under Henry VIII and Elizabeth" (p. 422). Philip, at any rate, accepted full responsibility for the deaths inflicted "for the good of the society over which *he had the right of life and death*" (*ibid.*: italics mine). "Alba had gone there to do certain things. He had done them. He had made what he considered just enough show of force to uphold his King's authority, to frighten the Calvinists, Anabaptists, Jews and other agitators into flight or silence, to inflict just punishment on the ringleaders, and then, when peace and authority were fully restored, to grant a general pardon. Coolly and dispassionately he had rounded up people guilty of burning or sacking churches, desecrating the Host, or taking arms against the King or his officers. As Cabrera says, reflecting the Spanish point of view, 'he began to dispense justice with moderation, that none might be scandalized'… Alba was not a cruel man by nature, but he was a soldier…" (p. 469).

The last comment of Dr. Walsh's to be quoted in connexion with the Duke is perhaps one of the most amazing in its one-sidedness. "While Alba fought *and suffered* in the Netherlands, while Requesens and Don Juan and Alessandro Farnese were *broken on that cross*, the Council of Trent was able to meet, deliberate, and complete the Reform" (p. 707 – italics mine). Yet who can read the story of Alva in the Netherlands, and be impressed by *his* sufferings? Under Requesens (1573-76), after his attempt at negotiation had broken down owing to the sustained refusal of the Spanish government to concede freedom of conscience and other elementary rights, war was renewed; and in 1575 the towns of Oudewater and Bommenede were taken by storm, and the garrisons and most of the townspeople slain. "Requesens received repeated orders from Madrid to find some means of despatching both William and Lewis of Nassau; and, far from demurring, the Grand Commander only expressed regret 'that there was small hope of success unless God should help him.'"[19] The worthy governor died of fever in March 1576. Don John of Austria (1576-78) was never strong enough to effect much: but the policy of the king he served, and his treacherous seizure of Namur (1577), indicate pretty clearly the line he would have followed, had he had the power. Like Requesens, he too was urged on Philip's authority to have Orange assassinated. He died in October 1578. Alexander Farnese, despite his soldierly virtues, sacked Maestricht in 1579; and his soldiers tore women limb from limb in the streets of the town after its capture. He was privy to Gérard's plot to assassinate William of Orange, and had earlier hired other men to attempt the deed. Prior to the Spanish Armada, he carried on long and utterly mendacious negotiations with Queen Elizabeth, in order that she might be the more taken by surprise.

---

19. G. Edmundson in *Camb. Mod. Hist.*, vol. iii (1904), p. 238.

He also died in harness, in 1592. The characters of these three men were not without their noble features: but to speak of them, in connexion with the struggle in the Netherlands, as being "broken on that cross", thus suggesting an analogy or comparison between their evil deeds and our Lord's sacrifice on Calvary, cannot but strike the mind of any Christian possessing any knowledge of the facts as profoundly shocking.

As for the Duke of Alva, further comment on Dr. Walsh's eulogies is, in view of the facts we have mentioned, hardly necessary. The only further observation I wish to make is this: if Alva was not cruel and bloody, then I know of no cruel and bloody man who has ever existed on this earth from the beginning of history until now.

Chapter Six

The Personal Character of Philip II

It may possibly occur to some of my readers that, in insisting at the end of the last chapter that the Duke of Alva was a cruel and bloody man, I have been guilty of forgetting the self-denying ordinance which I imposed on myself at the beginning of this book (pp. 10-12), namely, that I would confine myself to a characterization of evil deeds only and not venture to cast blame on the doers of them. It is a fair question whether to call a man cruel and bloody does not amount to a personal condemnation of him. It certainly does approach very near to that. Yet on the whole I am disposed to defend myself against the charge of breaking my own rule. I can recall a prominent Biblical character who is said to have "shed blood abundantly", but is yet called "a man after God's own heart"! As for cruelty, I am at a loss to know how we can refuse to describe Alva's *actions* as cruel – and equally at a loss to see how cruel actions can be done by one who is not himself cruel. But I have not presumed to pass any sort of final judgment on the man himself. His personal piety is, of course, unquestioned; and his own reading of the duty that lay before him must be assumed to have been conscientious. If he needs to be condemned in the sight of God, it is for God to pronounce the verdict. To describe him as cruel and bloody in his actual deeds is not necessarily to usurp that function.[1]

The same distinction must be kept in mind as we discuss the character of Alva's royal master. I shall try to limit myself to describing those features of Philip's character which can be observed in, or inferred from, his known actions, without undertaking to administer moral blame. I should endeavour to observe this self-restraint even if the *whole* of these knowable features were repellent: loyalty to it is still more incumbent upon me seeing

---

1. Even Professor Butterfield, averse as he is to the passing of moral judgments in history, concedes to the historian the right of describing, "subject to obvious limits", the characteristics of historical personalities, and even allows him to "concern himself with… the effect which the promulgation of slipshod ideas on moral questions may have had at any time upon human conduct", and so on (*The Whig Interpretation*, etc., pp. 125 f.).

that there is admittedly much in the picture which is not repellent. The general view of Philip traditionally taken by Protestants – a view founded on the horror which so much of his activity naturally rouses in Protestant bosoms – is one of unrelieved condemnation.[2] It is only fair that we should be willing to take note of other aspects of his life, those not directly connected with the suppression of Protestantism, which – looked at in isolation, and judged on their own merits – permit a much more favourable judgment to be passed.

It must for instance be patent to anyone at all closely acquainted with the details of Philip's reign that he was a deeply religious man, sincere and assiduous in his worship and possessed of a strong trust in the Providence of God and a very high sense of personal duty. It is true that his religious devotion involved a profound veneration for relics of the saints: but this was an aberration inseparable from a strong adherence to the Catholic view of things, and one from which Philip's education could hardly be expected to have freed him.[3] He exercised an extraordinary self-control over his feelings: very rarely was he seen in a rage; and the patience he displayed under his disappointment at the failure of the Armada and under the terrible sufferings of his last illness was truly amazing. He had a love of social justice as he understood it; and he endeavoured to secure it for his subjects. The confession made on his death-bed that he was not conscious of having ever wilfully wronged anyone, could not but have been uttered in complete seriousness; and it serves therefore at least to illustrate what his own intentions and aspirations had been.

As a family-man he was affectionate. He has been accused of having caused his eldest son Don Carlos to be put to death: but there is no conclusive evidence that he did so. The exceptional

---

2. Typical examples may be seen in J.G. Rogers's lecture on "Clericalism and Congregationalism", printed in *Jubilee Lectures* (1882), vol. ii, pp. 202-205, and, of course, in Motley, *United Netherlands* (ed. 1875-76), vol. iii, pp. 481-510. Merriman says (*Philip the Prudent*, p. 599, n. 2): "There can be no doubt that the words and writings of Pérez went far towards creating that hostile conception of Philip II which continued to prevail north of the Pyrenees till the middle of the nineteenth century…" (for Pérez, see below, pp. 123 f.). There were, however, plenty of other grounds for the customary view.

3. Dr. Walsh (*Philip II*, p. 196) is at pains to contend that Philip was less superstitious than certain militant Protestants of his time: but then he does not regard belief in the efficacy of relics as superstitious (cf. pp. 333, 335).

measures he took with regard to him (depriving him of his freedom, and so on) can be readily explained by the peculiar difficulty with which the morose and degenerate character of the prince faced him.[4] When no reasons of state called for severity, he was kind-hearted and charitable to those in need. He behaved with generosity in the Flemish famine of 1556, and on occasions of public calamity in Spain. When St. Quentin was sacked in 1557, he ordered that the women and children should be spared. He washed and kissed the feet of the poor. He regretted the sufferings needlessly inflicted on the unfortunate Moriscos[5] and on the inhabitants of captured Maestricht.

The habitual solemnity and taciturnity of his demeanour was naturally accentuated at times of defeat or bereavement. Hence has arisen the customary Protestant idea of him as a morose and gloomy recluse. This is no doubt an exaggeration; for Philip, though his manner was not characteristically genial, was a patron of art, literature, and music; he played the guitar, loved flowers and scenery, and was fond of dancing and hunting. Dr. Walsh is at great pains to correct the Protestant impression by adducing evidence along these lines; and we may accept his verdict – though the instances he quotes shed a rather strange light on the ethical judgments both of hero and of biographer. In proving, for instance, what a good hearty fellow the king really was, he describes how he once asked for a boar to be let loose in an enclosure, how he went hunting it in a coach, how monks watched the fine sport from the windows, and how "the boar gave a good account of himself, and disembowelled a horse with one of his tusks before he was slain".[6] He could, moreover, write simply and sweetly to children. During his stay in Portugal in 1581-83, he wrote delightful letters to his two young daughters, Elizabeth and Catherine, in Castille, telling them on one occasion about a nice auto-de-fé that he had witnessed at Lisbon, and how he had been in the same house as the secular

---

4. Dr. Walsh, though holding Philip innocent of putting Don Carlos to death (*Philip II*, pp. 449, 451: cf. R.T. Davies, *Golden Century*, p. 119), maintains that, as king, he would have been fully within his rights in doing it, had he considered it necessary in the public interest (pp. 452 f., 456).
5. Though their revolt had been caused by his own intolerable oppression (cf. M. Brosch in *Camb. Mod. Hist.*, vol. iii [1904], p. 131).
6. Walsh, *Philip II*, pp. 651 f.: cf. pp. 324, 669 (hunts cranes with a musket), 680 (hunts rabbits *with his children*), 718 (boar-hunt at the age of seventy).

judge who was going to sentence those condemned by the Inquisitors to be burnt. He had come away as soon as the sentences were read, and had not been over-tired by the labour of watching and listening.[7]

Conscientious and diligent in discharging the affairs of state, he was painfully slow and inefficient in his methods. Nearly all negotiations between himself and his ministers were carried on in writing. Instead of delegating large authority and responsibility to competent administrators, he kept far too much of the departmental duties of government under his own personal control. The absolute character of his rule discouraged the spirit of inventiveness and initiative in his subordinates. Furthermore, he was at times unwise and unfortunate in the choice of his agents – a fact illustrated by his insisting on the appointment of the inexperienced Duke of Medina Sidonia to the command of the Armada. Closely allied to the temperamental defects just mentioned was the cynical distrust and jealousy which he felt and displayed towards the more gifted of his servants, and his lack of a sense of gratitude towards those who had rendered him signal service. Without presuming to decide whether or not Don John's death was due to Philip's contrivance, as has been believed by many, we observe that even Dr. Walsh (p. 678) realizes that Philip was jealous of the loyal Duke of Parma, who, though never given a free hand, had virtually saved the southern half of the Netherlands for him.

It must in fairness be reckoned to Philip's credit that, unlike his father (who, however, warned him against the evils of war), he was an habitual lover of peace. He constantly endeavoured to gain his ends by persuasion and bribery rather than by appealing to arms. It may, of course, be plausibly suggested that he shrank from waging war, not so much from feelings of humanity, as from a cautious and parsimonious dislike of the expensiveness and risks of armed strife. And it is clear that, when roused, he did not shrink from bloodshed. Yet some measure of credit may fittingly be allowed to him for preferring normally to exhaust the gentler means of political pressure before resorting to arms.

---

7. Walsh, *Philip II*, pp. 610-613. Cf. R.T. Davies, *Golden Century*, p. 119.

Something perhaps should now be said about Philip's relations with women. In November 1543, when he was not yet seventeen, he was married to his cousin Maria Manuela of Portugal, who in July 1545 bore him the misshapen pervert Don Carlos, and died a few days later. Between this time and his marriage with Mary Tudor in 1554, Philip lived for several years in adultery with his mistress Doña Isabel de Osorio, by whom he had several children.[8] In July 1554 he married Mary of England, who was then thirty-eight years old – eleven years his senior. Whatever may have been the bride's feelings towards her husband, on Philip's side the union was certainly no love-match. He entered into it, in compliance with a scheme devised by his father the Emperor, for the purpose of strengthening the Hapsburg-monarchy and the Roman Church: and although, with Stoic self-control, he did while in England all that could be expected of a newly-married husband, his heart was not in it. During his prolonged sojournings in the Netherlands later in Mary's reign, stories were afloat of his gallantries with the young women of the country; and there was enough verisimilitude about them to arouse the poor queen's jealousy. Allowance must, of course, always be made for the unreliability of gossiping rumour, "upon whose tongues continual slanders ride"; and on this ground some of Philip's apologists are disposed to acquit him of all or virtually all extra-marital immorality. On the other hand, gossip is not always untruthful. Moreover, Philip was a handsome young Spaniard, living in an age when royal irregularities with women were common and were easily condoned; and he is well known to have been extremely fond of dancing and of female society.[9] It must therefore be regarded as more probable than not that his life in the Netherlands between 1555 and 1559 was marked by some licentiousness of conduct.[10] Mary

---

8. In stating this as a fact, I am following the majority of modern authorities: e.g., M. Hume, *Two English Queens and Philip* (1908), p. 22 n. 1, p. 27, *Philip II*, p. 26; *Encyc. Brit.*, vol. xxi (1911), p. 384 b; R.T. Davies, *Golden Century*, p. 119. Dr. Walsh (*Philip II*, pp. 102, 115) prefers to regard the allegation as unverified. Other amorous attachments during this period are assigned to Philip on less specific evidence.
9. Walsh, *Philip II*, pp. 113, 137.
10. P.J. Blok (*Netherlands*, vol. ii [1899], p. 289) holds a favourable view of Philip's purity. M.A.S. Hume (*Philip II*, pp. 17, 26) thinks he was not blameless, but a good deal better than most contemporary monarchs. H.C. Lea (in *Amer. Hist. Review*,

died in November 1558. In 1560, shortly after his final return to Spain, he married Princess Elizabeth (or Isabel) of France, who was then fourteen or fifteen years old. He was very fond of her, and she gave him two daughters (the children to whom he wrote from Portugal). To his great sorrow she died in October 1568. The rumour embodied in William of Orange's "Apology" of 1580 to the effect that Philip had had her poisoned is unconfirmed and improbable. It was, however, very shortly after this bereavement that, for the sake of having a male heir (the impossible Don Carlos having recently died), he agreed to marry his niece Anne of Austria: the marriage took place in November 1570. Anne bore several children, including the prince who succeeded his father as Philip III. She died in October 1580. "The widower", writes Dr. A.W. Ward, "with characteristic promptitude offered his hand to her younger sister Elizabeth…"[11] – a fact which, I think, Dr. Walsh does not mention. No further marriage, however, took place. Late in 1590 rumours were afloat at the French court to the effect that Philip's ambassador at Rome had begged Sixtus V (who had died in August that year) to allow Philip to marry his own daughter Isabel Clara Eugenia – a union which would have fitted in well with his claim to the crown of France (Isabel's mother having been Elizabeth of Valois). Torn between the inherent improbability of so incestuous a plan, and the implications of belief in it on the part of at least two French ambassadors, we may perhaps give Philip the benefit of the doubt, and not press the appalling charge against him.

The character of Philip, therefore, as so far considered, while not wholly admirable, was not without its estimable features. When, however, we attempt to isolate for special study those practices of his which arose directly from his aims and purposes as a Hapsburg and a Catholic, the picture is far less pleasing. Considerable allowance must of course be made for the immense

---

vol. ix, p. 242 [January 1904], says that "if his favorite vice was licentiousness", that is no reason for doubting his religious sincerity. R.B. Merriman says "there can be no doubt that in his earlier years he had various mistresses…" (*Philip the Prudent*, pp. 30 f.) – also that he was much perturbed by the prevalance of unnatural vice at his court in 1588 (*op. cit.*, p. 29, n. 5). Dr. Walsh discusses Philip's sex-morals, and decides on the whole in his favour, defending him at least against the more violent accusations brought against him, but granting also that he did not come through his temptations unscathed (*Philip II*, pp. 114-116, 550).

11. In *Camb. Mod. Hist.*, vol. iii (1904), p. 699.

bias imparted to his mind by heredity and education.[12] Over and above that, there comes the peculiar character of political responsibility, which never makes it easy for the holder of it to act on precisely the same principles as those which bind him in his private capacity. Political ethics constitute a thorny and difficult problem; and most rulers, however conscientious and charitable they may be, find themselves faced with ethical dilemmas of a kind that does not usually trouble the ordinary man. Many of these dilemmas, though by no means all, are connected with the *coercive* activity incidental to all political administration. That is why the records of nearly all rulers, including many possessed of great personal virtue, are marred by acts of severity and deceit and by other moral blemishes.

To this general truth Philip II was no exception. On the contrary, his very conscientiousness lent such strength to his political and religious convictions that they led him into violations of the moral law even greater than a less thorough doctrinaire would have ventured to commit. His ambition was in a word both conscientious and boundless. He was ambitious to preserve and increase his rights as an absolute sovereign. He was ambitious to promote the interests of Spain, to cover the house of Hapsburg with glory, and – by annexing neighbouring states to his crown and family – to enlarge the area of his dominions. He was ambitious to strengthen the hold of the Roman Church on the minds of men, and to destroy whatever might tend to undermine it. These ambitions were so sacred to him that, in pursuance of them, he was prepared not only to do things from which a private person ought certainly to refrain, but to go to extremes which less serious rulers would never have had the hardihood to reach.[13]

---

12. This is H.C. Lea's great plea in his paper on "Ethical Values in History" in *Amer. Hist. Review*, vol. ix, pp. 238-242, 244 f. (January 1904). See above, pp. 4 f.
13. Dr. Walsh (*Philip II*, pp. 255 f.) quotes in extenso a passage translated from Machiavelli's *Il Principe*, in which it is explained that a prince "cannot observe all those rules of conduct in respect whereof men are accounted good, being often enforced, in order to preserve his Princedom, to act in opposition to good faith, charity, humanity and religion…" He then goes on: "The enemies of Philip would say that here Machiavelli had painted his portrait. It would be more just to call it a caricature, for it leaves out of account the very real piety of the man. There is truth in it, however, to the extent that it does express a tendency that appeared from time to time in his policy. It was a tendency inherited from the government of the Emperor. It was only one of many bequests".

Of these more glaring transgressions, we may mention first Philip's various illegal acts. Allusion has already been made to the repeated violation of his twice-taken oath to observe the ancient charters guaranteeing local liberties and privileges in sundry cities and districts of the Netherlands (see above, p. 85). But breaches of the constitutional law were continually occurring in Spain also, and were a constant topic of protest on the part, for instance, of the Cortes of Castille.[14]

It is, however, in his capacity as a persecutor that he exhibits his ruthlessness most conspicuously. We have discussed at an earlier point in this study the question as to whether his motives in persecuting were religious or political (see above, pp. 45-47); and I have hazarded the opinion that they were at least in large part religious. Yet it is also certainly true that they were in part political. The idea then current was that kings were appointed and established by God: and it was easy, therefore, for Philip to get the idea fixed in his mind that it was God's Will, not only that he should be king of Spain and master of its dependencies, but that his monarchy should be as strong and glorious as he, with God's help, could make it. But to attempt to disentangle the religious and political elements in his passion as a persecutor is for that very reason a hopeless and artificial task. Not only was he the king of Spain; he was also a firmly convinced Catholic: and the two ideals coalesced into a dominating unity. Spain was to support the Catholic Church, and the Catholic Church was to support Spain: both causes were dear to the Almighty's heart. As we study Philip's persecuting measures, we see now and then the political motive dominant, perhaps more frequently the religious: but they are conjoined in the closest possible manner; and it is only occasionally that anything like a tension between the two is discernible (see above, p. 46). He felt conscientiously certain that God had charged him with a sacred mission – to glorify the House of Hapsburg, and to destroy Protestantism.

With such ideals fixed in his mind, he drew the conclusion that no considerations of mercy (which, had nothing else been

---

14. It is, however, only fair to mention that some of the traditional liberties of Aragon were very bad, and that the suppression of them by Philip in 1591-92 was a distinct social improvement (Merriman, *Philip the Prudent*, pp. 434, 568, 594, 598).

at stake, would doubtless have weighed with him)[15] could be allowed to stand in the way of the zealous fulfilment of his divinely-given mission. Nay, nothing less than the full range of the coercive power of despotic rule was to be employed in its service. It is this thoroughgoing policy which makes the story of his reign such terrible reading; and all the efforts of his apologists to emphasize his more amiable qualities, and to depreciate the character of his enemies, do not avail to render his severities other than most repulsive. However kind-hearted he might be in his immediate personal relationships, yet where the interests of his monarchy or the interests of the Roman Church were involved, he was utterly merciless. Within the frontiers of Spain he revived and vigorously maintained the Inquisition – an institution whose hideous cruelties and calamitous results have been described in an earlier chapter. He several times attended the auto-de-fe: whether he personally witnessed the burnings (as some Protestant writers have perhaps rashly assumed) or always withdrew before the sentences were carried out (as Dr. Walsh is at great pains to represent as probable – pp. 232-236, 358), makes little difference. The burning was done in the presence of large crowds, and with the king's knowledge and full approval. At an auto held at Valladolid in October 1559, one of the victims – as he was being led away to be burnt alive – shouted out a protest to the king. Philip replied, "If my son were as wicked as you are, I would fetch the wood to burn him myself". The story of how he drenched the Netherlands with blood has already been summarized (see above, pp. 76 ff.). In other countries he fomented civil strife, not shrinking from the misery and desolation he was thus promoting. To the enormous volume of human suffering thus occasioned, he seems to have been totally indifferent. Not only did he urge Catherine de' Medici to chop off the heads of the leading Huguenots in her kingdom;[16] but when, twelve years later, many thousands of Huguenots were brutally slain in the massacre of St. Bartholomew, Philip rejoiced on hearing the news.[17]

---

15. One must not forget that Philip was a humanitarian in his own way" (Merriman, *Philip the Prudent*, p. 568).
16. Walsh, *Philip II*, p. 287.
17. Walsh, *Philip II*, pp. 536 f. He thinks it probable that Philip for once in his life came near to roaring with laughter.

Other sovereigns have felt themselves under the necessity of coercing and punishing troublesome subjects. But without forgetting this, or departing from our recognition of the religious basis of Philip's policy, I do not see how, with the facts before us, we can do other than describe him as a cruel and intolerant bigot. He was totally unable to understand or respect any convictions that differed from his own. If that does not constitute a man a bigot, what does the word "bigot" mean? How far, if at all, he was to blame for being so, I do not undertake to say: but the fact cannot, I submit, be truthfully denied. Similarly, if his ruinous proceedings do not deserve to be characterized as cruel, I know not where in history cruelty is to be seen.

Murder, says the Christian conscience, is always a crime: but, it normally adds, not all killing is murder. The mutual slaughter of armed men in war, for instance, even when condemned by pacifists on moral grounds, is not for the most part seriously equated even by them with murder. As for the non-pacifist majority, the normal member of it would agree with Iago in confessing:

> *"Though in the trade of war I have slain men,*
> *Yet do I hold it very stuff o' the conscience*
> *To do no contrived murder:…."*

The judicial execution of the legally sentenced criminal is another widely recognized instance of "killing no murder". In ancient Greece, to kill a "tyrant" (i.e., a man who by force established himself in supreme political control of a community, in defiance of the laws), whether it would have been normally designated φόνος or not, so far from being censured or criticized as a moral offence, was lauded to the skies as a conspicuous act of virtue and heroism. Whether tyrannicide was morally right or wrong was one of the great questions which exercised the minds of Churchmen and others during the Middle Ages. The death of the usurping Duke of Orléans in 1407 by contrivance of the Duke of Burgundy effectually stimulated the discussion. Opinion remained divided: but the fierce antipathies roused by the ecclesiastical strife of the sixteenth century both multiplied instances of assassination, and called forth at the same time – especially on the Catholic side – a willingness to defend the morals of the practice.[18] A Spanish Jesuit, Juan de Mariana, wrote an elaborate treatise, entitled *De Rege et Regis Institutione*, which he published in 1599 and dedicated to Philip III, and in which he justified tyrannicide. To pass from regarding a monarch as a heretic to regarding him as a tyrant was an extremely easy step: and if heresy justified killing a king, how much more would it justify killing a person of inferior rank.

Here then was one chain of reasoning which might well convince a man of Philip's mentality that, if he could compass the assassination of persons like William of Orange, Elizabeth of England, and Henry IV of France, he would be offering service unto God. But there was another consideration which chimed in with this general acknowledgment of the justifiability of killing heretics – and that was the absolute monarch's presumed autocratic right of inflicting the death-penalty upon a guilty subject. As the fountain of justice, the king was regarded as fully entitled to order, on his own authority, a private execution as the judicial penalty of a legal offence.

Mr. Trevor Davies says: "Philip, no doubt, shared with nearly all his contemporaries a belief that assassination for reasons of State was justifiable".[19] Now in a period of desperate conflict, a scheme of assassination is liable to suggest itself at almost any time to one or other of the parties involved: and instances of such schemes may be cited from almost any epoch of history. During the sixteenth century, when – in the cause of ecclesiastical loyalty – the most passionate feelings were aroused, the instances are rather more frequent than at other times. But even so, I should regard it as an overstatement to say that at that time the "belief that assassination for reasons of state was justifiable" was accepted by nearly all Philip's contemporaries. It was, even in that sanguinary age, a desperate

---

18. Cf. A.M. Fairbairn, in *Bicentenary Lectures* (1889), pp. 37 f.
19. R.T. Davies, *Golden Century*, p. 198. Miss Putnam (*William the Silent*, etc. [1911], p. 472) holds a similar view: she cites Montesquieu as the first – in 1748 – to condemn on principle the incitement to assassinate. Mr. Davies adds in a footnote: "*E.g.* Coligny, Henry III of France and Queen Elizabeth of England, who was not averse from the removal of Irish chieftains by poison". Cf. the anonymous author of the article on "Philip II" in *Encyc. Brit.*, vol. xxi (1911), p. 385 a ("This was but in accordance with the temper of the times. Coligny, Lord Burghley and William the Silent also entered into murder plots"). Of those here accused, Henry III is obviously guilty, and Elizabeth probably so: as regards Coligny and Lord Burghley I am without confirmation: the case of William of Orange is considered below, p. 196.

expedient, to which recourse was had only in most exceptional circumstances, and which was usually shielded with care from the public eye, not only for the purpose of ensuring success, but also because it was realized that a certain moral stigma was widely felt to cling to it.

Philip's own record in the matter is hard to grasp with any fullness and precision, chiefly because of the secrecy in which he would naturally wish to shroud all such proceedings. A certain number of schemes of assassination are laid to his charge, of which it is impossible to prove him guilty, and some of which are definitely improbable. Examples are the deaths of his wife Elizabeth of Valois and of his son Don Carlos (see above, pp. 112 f, 116). A court of law would have no option but to acquit him on these charges. But the historian's responsibility is not quite that of a court of law. While the historian must not categorically affirm that a man has committed an evil act unless there is fairly convincing evidence that he did commit it, it cannot reasonably be demanded of him that, before he records his judgment, the evidence should be of the same degree of cogency as a juryman in a murder-trial would rightly insist upon. On the other hand, it is not open to him, as it is to the juryman, to say "Not guilty" whenever the data, though suspicious, fall short of legal proof.[20] In such cases, his duty – unlike the juryman's – may well be to say "Probably guilty". Some of the instances charged against Philip are of this nature. Philip's general character, attitude, and policy are, for the historian, part of the evidence bearing on each particular case. Thus, granting for the sake of argument, that he did not, in point of fact, contrive the deaths of Elizabeth his wife and Carlos his son, we may well ask the question, Is nothing whatever as to his views on assassination to be inferred from the fact that his contemporary William of Orange thought it wise, in a document laid before the eyes of the world, to charge him with murdering them? William's alleged spite or savagery in making the charges is on this precise issue not to the point. The fact that even false charges were made under such circumstances, while it does not make

---

20. Merivale clearly had this distinction in mind when, referring to Seneca's possible responsibility for Nero's murder of Britannicus, he says: "Posterity, while it shrinks from condemning, must not venture to acquit him" (*Romans under the Empire*, vol. vi, p. 288).

them true, is – in view of other things known about Philip – not without its significance for history. We may safely say that there is nothing inherently unlikely in Philip having secretly had *any* person put out of the way, whose life he regarded as prejudicial to the security and well-being of his throne, his person, or his Church.[21]

I have already described at an earlier point in this study (p. 80) the secret destruction in a Spanish prison in 1570 of the life of the Baron of Montigny, whose death was then publicly declared to have been due to fever. Nominally it was a judicial execution, for Alva had already condemned the man to death in his absence. But the secrecy of the proceeding, and the lying report published about it, indicate surely that Philip shrank from the judgment which public opinion would pass on it.

On March 31, 1578, Escovedo, secretary and envoy of Don John, was stabbed to death in a street in Madrid, by contrivance of his friend Antonio Pérez, the King's confidential agent. In later life, Pérez asserted that he had acted on the king's orders, but that Philip nevertheless persecuted Pérez, because both of them were in love with the widowed Princess of Eboli. A large literature has grown up around the question as to Philip's guilt or innocence regarding Escovedo's death. There are indeed strong grounds for suspecting his privity:[22] but it would be foreign to our purpose to undertake a discussion of the mysterious problem. Nor can we investigate the question whether Philip did or did not cause the premature death of his illegitimate half-brother Don John in October 1578 (see above, p. 114). The incidents are covered by our remarks on the previous page. Pérez's escapades, however, led to a clash between the Aragonese and the Inquisition. The rebellion was crushed; and Philip ordered the Justicia of Saragossa to be executed in defiance of

---

21. Mr. Armstrong says of Charles V, "Unlike his son Philip, he never let an old servant fall into disgrace; his smile was not as Philip's the prelude to the dagger" (*Charles V* [ed. 1910], vol. ii, p. 372).
22. It is accepted by M. Hume (in *Camb. Mod. Hist.*, vol. iii [1904], pp. 514 f.), Geyl (*Revolt*, etc., p. 160), and even Walsh (*Philip II*, pp. 584, 754 f.); but it is regarded by Mr. Trevor Davies (*Golden Century*, p. 198) as "in the highest degree unlikely". R.B. Merriman significantly remarks (*Philip the Prudent*, p. 327, n.): "... to maintain that Philip was morally incapable of such an act – and this after all is the fundamental contention of [two of his apologists] – seems to us absurd.... The absence of conclusive evidence of his guilt would doubtless make it impossible to convict him to-day in a court of law; but it is certainly difficult to believe that he was wholly innocent".

the law entitling him to be tried by the Cortes of Aragon. Later he made several efforts to get Pérez himself assassinated.

In the case of William of Orange, Philip made repeated efforts to get him put to death by the hands of an assassin: and, in view of the part William took in organizing resistance to the king, and in view of the way Philip would inevitably feel about it, one can hardly be surprised. Allusion has already been made to Requesens' part in these schemes (see above, p. 109). In 1577, when Don John was in the Netherlands, the king approved of a suggestion sent by Pérez to Escovedo that the latter should think out some means of getting the Prince of Orange put to death. In 1580, at the suggestion of Cardinal Granvelle, Philip signed and caused to be published in the Netherlands a royal proclamation denouncing William as a traitor, miscreant, and enemy of his country, encouraging anyone who could to injure him in property or life, and offering 25,000 crowns, noble rank, and a free pardon of any crime, to any one who would deliver him to the king alive or dead.[23] Under the stimulus of this ban, several plots were laid against the Prince's life: one nearly successful attempt was made in 1582; the last was made in 1584, when he was shot dead at Delft by a man named Balthasar Gérard. The assassin had been moved both by Philip's ban, and by the desire to rid the world of a dangerous heretic: and both Alexander Farnese and representatives of the Church were privy to his plot. He was tortured to death for the deed; but his surviving relatives were richly rewarded by Philip with a patent of nobility and a large gift of landed property.[24]

There can be no doubt that Philip was privy to several attempts to poison or assassinate Queen Elizabeth. On the other hand, he disapproved of the proposal, as part of the Babington plot, to include Lord Burghley among the victims. Others against whom murder-plots were with Philip's authority or approval contrived during the latter years of his reign were Maurice of Nassau

---

23. Dr. Walsh (*Philip II*, pp. 617 f.), after blackening William's character, says that Philip "succeeded in having him placed under the ban of the Empire" (sic), "with a price of 25,000 gold crowns on his head", and seems to regard the murder as legally and morally justifiable.

24. Dr. Walsh (*Philip II*, p. 618) does not mention the actual rewarding of Gérard's relatives; nor, strangely enough, does the name of the worthy murderer find a place in his otherwise excellendy full index.

(William's son), John of Oldenbarneveld, St. Aldegonde, and King Henry IV of France.

How, then, in the face of this mass of mingled evidence and rumour, are we to sum up Philip's record as an assassin? It must, I think, be granted that comparatively few politicians of that period would have held that under no conceivable circumstances was it ever permissible to plot the death, by guile, of a harmful individual, whose misdeeds could not otherwise be curbed. But that is not to say that assassination was a widely approved or generally recognized method of exerting political pressure. So far as the general sentiment is concerned, it was held in reserve as a last resort, the use of which could be justified only once in a way, if at all. Only so could the moral stigma, which always in some measure clung to it, be risked or tolerated. What seems to be peculiar about Philip, and is moreover completely consistent with the ethical tone which normally characterized his political behaviour, is that he seems to have imposed on himself very little moral check in the use of this unlovely instrument of kingcraft. The man who could allow the unstinted bloodshed committed by Alva, and who withstood all the Emperor's efforts to hasten its end, would not be likely to have any qualms about secretly contriving the death of any individual obnoxious to him as a Catholic and a Hapsburg: and the evidence, as we have seen, amply warrants us in drawing this inference.

The duty of speaking the truth and keeping one's word – like the duty of having respect unto one's neighbour's life – is one that is imposed alike by secular ethics and by the dictates of the Christian religion. But here again man, and particularly man qua political ruler, has become accustomed to allow himself a margin – more or less liberal – of exceptions. He has not always realized that the practice of lying, in politics as elsewhere, since its object is always that the lie may be believed, is one that is apt to become useless after the first few occasions of employing it; for sooner or later the existence of the practice becomes known, and thereupon men's willingness to believe disappears. The expediency of the moment, however, is usually so clamant, and man's foresightedness is usually so limited, that the self-defeating character of mendacity, not to mention its moral obliquity, has been unable to prevent men from more or less frequently resorting to it. Duplicity and dissimulation have been normal practices on the part of many rulers and their agents; and during our period as well as during others, even solemn treaties were commonly understood to be binding only as long as no tangible advantage seemed to be obtainable by breaking them.

Thus it was that European sovereigns of the sixteenth century and the agents charged with negotiating their affairs did not shrink from the occasional use of falsehood. Henry IV of France and Elizabeth of England (whose mouth, says Dr. Walsh [p. 158] was "apt for lies") were no exceptions. Of William of Orange's alleged duplicity we shall speak later (see below, pp. 196 ff.).

Yet there is lying and lying, just as there is homicide and homicide. Clearly there can be great differences between one lie and another, in regard to (*a*) barefacedness, (*b*) frequency, and (*c*) provocation by circumstance. There are many ways of keeping confidential facts unknown to others, besides mendaciously and explicitly denying them. It is one thing to lie or dissimulate once a year; another to do so every week or every day. It is one thing to lie or dissimulate when one is in an exceptionally tight corner; another, to do so when there is really nothing to be gained by it. Moreover, a general loyalty to truthfulness and to one's pledged word is to be found in many individuals even in an age when dishonesty is very rife. And for all their shortsightedness, men and even politicians are often aware that honesty is the best policy. Whatever may have been the personal practice of William of Orange, for instance, it may safely be said that the Dutch were, on the whole, far more truthful and straightforward in their diplomacy than were the Spanish and Italians.

Now in this matter of mendacity and promise-breaking, as in the last-discussed question of assassination, Philip stands out, amid a galaxy of politicians of whom few or none were wholly innocent, as indulging in the evil practice more frequently and more willingly than did they. It was not that in the abstract – and concretely, in the case of the conduct of his fellow-men – he did not realize the value and claims of truthfulness and good faith. Dr. Walsh quotes him (p. 492) as writing thus to Don

John in 1568: "Truth in speaking and fulfilment of promises are the foundation of credit and esteem among men, and that upon which the common intercourse and confidence are based. *This is even more necessary in men of high rank and those who fill great public positions, for on their truth and good faith depend the public faith and security.* I urge it upon you most earnestly, that in this you take great care and heed, that it be well known and understood in all places and seasons that full reliance may be and ought to be placed on whatever you say…" (italics mine). What could be finer than such counsel? Any insincerity or untruthfulness in his friends and ministers Philip rebuked with the utmost severity. He "hated lies and liars".[25]

Yet when we examine his own conduct, we find him more or less habitually speaking and writing untruthfully and failing to keep his word. Thus, when he left his wife Mary Tudor at the end of August 1555, he promised her, in response to her urgent petition, to return within a month, "though to his own Spanish confidants he said that if once he set foot in Spain again, he would never leave it on so poor an occasion".[26] In December he sent her a promise that he would come at once – a promise which he repeated a little later. He actually came back to England in March 1557, and left it for the last time in the following July. During 1558, when Mary's health was failing, "Philip sent her affectionate messages, and promised repeatedly to visit her; but he never did. It is not quite clear how much sincerity there was in his promises. It would seem that he could have managed to get across the channel for a few days at least, had he really desired to do so;…"[27]

While concluding the Truce of Vaucelles with France in February 1556, and impressing the French king with his sincerity, Philip was demanding from Mary that England should join him in a war against France. "Perhaps", says Dr. Walsh (p. 176), "the French king should have praised Philip's precocious powers of dissimulation, instead of his sincerity". In the spring of 1559, he instructed Feria, his ambassador in England,

---

25. Walsh, *Philip II*, pp. 336, 526, 548.
26. M. Hume, *Two English Queens*, etc., p. 124: cf. p. 127 ("Like a courteous highbred gentleman, smiling and debonair, he bade a fond farewell for a month to his faded wife, whom, if he could have had his way, he wished never more to see"), 132.
27. Walsh, *Philip II*, p. 200; cf. pp. 202, 222.

to supply the leading Catholics there with money surreptitiously, and to speak the Protestants fair, so as to put them off their guard and prevent them from appealing to France. While toying with the idea of invading England, he wrote a conciliatory letter which Feria could show to Elizabeth. On leaving the Netherlands in August 1559, he promised to withdraw the Spanish troops from that country within three or four months: he did not do so; and such was the hostility which their presence aroused that in January 1561 Granvelle and the Regent deported them to Spain without his orders. As has been pointed out above (p. 85), his whole policy in the government of the Netherlands involved the violation of his twice-sworn oath to respect the charters and liberties of the country. In 1562 he definitely advised Granvelle to dissimulate in the face of his enemies and accusers. In 1564, when he had at last come to the conclusion that Granvelle must be removed, he engineered his retirement by means of an elaborate system of false pretences, in order to avoid giving the impression that a concession was being made to popular clamour. When forced, by the violence of local feeling in 1566, to grant pardon and toleration in the Netherlands, to withdraw the Inquisition, and to suspend the placards, he formally but privately declared in writing that this pardon was granted only under duresse and that he would not therefore be bound by it; and he informed the pope that his withdrawal of the Inquisition was a mere form of words (see above, pp. 78 f.). This was the year before he sent Alva into the country with an army. He gave it out that he intended to visit the Netherlands himself, and that Alva was simply going to prepare the way for him: but he never went, and in all probability never intended to go.[28] In 1568 he wrote to the pope what Dr. Walsh himself (p. 465) describes as an "obviously insincere letter" about his son Don Carlos. The Marquis of Berghen and the Baron of Montigny came to Spain in 1566 in order to negotiate with Philip, and were received with cordiality: but neither of them was ever allowed to return. The former died in Madrid. The latter was put off with deceitful excuses, was eventually imprisoned, and, after being in his

---

28. Pirenne, *Belgique*, vol. iv (1911), p. 5: "Pourtant il est bien décidé à ne pas bouger. Il ne veut pas présider à l'annulation des privilèges qu'il a juré de maintenir, assister aux exécutions qu'il a ordonnées, voir couler le sang, entendre les supplications de son peuple".

absence sentenced to death by Alva at Brussels, was by Philip's orders secretly strangled in October 1570, his death being publicly declared to be the result of fever (see above, p. 80). Not only did Philip rejoice over the massacre of the Huguenots in France in 1572, but he spoke appreciatively of the "long dissimulation" practised in connexion with it. In 1575 he repudiated his debts. He dissimulated with his bastard brother Don John and the latter's secretary Escovedo (1576-78). In 1578 he agreed to pay the 600 Italian mercenaries whom the pope was sending to Ireland, "but wanted the fact kept secret, in order to avoid offending Queen Elizabeth".[29] He instructed Mendoza to bribe the English ministers.[30]

Along with the deceitfulness of the king went necessarily the deceitfulness of his agents. The Duke of Alva advised his sovereign to dissemble temporarily until he should be strong enough to behead the troublesome nobles of the Low Countries (see above, p. 93). Alva himself effected the arrest of Counts Egmont and Hoorn only after allaying their suspicions by a hypocritical display of kindness (see above, p. 95). In 1572 he was encouraging Philip to temporize with England pending the conquest of the Netherlands, so that he could deal with England at his discretion later. But perhaps the most extraordinary example of diplomatic deceitfulness practised conjointly by Philip and one of his agents was one which went near to bringing England into complete subjection to Spain. For approximately two years before the Armada sailed, the Duke of Parma was, with Philip's full knowledge and consent, carrying on a series of elaborate peace-negotiations with England, for the sole purpose of deluding Elizabeth, convincing her of Philip's friendliness, putting her off her guard, and so gaining time for the preparation of the already fully-intended Spanish invasion. On the side of the Queen, her representatives, and most of her ministers, the consultations were sincere, subject to the usual margin of secretiveness and camouflage incidental to the diplomacy of that period; and a genuine desire and hope of coming to terms was felt. On the Spanish side, the whole affair from beginning to end was a protracted piece of hypocrisy and lying, a mere "ruse

---

29. Walsh, *Philip II*, p. 577.
30. Walsh, *Philip II*, pp. 589 f.

de guerre". While it was in progress, similar but less elaborate deceit was practised on France, in order that she might be kept occupied with her own internal broils, might rest confidently on Philip's untruthfully professed friendship, and so not go to England's help. Similar duplicity continued to mark the Spanish diplomatic relations with France, even after the death of Henry III in 1589. At least one further attempt was made on England under the mask of indirect assurances of Spanish friendship. When, after years of magnificent service, Parma at last incurred the suspicion and jealousy of his royal master, the latter masked his real sentiments and intentions by means of a series of flattering lies. Parma's death in December 1592 put him beyond Philip's power to wrong him further. In 1596 the king again repudiated his debts.

Surely we have here a life-long practice of falsehood and deceit far exceeding that more or less normal secretiveness and lack of candour which is apt to mark all diplomacy, and which certainly characterizes much of the intercourse between European states in the sixteenth century. Up to a point, I suppose one may say, it was so common that it deceived nobody. But Philip's record shows a love of "by-paths and indirect crook'd ways" which puts the deceitfulness of his contemporaries completely in the shade. We may or may not wish to make our own Motley's strong characterization of Philip as "the great father of lies who sat in the Escorial":[31] but, rhetoric apart, the phrase is not substantially incorrect. Dr. Walsh does not use such strong language about it: but what else *in substance* is conveyed by his repeated allusions to Philip's masterly dissimulation?[32] Mr. G. Edmundson says of him: "He had great belief in his powers of tortuous diplomacy; and, instead of taking the prompt measures which are essential in a crisis, he sat brooding in his cabinet at Segovia, and slowly evolving by what course of action he could

---

31. Motley, *United Netherlands* (ed. 1875-76), vol. ii, p. 338: cf. vol. i, pp. 109, 474, vol. iii, pp. 177, 507 ("Falsehood was the great basis of the king's character.... Certainly Nicholas Macchiavelli could have hoped for no more docile pupil...").
32. Walsh, *Philip II*, p. 336 ("... the dissimulation at which Philip became a past master in dealing with treacherous enemies and questionable friends"), 457 ff. ("The Subtle Diplomacy of Philip"), 483 ("... those smiles of dissimulation at which the King had become so skilful, and those evasive answers..."), 673 (Henry IV's dissimulation, "an art in which he was scarcely less skilful than Philip II"), 720 ("The face that had, masked from curious eyes so many deep policies...").

best circumvent his difficulties, cajole his adversaries, and, it may be added, deceive his friends".[33]

No one will deny that his frequent recourse to mendacity and deceit was practised in the steady pursuit of a dominating ambition or, let us say, two dominating ambitions – to enhance his own royal power, and to defend Catholicism. But of the fact that he did actually and habitually practise deceit the record of his doings, even as his panegyrist presents it, leaves not the slightest room for doubt. Dr. Walsh, therefore, stultifies his own narrative, when he writes of Philip (p. 705): "His magnanimity and Christian charity make a contrast with the duplicity of Henry and with the cold calculating malice of the Cecils..." With the story of the long-drawn-out peace negotiations preceding the Armada before our eyes, we deem this author to be but playing with facts when he writes (p. 589): "Philip... suffered... from another kind of blindness from which Elizabeth was singularly free: with an almost childish trust, he was constantly under-estimating his enemies and their power to do him harm. In this he was anything but Machiavellian..." The names of the two sovereigns need rather to be interchanged here – at least if regard is to be had to the diplomatic episode to which I allude. Dr. Walsh's reviewer in *The Times Literary Supplement* for February 19, 1938 (p. 118) is as inaccurate as Dr. Walsh himself. "Certainly by contrast with the widespread opportunism and duplicity of his time", he writes, "Philip II's character stands out nobly. It had extraordinary consistency". But consistency in ambition is by no means incongruous with opportunism and duplicity. As regards these latter, Philip appears, not better, but consistently worse, than most of his contemporaries. Nor can I at all understand how a scientific historian like Mr. Trevor Davies, aiming to "steer an even... course between the Scylla of Protestant, Liberal and Anti-clerical prepossessions and the Charybdis of Roman Catholic partisanship", can bring himself to write of Philip (p. 120): "Duplicity and even crime are possibly, though by no means certainly, to be found as incidents in his diplomatic and political life; but such things were no part of his

---

33. In *Camb. Mod. Hist.*, vol. iii (1904), p. 200. Cf. Pirenne, *Belgique*, vol. iii (1912), pp. 387 f., 398.

normal behaviour. Those who knew him best recognised him as truthful,…"

It is no easy task to sum up the evidence for Philip's character with justice and accuracy, even when we remember that our business is to describe the character, and not to acquit or convict the man, and also that a monarch has sharper ethical problems to face than those which challenge ordinary humanity. There is in Philip's case a further fact to be reckoned with, to which allusion has not yet been made. His family was tainted with insanity. The cause of this was probably the chronic in-breeding which marked its matrimonial history. Philip's grandmother died at the age of seventy-six, after having been hopelessly mad for fifty years. The epileptic Don Carlos, son of Philip and his first cousin, was as degenerate in mind and character, as he was obviously misshapen in body. Philip's successors on the Spanish throne exhibited both physically and mentally the abnormalities of their heritage. Philip himself was the child of first cousins. His mother was the offspring of several generations of consanguineous marriages, and her two younger sons died in early childhood of epilepsy. How far he himself may have been affected by the taint it is impossible to say, even though his normal thinking powers never betrayed any signs of it.[34]

No doubt his modern apologists are right in insisting that the detestation in which he was long held in Protestant countries engendered a traditional view of him which did less than justice to his piety and his private virtues. But the traditional horror felt towards him is not necessarily on that account to be regarded as groundless, or as due simply to religious narrow-mindedness. The unrestricted and extensive use which he made of falsehood and bloodshed in order, not only to serve the Roman Church, but also to defend and increase the glory of his throne and dynasty, though not inconsistent with earnest religiousness and with certain personal graces, naturally and inevitably blackened his reputation, and amply explains and goes far to justify the

---

34. Cf. M. Hume in *Camb. Mod. Hist.*, vol. iii (1904), p. 522: "As in the case of his father, the taint of neurotic dementia in the blood of Castile had brought with it the morbid spiritual introspection, the yearning for relief from the things of the world, that had led the great Emperor to a cloister, and now made Philip long for his rest".

opinions customarily entertained regarding him. It is no Protestant fanatic, but so sympathetic an historian as Mr. Edward Armstrong, who writes: "Given the character of Philip II, the personal union of Spain and the Netherlands was an unmixed evil,…"[35]

---

35. Armstrong, *Charles V* (ed. 1910), vol. ii, p. 89: cf. Merriman, *The Emperor*, pp. 225 f., 394, 405 f., *Philip the Prudent*, pp. 661 f. (he calls Charles's attachment of the Netherlands to Spain the worst mistake he ever made), 672 f.

Chapter Seven

The Popes of the Period

A useful side-light is thrown on the history of Philip's reign by noting the part taken in the events of the period by the successive bishops of Rome. Before we begin such a survey, it will be well for us to bear in mind that, alongside the great struggle between Catholicism and Protestantism, there were three other important antagonisms rife in Europe, based on different interests and serving to complicate the progress of the ecclesiastical conflict. The House of Hapsburg was one of the great foes of Protestantism: but it happened to be also the rival of the papacy, the enemy of France, and the sworn defender of Christendom against the Turks. So formidable was its power, and so menacing its domination, that some measure of sympathy and co-operation was likely to show itself from time to time between any two of its four great opponents – Protestantism, France, the Papacy, and the Crescent – however fiercely these might be opposed to one another on religious or other issues.

Giovanni Pietro Caraffa was elected Pope, in defiance of Charles V's opposition, in May 1555, and took the name of PAUL IV. A Neapolitan of the age of seventy-nine, he had all along been a hater of Spain and the Emperor, and resented the domination which they had secured in Italy at the expense of the French. He zealously desired to reform the Church; but he still more zealously desired to see the Spanish power humiliated. He regarded the Emperor as a favourer of heretics – because Charles, in his inability to crush the German Protestants, felt compelled at length to come to terms with them. The provisional Peace of Augsburg, which Ferdinand agreed to on his brother's behalf in September 1555, and which allowed each German prince to decide whether his princedom should consist of Catholics or Lutherans, greatly shocked the pope; and he began to draw near to France. He arrested or put to flight the imperialist cardinals, promoted his worldly and warlike nephew Carlo Caraffa (who shared his hatred of Spain) to the rank of cardinal, and prepared for hostilities. Already in 1556 the struggle exhibited the cross-currents which the complexity of the situation set up; for while the devout Catholic Alva swore that he would force the pope to make himself worthy of his title of "Holiness", and proceeded to invade the papal states from Naples with that end in view, the pope defended himself with Protestant troops hired from Germany, and even begged the Turks to give up their attack on Hungary and turn their arms against Philip in Sicily and southern Italy. Disappointed and angered by the Truce of Vaucelles between France and Spain in February 1556, the pope was assisted at the end of the year by the Duke of Guise with a French army. Cardinal Caraffa, as papal legate, succeeded in rekindling the war between France and Spain. But the defeat of the pope's troops by the Spaniards in Italy in April 1557, and especially the complete victory won by Philip's army at St. Quentin in August, spelt the total collapse of Paul IV's plans. The irascible old pontiff had perforce to simmer down. He graciously pardoned Alva: and although the ill-will between himself and Philip continued, he gave up all hope of engineering any violent opposition to him. He granted the king a bull authorizing, in the teeth of popular dislike, a more numerous episcopate in the Netherlands. He discarded his anti-Spanish nephews, and gave his attention almost exclusively to the reform of the Church.

This involved an extension of the Roman Inquisition – an institution which Paul IV himself in earlier days (1542) had been mainly instrumental in reviving. His government was a reign of terror. So inhuman and severe were the severities practised by the Inquisition in his time that on his death violent riots broke out in Rome. In January 1559 he forbade the printing, perusal, or even possession of any translation of the Bible into a vernacular language, without the licence of the Office of the Roman Inquisition.

His overbearing attitude in his relations with England was largely responsible for the ultimate failure of Catholicism in that country. He was the bitter enemy of Cardinal Reginald Pole, whom his penultimate predecessor, Pope Julius III, had appointed papal legate in 1553, and who, since November 1554, had led the Catholic reaction in England under Philip and Mary; and he endeavoured to disgrace him. Contrary to the understanding agreed upon by the various parties concerned, he demanded that all property alienated from the Church of England since the beginning of the great turnover in Henry VIII's time should be restored to her. When Elizabeth succeeded to the throne in November 1558, he demanded that she should submit her claims to his judgment, since he regarded himself as the master of princes; and it was only under the urgent pressure exerted by Philip himself (who feared a possible union of England with France) that he refrained from taking still more violent steps against her on behalf of the English Catholics. His successor recognized that it was he who lost England for Rome.

In February 1559 he published the bull *Cum ex apostolatus officio.* In this he described the pope as ruling over the lands in the capacity of God's and Christ's vicegerent, as possessed of full authority over nations and kingdoms, as judge of all, but subject to the judgment of none. He solemnly pronounced all heretical or heresy-favouring prelates and secular rulers to be ipso facto deposed, and liable to punishment by the secular arm. He mentioned no names; but it was moderately obvious that the pronouncement was directed against Elizabeth.

At his death, as has already been intimated, a wild outburst of popular anger against him took place in his capital city.

His successor was Giovanni Angelo Medici – PIUS IV (1559-65). A sexagenarian of lowly origin, unconnected with the great Medici-family of Florence, he formed a striking contrast to Paul IV, to whom he had indeed been an object of dislike. He was a kind-hearted and unassuming man, favourable to Spain and the Emperor, a lover of peace, and disliking the severity of the Inquisition. He recognized Elizabeth's royal title, and concurred in Philip's policy (based on the political needs of the moment) of not attacking her for the present. He punished his predecessor's nephews, executing several of them – including Cardinal Carlo Caraffa – for their crimes. The only nephew of his own whom he promoted was the saintly Carlo Borromeo of Milan.

But mild as the pope was, it was impossible for the contest between the representatives of the two religious systems to be altogether quiescent. In 1561 Cecil scandalized the Spanish ambassador by telling him that the pope had no right to partition the earth and to give away kingdoms as he liked. But the most significant episode in the Catholicism of Pius IV's time was the resumption and conclusion of the great Council of Trent. The last preceding session, the sixteenth, had been held in 1552. The Council reassembled in January 1562, under altered conditions. There was no hope now of reconciling the Protestants, though Protestant delegates were – as a matter of form – invited and promised safe-conducts, and Ferdinand the Emperor was in favour of conciliation. The violent antagonism between pope and emperor had passed away. A few doctrines remained to be defined, a few reforms to be effected. Breaches of sympathy between the Catholic powers were to be healed. Spain, France, and the Empire all desired reforms: but the pope, in dread of these, evaded them by skilfully playing off the parties against one another. The twenty-fifth and last session was held in December 1563; and the Council was dissolved with a great flourish of trumpets, but with no thorough reform of the Curia and no diminution of the papal power.

Some tension had indeed arisen between Philip and the pope as regards the privileges and the excessive severity of the Spanish Inquisition: but the all-round reconciliation between the papacy and the Catholic monarchies imparted to European Catholicism a new sense of solidarity and power. At an earlier date, Pius IV had dismissed the suggestion that he should support a general attack on Geneva: but at the close of his reign it seemed not unlikely that some great Catholic effort might be made to suppress Protestantism everywhere. The conflicting temporal interests of the various royal houses, however, prevented the idea from taking shape. What the year 1564 did see was the resumption of the Roman Inquisition and the promulgation of two important bulls – *Benedictus Deus*, confirming the Tridentine Decrees, and *Injunctum nobis*, embodying the short permanent summary of Catholic belief known as *Professio Fidei Tridentince*, or, in English, *the Creed of Pius IV*.

The little finger of Michele Ghislieri, who succeeded to the tiara as PIUS V (1566-72), proved to be thicker than his predecessor's loins, The latter could hardly be said to have chastised heretics with whips: the new pope visited them with scorpions indeed.

It must be stated in all fairness that Pius V was an extremely devout man – so devout, in fact, that in 1712 it was deemed fitting that he should be canonized. So he goes down to history as *"Saint Pius V"*. He was personally religious, dutiful, unselfish, pure, charitable to the poor, and unostentatious. He avoided nepotism. He advocated and promoted a higher standard of morals in Italy; and it is imputed to him as a merit that he hung Niccolo Franco, the rival of Pietro Aretino in obscenity. He cleansed the papal court of all insobriety, and drove the prostitutes from Rome. He effected a number of Church-reforms – of which the most important historically was the compilation and publication in 1566 of the *Catechismus Concilii Tridentini*, a systematic and complete summary of Catholic teaching on the basis of the decrees of the Council of Trent.

Catholic and catholicizing historians speak of this pope with deep respect. Pius V, says the Anglo-Catholic scholar, Dr. B.J. Kidd, "was a great saint; deservedly canonized, 1712".[1] Dr. Walsh describes him as "one of those rare Christians who take all the words and examples of Christ literally, without exception or reservation, and so move through the world like a light in a dark place. He spoke little, save of the things of God..." (p. 374). He calls him "a truly great and saintly character" (p. 394). He attributes Don John's great victory over the Turkish fleet at Lepanto in 1571 to the prayers of "the old saint in the Vatican" (pp. 516, 528, 570).

It had not, however, apparently occurred to Pius V that this literal obedience to the teaching and example of Christ involved any obligation to refrain from cruelty or to moderate justice with mercy. He exemplifies better than any other historical individual known to me the general description which Lecky gives of the character of the class to which he belongs. "The monks, the Inquisitors, and in general the medieval clergy", wrote Lecky, "present a type that is singularly well defined, and is in many respects exceedingly noble, but which is continually marked by a total absence of mere natural affection. In zeal, in courage, in perseverance, in self-sacrifice, they towered far above the average

---

1. Kidd, *The Counter-Reformation* (1933), p. 163.

of mankind; but they were always as ready to inflict as to endure suffering. These were the men who chanted their Te Deums over the massacre of the Albigenses or of St. Bartholomew, who fanned and stimulated the Crusades and the religious wars, who exulted over the carnage, and strained every nerve to prolong the struggle, and, when the zeal of the warrior had begun to flag, mourned over the languor of faith, and contemplated the sufferings they had caused with a satisfaction that was as pitiless as it was unselfish. These were the men who were at once the instigators and the agents of that horrible detailed persecution that stained almost every province of Europe with the blood of Jews and heretics, and which exhibits an amount of cold, passionless, studied and deliberate barbarity unrivalled in the history of mankind".[2]

Of such quality, without a doubt, was the sainthood of the man who was, in Dr. B.J. Kidd's opinion, "deservedly canonised, 1712". Before he became pope, he had distinguished himself by his severity and thoroughness as an Inquisitor. The opposition he aroused at Como in 1550 necessitated his recall. Paul IV advanced him, making him a cardinal and finally Grand Inquisitor. This office he discharged with such rigour as to make his very name a terror, and to involve him in the displeasure of Pius IV. His regard for Paul IV was expressed in his reversal, as pope, of the judgment against the Caraffa-family, and the rehabilitation and restitution which he caused to be granted to them. Dr. Walsh writes significantly (p. 374): "Before his election he had been Grand Inquisitor for all Christendom, a circumstance for which the enemies of Christianity have never forgiven him. They still write of his pride, cruelty and arrogance". The authorities are at one in regard to the rigour and severity of his attitude to heretics of every sort and kind – as to offenders generally – during his tenure of the supreme authority.[3] "The utter extinction of heresy", writes Dr. T.F. Collier, "was his darling ambition, and the possession of power only intensified his passion. The rules governing the Holy Office

---

2. Lecky, *Rationalism in Europe* (ed. 1872), vol. i, pp. 326 f.
3. Von Pastor says (*Popes*, vol xvii [1929], p. 101): "A circular addressed to the governors of the Papal States in August, 1568, urged them to employ nothing but severity, and to show no mercy. It was estimated that more executions took place at that time in a single month than in four years under Pius IV".

were sharpened; old charges, long suspended, were revived; rank offered no protection, but rather exposed its possessor to fiercer attack; none were pursued more relentlessly than the cultured, among whom many of the Protestant doctrines had found acceptance;... greater thoroughness [was] introduced into the pursuit of heretical literature.... Thus heresy was hunted out of Italy: the only regret of Pius was that he had sometimes been too lenient.... He urged a general coalition of the Catholic states against the Protestants;..."[4] "He bore the very bitterest hatred", writes Von Ranke, "to all who would not accept his tenets. And how strange a contradiction! the religion of meekness and humility is made the implacable persecutor of innocence and piety! But Pius V... was incapable of perceiving this discrepancy; seeking with inexhaustible zeal to extirpate every trace of dissent that might yet lurk in Catholic countries, he persecuted with a yet more savage fury the avowed Protestants, who were either freed from his yoke or still engaged in the struggle.... How wonderful is this union of upright purpose, elevation of mind, austerity towards himself, and devout religious feeling, with morose bigotry, rancorous hatred, and sanguinary eagerness in persecution!"[5]

To Dr. Walsh, all this readiness to inflict suffering constitutes part of the pope's claim on our regard, being presumably part of his literal obedience to the words and example of Christ! Thus (p. 374: cf. p. 500), "Since he saw clearly the challenging, uncompromising truth of Christianity, he had no tolerance for those perversions or travesties of it that were called heresies". Again (pp. 530 f.), "He encouraged and fortified Catholics against Protestants and other enemies in all parts of the world.... His administration was like a strong medicine to restore the health of Christendom. Its reaction on unhealthy tissue was often unpleasant, but it accomplished its purpose.... Saint Pius, like all the Roman pontiffs, was the heir of that august power in the new dispensation of Christ. Its burden sometimes drew tears from him. He exclaimed that God had placed it on him in punishment for his sins (for he had never

---

4. In *Encyc. Brit.*, vol. xxi (1911), p. 685 b.
5. Von Ranke, *Popes*, vol. i, pp. 285 f.

wished to be Pope); but he used it unflinchingly as his conscience commanded".

Let us glance at some of the examples of this supposedly healing policy.

He loudly protested against the toleration of Protestantism in the Empire. He commanded the complete extermination of the Huguenots in France; and in despatching an armed force to aid the French Catholics, he gave their leader orders to take no Huguenot prisoner, but instantly to slay every one of them who should fall into his hands. There is no reason to believe that he was privy to the plans for the massacre of St. Bartholomew; but there can also be no doubt that he shares in the moral responsibility for it.[6]

As long as he could believe that Mary Queen of Scots, intended to restore Catholicism in Scotland, he enthusiastically encouraged and helped her: but when it became clear that she had no intention of suppressing Protestantism (as indeed she had no power to do), and above all, when she married the Protestant Bothwell after the death of Darnley, he ceased to support her.

Elizabeth of England was, however, the chief thorn in the saintly pontiff's side. One of his great longings was for her dethronement: and to this end he secretly instigated the northern Earls to rebel in 1569. The following year he launched his famous bull, *Regnans in excelsis*, in which he declared Elizabeth a heretic and as such possessed of no right to rule, absolved all her subjects from their oaths of allegiance, and forbade them under pain of anathema to obey her orders.[7] The bull was not allowed to be published in either France or Spain; and it was only with some difficulty that a copy of it was fastened to the Bishop of London's door. Its main effect, after the first alarm had died down, was to make England more Protestant and Elizabeth more popular than before, and to cause the oppression

---

6. For Pius V's vehemence against the French Huguenots, and his displeasure at the conclusion of terms of peace with them, see Von Pastor, *Popes*, vol. xviii (1929), pp. 125 ("... nothing was more cruel than compassion for the wicked and for those who had deserved death"), 128-130. At the same time, he seems to have disapproved of *assassination* as such (pp. 154 f.). His view seems to have been that the heretics should be destroyed only by means of open, merciless, and truceless war.

7. The text of the document is printed in Mirbt, *Quellen zur Geschichte des Papstums* (ed. 1924), pp. 348 f.

of English Catholics to become more severe. It is, however, noteworthy that no Catholic was put to death in Elizabeth's reign in England until *after* this aggressive bull had been published.[8] The following year the pope urged Philip II to assist in the execution of the Ridolfi-plot, a scheme which included a plan for the Queen's assassination.

Concern for the cause of Christ made Pius V a close ally of Philip II, and Philip II a strong supporter (on the whole) of Pius V.[9] The pope urged the worried king to overcome the heretical resistance to his rule in the Netherlands by means of armed force. The result of Philip's following this advice was the shocking episode of the Duke of Alva's six years in the country. The pope had wished Alva to diverge on his march, and destroy Geneva en route. How the Duke spent his time in the Netherlands we have already seen (pp. 93-110), so that the reader will be in possession of our grounds for referring to the episode in question as "shocking". But it was, at least in its earlier stages, very far from shocking to the saintly pope. In its large-scale destruction of Protestant life, he sensed nothing incongruous with Christian practice; and in expressing his hearty approval of it he was unaware of any infringement of his duty to "take all the words and examples of Christ literally". Over Alva's defeat of Count Louis of Nassau at Jemmingen he performed three processions of thanksgiving. He approved of the execution of Egmont and Hoorn. He wrote cordially to the Duke of Alva, praising him for his proceedings, congratulating him on his success, and sending him as a mark of honour the consecrated hat and sword. He expressed, to Philip's ambassador the hope that, when the Netherlands were subdued, the king would undertake to capture Geneva and burn it to the ground.[10] In 1569, when resistance had for the time been quelled, the pope advocated an amnesty for such Netherlanders as would now peacefully and penitently submit to the Church (see above, p. 98). But in 1571 he granted Philip financial help for the maintenance of Catholicism

---

8. See some judicious remarks of Dr. Norman Sykes on this subject in *The Journal of Theol. Studies*, vol. xliv, pp. 92-94 (January-April, 1943).
9. There was however, not infrequently, some tension between them – chiefly in the form of offence on the part of the pope at Philip's encroachment on papal and ecclesiastical prerogatives (Walsh, *Philip II*, pp. 484-487, 501 f., 511, 525).
10. Von Pastor, *Popes*, vol. xviii (1929), pp. 100 f.; Walsh. *Philip II*, p. 464.

in the Low Countries; and in 1572 (after the fall of Brill) he lined up again with Alva.[11]

We may conclude our notice of Pius V with a reference to his relations with the cruel and immoral Cosmo I, the despotic Duke of Florence (1537-74). Though at first an opponent of the papacy, the Duke later, in the hope of receiving its political support, was obsequious in complying with the pope's wishes. Thus it was that, in obedience to Pius V's orders, he allowed to be arrested (some said at his own table) his personal friend Pietro Carnesecchi, who had ventured back to his native city. Taken to Rome, Carnesecchi was put on trial by the Inquisition, not for his published views, but for certain privately expressed opinions. On most of the charges he had been acquitted under a former pope. His life was morally blameless, nor had he ever rebelled against the Church. He was tortured, imprisoned for many months, and finally, in October 1567, beheaded and burnt. Two years later the pope crowned Cosmo as Grand Duke of Tuscany.

It is thus not without good reason that Dr. B.J. Kidd, despite his view that Pius V was "deservedly canonised", and that by his actions he sealed the fate of Protestantism in Italy, thus saving the country from a devastating religious war, observes, with reference to his rule, "We could not now approve the horrible barbarity of the Inquisition".[12]

Within a fortnight of Pius V's death, the septuagenarian Cardinal Hugo Buoncompagno was elected to the papal throne, and ascended it as GREGORY XIII (1572-85). Like his predecessor, he was zealous for the suppression of heresy, and refrained from excessive nepotism: on the other hand, he lacked Pius's extreme rigour and sanctimoniousness: he was, moreover, the father of an illegitimate son, born to him before he became a priest. This son was, from time to time, the cause of a little embarrassment. The pope sought out various honours for him, and induced the Republic of Venice to enrol him among its "nobili". Uncertainty being felt as to how the young man had best be designated, the Venetian ambassador asked the Cardinal

---

11. Von Pastor, *Popes*, vol. xviii (1929), pp. 101, 104.
12. Kidd, *The Counter-Reformation* (193 3), p. 177.

of Como whether it would be in order to describe him as the pope's son. The cardinal in reply suggested that perhaps it would be better to refer to him as "Signor Giacomo Buoncompagno of Bologna, closely related to his Holiness".

Gregory XIII laid posterity under an obligation by effecting a reform of the calendar (1582). One of his most important ecclesiastical measures was the lavish support which he gave to the educational institutions of the Jesuits in Rome and elsewhere, for the purpose of training defenders of the faith. The Jesuits, it will be remembered, were Rome's most active agents in the work of the Counter-Reformation. They toiled to undo the achievements of Protestantism in every country where traces of it still survived. "In Germany, Poland and England", writes Dr. Walsh (p. 531), apparently not meaning to be sarcastic, "other Jesuits, willing to shed no blood but their own, were engaged in a titanic struggle for the souls of whole nations".

Within a few months of Gregory's accession, there occurred in France the blackest Catholic crime of the century. Catherine de' Medici, mother of the young French King Charles IX, was terrified at the danger of her son falling under Huguenot influence. She therefore took advantage in August 1572 of the presence of an exceptionally large number of Huguenots in Paris, to instigate a wholesale massacre of them. In this she had the consent of the king and the approval and assistance of several ecclesiastics and, of course, of the powerful family of the Guises. The massacres lasted in Paris from August 24 until late in September: in the provinces they began before the end of August and lasted until the beginning of October. Estimates of the numbers slain vary considerably: a modern historian leans to about 30,000: Charles IX himself reckoned it at about 70,000. For this deed Catherine received the congratulations and plaudits of the whole Catholic world. Gregory XIII, as soon as he heard the news, celebrated a special high mass of thanksgiving, proclaimed a jubilee for all Christendom, had bonfires lit, guns fired, and a medal struck bearing the inscription "Ugonottorum strages". He summoned the painter Vasari from Florence, and commissioned him to depict the massacre in a series of frescoes. Towards the close of the year, by which time, of course, the dreadful facts were fully known, Cardinal Orsini was sent to Paris as papal legate.

While there, he absolved a number of the murderers; and on behalf of the pope, he urged the king to continue his policy of extermination.[13] In the course of 1573 the pope sent Charles a consecrated sword and cap; and on St. Bartholomew's day at Avignon, the anniversary of the commencement of the massacre was celebrated by an ecclesiastical procession.

In eloquent contrast to the grateful jubilation with which the horrid deed was at the time welcomed and applauded by Catholic Christendom is the attempt repeatedly made by modern Romanist writers to relieve the papacy of all responsibility for either causing the massacre or even rejoicing over what had really taken place. But apart from the habitually sanguinary counsels of Pius V, that pope had already received from the French court dark hints as to what it one day hoped to effect. As regards Gregory XIII, the former Catholic plea that, when he rejoiced, he had heard only that a Huguenot plot against Charles IX's life had been frustrated by the slaughter of a comparatively few ringleaders, is completely refuted,[14] firstly, by the dates concerning the movements of Vasari and Cardinal Orsini, and secondly, by the total absence of any modification in the pope's attitude when ample time had elapsed for the real facts to become completely known. No doubt, it was not the Church, but Catherine de' Medici, who took the decisive step; no doubt, her motives were mainly political, not religious; no doubt, Protestants may get, and sometimes have got, erroneous notions as to the details of what happened. But the damning facts as regards the ethics of the Roman Church in general, and of the papacy in particular – at this juncture in history – can safely be left to speak for themselves.[15]

---

13. Von Pastor (*Popes*, vol. xix [1930], p. 516) says: "Then Orsini turned the conversation to the complete destruction of the Huguenots, reminding the king of the words which he caused to be written to the Pope by the nuncio, to the effect that within a few days there would not be a single Huguenot left in the kingdom".
14. Von Pastor abandons it (*Popes*, vol. xix [1930], p. 505, n. 2).
15. Dr. Sylvia L. England, in her book, *The Massacre of Saint Bartholomew* (1938), gives us an up-to-date, impartial, and well-documented version of the story: she con-jecturally puts the number slain at about 30,000 (p. 180: Von Ranke *[Popes*, vol. i, p. 441] had given it as 50,000). Her closing chapter (pp. 239-257) on "Judgment" well illustrates the difficulty of justly synthetizing horrified indignation with the desire to make all reasonable allowances. A detailed and well-documented study of the part taken by Rome is contained in C. Poyntz Stewart's *The Roman Church and Heresy* (London: Thynne and Jarvis, 1925). Cf. my own *Catholicism and*

Gregory XIII's whole policy in western Europe was directed to the suppression of Protestantism by forcible means. Though unable to secure a continuation or repetition of the massacre of St. Bartholomew in France, he aided the Catholic "League" formed there by the Duke of Guise. Though devoid of all sympathy with Philip II's dynastic ambitions, he valued him as a champion of Catholicism, and subsidized him in his wars in the Netherlands. He tried to effect a league of Catholic sovereigns, for the purpose of grappling both with Protestants and with Turks.

Of special interest to us are his prolonged and repeated schemes for the overthrow of Elizabeth of England, the strongest political figure on the Protestant side. In 1576-78 he encouraged Don John of Austria, then governor of the Netherlands, to aspire to the conquest of England and a marriage with Mary Queen of Scots. The pope sent a nuncio to Philip to urge him to approve of this ambitious scheme: but Philip's caution led to its eventual abandonment. Gregory, however, renewed Pius V's bull of excommunication and deposition against Elizabeth, and patronized several attempts to raise armed rebellion against her in Ireland. In 1580 began the invasion of England by Jesuit priests from the seminaries of Douay, Rheims, and Rome.[16] We may readily grant that the motives of many of these

---

Christianity (1928), pp. 569 f., 600. Von Pastor (*Popes*, vol. xix [1930], pp. 505 ff.) gives an objective account of the rejoicings at Rome, but pleads (1) that they had reference, not to the atrocities (which he regards as intelligible, though not excusable, p. 510, n. 1), but to the advantage accruing from the event to Catholicism, (2) that Gregory deplored the illegality of the means used, and (3) that the Huguenots' cruelty to the Catholics had been extreme, and that they were a most serious danger to the Catholic religion.

In 1612 the English poet George Chapman, in his tragedy *The Revenge of Bussy d'Ambois* (Act II, scene i, 11. 196-234) makes Clermont d'Ambois defend the Duke of Guise as the prime author of the massacre on the ground that spirit matters more than flesh and that those really responsible were the Huguenots. Clermont is made to conclude:

"Had faith and true religion been preferr'd
Religious Guise had never massacred".

In a note, Chapman's editor, T.M. Parrot (ed. 1910, p. 581) observes that this and other passages (see above in this book, p. 47) have been interpreted as indications that Chapman was leaning to Romanism; but he himself thinks that they are to be attributed to his love of paradox and his habit of flouting received opinion, the spirit of his work being mainly that of a free-thinker of the Renaissance.

16. Before they left Rome, Campion and Parsons obtained from the pope an explicit statement to add to their instructions, to the effect that the bull of 1570, although already binding on Elizabeth and her adherents, was not binding on her Catholic subjects, so long as the existing state of affairs continued. It would become binding

emissaries were predominantly, or even solely, religious: but the attitude taken by the pope and the Catholic powers, not to mention the avowed hopes and schemes of many of the missionaries themselves, rendered it impossible to keep the confession of treason and the simple confession of Catholic propaganda legally distinct. Several very serious plots to assassinate Elizabeth were laid. Catholic nobles, itinerant priests, continental rulers, and high ecclesiastics, were intermittently active behind these murderous schemes; and Pope Gregory XIII has been proved to have given them more than once his personal approval. It is not therefore to be wondered at that the anti-Catholic legislation in England became increasingly oppressive; and that a considerable number of capital sentences followed.[17]

The need of money for financing his various building-operations and launching his Jesuitical seminaries, and for his general liberality and extravagance, caused the pope great financial difficulty. The extraordinary steps he took to meet these difficulties resulted in the social peace of the papal states being largely destroyed. The country became infested with bandits, and order could not be maintained even in the capital. It was left to the pope's successor to grapple as best he could with the chaos that had been produced.

That successor was Felice Peretti, who was sixty-four years old, and took the name of SIXTUS V (1585-90). There had been very little love lost between him and his predecessor Gregory; and he made no secret of his dislike when he found himself responsible for clearing up the situation the latter had bequeathed

---

on them as soon as it became practicable to put it into effect publicly – "catholicos vero nullo modo obliget rebus sic stantibus, sed turn demum, quando publica eiusdem bullae executio fieri poterit" (Von Pastor, *Popes*, vol. xix [1930], pp. 389 f.: cf. p. 468). Of these Jesuit missions, Professor F.M. Powicke says: "In the eyes of statesmen like Walsingham, ... these movements, often so secret, were dangerous and embarrassing enough" (*Reformation in England* [1941], pp. 125 f.).

17. For the evidence regarding Gregory XIII's views on the proposed assassination, see C.F. Keary's article on "John Ballard" in *Diet, of Nat. Biog.*, vol. i (1921-22), p. 1005 a; G.G. Coulton in *Anglican Essays* (1923), pp. 93 ff.; and Mirbt, *Quellen*, etc. (ed. 1924), pp. 351-353. It might indeed be reasonably presumed that the man who sang Te Deums, celebrated masses, sounded cannon, lit bonfires, struck medals, and had frescoes painted, over the massacre of several thousand Huguenots, would not be likely to boggle over the assassination of an individual heretic: we happen, however, in this case to have evidence in black and white touching his opinion. Mr. Theodore Maynard (*Queen Elizabeth* [1943], pp. 253 f.) softens his disapproval of the attempt to assassinate Elizabeth, by an appeal to what people's feelings would be if someone were to assassinate Hitler. It may be remembered that both the attempts on William of Orange's life – whereof the second was successful – took place during this pontificate, in 1582 and 1584.

to him. He set to work vigorously. Brigandage and social disorder throughout the papal states were suppressed with merciless rigour, and did not reappear until shortly before the end of the pope's life. With the help of a Jewish financial adviser, he managed to restore order to the public finances, and to amass a considerable treasure – but only by means which were financially unwise, were felt to be oppressive, and were productive of unpopularity.

His energy, however, was not exhausted in schemes of outward social efficiency, as represented by the security of life and property, the accumulation of money, and the construction of numerous buildings and other works of public utility. He also had an eye to the moral and religious dignity and zeal of his court; though along with the revived seriousness in religion there went some recrudescence of superstition. The mild nepotism which had become customary after the severe self-restraint of Pius V, was practised in its moderation by Sixtus V. He also made arrangements for the production of a standard edition of the Vulgate. The Council of Trent had declared the Vulgate to be the one authorized version of the Scriptures; but such texts of it as were available in print were in a very corrupt state. With the best intentions, but without proper equipment and assistance, Sixtus personally supervised the work of producing a corrected text: but on its completion it was found to be so faulty that after his death it was withdrawn from circulation on the pretext of printers' errors, and replaced later, in the time of Clement VIII, by an emended edition – which, however, still bore the name of Sixtus V![18]

Among the pope's major ambitions was the desire to re-win the Protestants for the Roman Church; but he regarded with disfavour and suspicion the Society of Jesus, which had done most in central Europe to further the Counter-Reformation. It was only death that prevented him from effecting drastic changes in the constitution of the Society. He interested himself but little in the affairs of Germany, while in Italy the severity of Pius V had virtually extinguished all heretical movement. His main concern was with Spain, France, and England: his foreign policy was on the whole conciliatory, and his dearest hope was that he

---

18. For fuller details see my *Catholicism and Christianity*, pp. 279 – 28

might unite the Christian powers of Europe in a grand attack on the Turks.

With Philip of Spain, indeed, he found it hard to avoid being in a more or less constant state of tension and mistrust. Possessed of enormous political power, and seeing little distinction between the good estate of his own royal dignity and the good estate of the Holy Catholic Church, Philip was inclined to arrogate to himself a disproportionate share of authority in ecclesiastical matters. An energetic and strong-willed pope like Sixtus V, elected in defiance of Philip's wishes, was little disposed to brook the pretensions of an earthly monarch, when they came into conflict with his own views. Yet neither of these two great leaders of Catholic Christendom could afford to fall out seriously with the other. The result was an uneasy alliance, tempered by a measure of chronic mutual suspicion and disapproval: and when Sixtus died, there were rejoicings in Spain.

While Philip was banking on his own vast resources and his schemes of conquest and annexation – primarily in the Low Countries, but also elsewhere – the pope, on the other hand, more than doubtful whether an extension of His Catholic Majesty's power would really be a good thing for the Catholic Church, was opposed to Philip's efforts to control France, and rested his hopes on the possibility of recapturing England. He felt considerable admiration for the stronger qualities in Elizabeth's character, was opposed to plans for her assassination or for the forcible reconversion of her realm, and seriously hoped that she could be won over by persuasion.

The progress of events, however, at length proved clearly to Sixtus, as it had already clearly proved to Philip, that nothing was to be hoped for from Elizabeth in the way of a return to Catholicism. For his part, Philip decided on the Armada, and pestered the pope for financial assistance. The latter could hardly do other than express approval of the scheme; but he was dilatory and niggardly as regards subsidizing it. He promised a sum of money; but none of it was to be paid until the Spanish force borne by the Armada had landed in England, and when the whole enterprise collapsed in defeat and disaster, he was not really very sorry.

At the time when Sixtus became pope, Henry III, the effeminate and unprincipled son of Henry II and Catherine de' Medici, had been king of France for nearly eleven years, and the Huguenot prince Henry of Navarre had for nearly a year been heir-presumptive to the throne. Eager to establish Catholicism as supreme in France without the help of Philip of Spain, Sixtus ere long (September 1585) excommunicated Henry of Navarre and pronounced him excluded for ever from the French throne. This action had the effect of strengthening French, or at least Huguenot, feeling on the side of legitimism, and on the other hand of leading the French king to think that he would be able to use the pope as a tool for his own ends. Philip, who was interested in the French succession for reasons not exclusively religious, was not prepared at any price to allow Navarre to ascend the throne; and in this he was powerfully supported by the Guise-family and the Catholic "League". Navarre took up arms in support of his claims, nominally against King Henry III, in reality against the forces of the League. The king's position became increasingly difficult, owing to the ascendancy of the Guises: and in December 1588 Henry III had Henry, the Duke of Guise, and his brother, Cardinal Louis, murdered. In May the following year, he was conditionally excommunicated by the pope; and in August he was assassinated by a Dominican friar, greatly to the pope's satisfaction.

It was all very well, however, for the pope to rejoice over the removal of this unworthy monarch: but it soon became apparent that his death had only accentuated the problem of the succession. For Henry of Navarre was now claiming to be recognized as the legitimate king; and the Republic of Venice, despite the pope's strong dissuasion and to his serious displeasure, congratulated him on his accession to the throne, and formally recognized him by receiving his ambassador. The victory which, about this time (September 1589), Henry won at Arques over the Duke of Mayenne, the murdered Guises' brother, coupled with the constant fear of Spanish domination, led the pope – though still greatly perplexed – to take up a less antagonistic attitude. For while the Guises and their partisans of the League took the same irreconcilable view as Philip, yet other French Catholics had shown themselves prepared to support Henry. Before the end of the year, Sixtus had been at least induced to give the Venetian ambassador his blessing.

In January 1590 the pope received graciously at Rome an envoy representing the French Catholic peers attached to Henry. These declared him to be ready to return to the bosom of the Church, if the pope would receive him; and the pope professed his willingness to do so. Now was seen the real ground of Philip's antagonism. He was not prepared to allow on the throne of France a Henry of Navarre reconciled to the Church any more than a Henry of Navarre unreconciled to the Church. He held that no conceivable submission Henry might make to Rome could possibly be genuine. He insisted on the pope refusing any offer of submission Henry might make; and he threatened, in the event of the pope persisting, to call a council, thus hinting at a possible schism on the part of the Spanish Church. Naturally enough, the pope very strongly resented this attempt of Philip to dictate to him. Meanwhile, Henry's fresh victory at Ivry in March 1590 and the ensuing siege of Paris brought the possibility of a heretic king appreciably nearer; and the consequent Spanish pressure succeeded in importing a considerable measure of vacillation into the papal policy. Philip, however, would be satisfied with nothing short of a complete compliance with his demands. He sent a new ambassador to Rome, who on August 7 delivered an ultimatum to the pope. Sixtus strode from the room in loud anger. The ambassador retorted by uttering threats in the presence of the assembled cardinals. The pope almost immediately fell ill, and died before the month was out – much to the satisfaction of the king of Spain.

Cardinal Giovanni Battista Castagna was elected to succeed him, and took the name of URBAN VII. He had been (as was so often the case) out of favour with his predecessor; and he would have supported the Spanish policy very much better than Sixtus had done. But as he died only twelve days after his election, i.e., on September 27, 1590, his tenure of the papal office made little difference to the course of affairs.

Philip of Spain now nominated seven cardinals, and required the conclave to elect one of them to the papal chair, declaring he would not recognize as valid the election of any other candidate. This pressure secured the tiara for yet another cardinal of the

Spanish party. This was Nicolo Sfondrato – GREGORY XIV. He was not elected until December 5, 1590; and during the interregnum, disorder and brigandage were rife in the papal states. The new pope was fifty-five years old. He was upright and devout in character, but ignorant of political affairs and completely subservient to the king of Spain. He gave his entire approval to the League, renewed the excommunication of Henry IV and declared him incapable of reigning, threatened his supporters, and aided his enemies with money and troops. This strong action, however, had the result of strengthening Henry's hands: for even convinced Catholics resented not only the aggression of Philip, but also the political pretensions of the pope, and remained on Henry's side in the confident hope of his early conversion to the ancient faith. Gregory, however, died in October 1591, after a reign of a little over ten months. He had spent a good deal of the treasure accumulated by Sixtus V in the Castle of St. Angelo in aiding the French schemes of Philip of Spain, instead of effecting the relief of his troubled subjects in Italy from the scourge of robbery, famine, and disease.

By once again exerting pressure, the king of Spain for the third time secured one of his own partisans as pope. The cardinal chosen was Giovanni Antonio Fachinetti – a weak old man of over seventy years of age. As INNOCENT IX he ruled the Church for two months, during which he faithfully supported the interests of Spain, particularly in the struggle still raging in France. But his death at the end of 1591 might have suggested that Providence was frowning on the control Philip was exercising on the papal elections: it did at all events suggest the need of choosing a man with a somewhat stronger hold on life.

Yet once more was Spanish influence set to work; and the saintly but very pro-Spanish Cardinal Santori Sanseverina, an intolerant inquisitor, was on the point of being elected, when a wave of independent feeling influenced the conclave to choose Cardinal Ippolito Aldobrandino, the least strongly pro-Spanish of those whom it was known Philip would tolerate. Though an unblushing nepotist, he was a good, pure-living, upright, and conscientious man; and his record compares well with that of several of his predecessors. He chose to be known as CLEMENT VIII (1592-1605). Being only fifty-seven years of age, he had some good prospect of a reign of reasonable length. The Spaniards were rebuffed – for Clement was a protégé of Sixtus V: but they could not help themselves.

Apart from the suppression of brigandage, the foremost task of the new pope was the settlement of the status of Henry IV of France. By the spring of 1593, Henry had come to the conclusion that he would never be able to reign peaceably over his kingdom unless he became a Catholic: he had therefore made up his mind to do so. Philip of Spain, still keeping up through his ambassadors an immense pressure at Rome, was determined to prevent at all costs any final reconciliation between Henry and the papal see. The pope, anxious not to give Philip any ground for offence, but anxious too to be eased of his tiresome domination, possibly also genuinely doubtful as to the sincerity of Henry's professions, played a cautious, waiting game.

At the start, Clement continued subsidizing the cause of the Catholic League, but took every opportunity of restricting the amount of aid he contributed. He refused to grant a public and official reception to Henry's first tentative deputation, and confined himself to private and unofficial generalities of a not-too-damning kind. He did not yet feel ready to go any further. In July 1593, Henry was formally received into the Roman Church by certain French ecclesiastics, who declared the validity of their act to be dependent on the ultimate sanction of the pope. The king now sent the Duc de Nevers to solicit absolution at Rome. Philip did all he could to intimidate the pope into refusing to receive the envoy or grant the absolution: but Clement, though seriously hesitating whether he ought to absolve a relapsed heretic, objected to being domineered over by a foreign ruler. He allowed the Duc de Nevers to see him in private; but he still refused to concede the favour which the French king sought.

It was impossible, however, to leave matters permanently in this unsettled state. In February 1594 Henry was crowned at Chartres; in March he entered Paris: the support he was receiving from various parties in the country and from other states was steadily growing. All this made it increasingly difficult to postpone a final reconciliation with the Church. And this in spite of the fact that, late in 1594, the attempt of Jean Chastel, a pupil of the Jesuits, to assassinate the king, viewed in the light of their well-known belief that "tyrannicide" was justifiable, drew forth an edict expelling them from France. At the same time, it so happened, they were (more innocently) in hot water in Spain also, for challenging what they regarded as the excessive determinism of the Thomist or Dominican doctrine of Providence. Yet Clement saw that he could do more for the Jesuits if he were reconciled with Henry; and Henry saw he could do more against Spain if he were reconciled with the Jesuits. Finally, with the alleged concurrence of over two-thirds of the cardinals, the pope, on September 17, 1595, publicly granted absolution to King Henry in the person of the latter's representative. The step was taken in the teeth of Spanish opposition, and had the effect of freeing the pope to a great extent from Spanish domination.

Certain measures favourable to Catholicism were stipulated for as a condition of papal favour. One was the publication and observance of the Tridentine Decrees; but Henry availed himself of an excepting clause largely to nullify this promise. Strangely enough, nothing had been laid down in regard to the suppression of Protestantism in France: and the Edict of Nantes, which was promulgated in April 1598, and secured tolerable conditions of life and liberty for the Huguenots, moved the anxious pope to make serious remonstrances. Clement was, however, instrumental in bringing to an end, at least for the time being, the long conflict between France and Spain: and in the next month of this eventful year the Peace of Vervins was signed. With the death of Philip on September 13 we pass into a new era.

A few more matters, however, have yet to be mentioned in order to conclude our summary of Clement VIII's pontificate. In 1592 the revised edition of the Vulgate version of the Bible was published (see above, p. 148): it has remained the official Bible of the Roman Church ever since. In 1599 occurred the famous trial of the members of the Cenci-family on the charge of compassing the murder of their father, Francesco Cenci. The pope refused to grant pardons: so Beatrice and her step-mother were beheaded; Giacomo, her eldest brother, was torn with red-hot pincers, killed with a mace, drawn, and quartered; Bernardo, her younger brother, was sentenced to perpetual imprisonment, but pardoned at the end of a year.

From time to time heretics were capitally punished in Rome.[19] In February 1600 there was burnt alive at Rome the philosopher Giordano Bruno. No full account of his teaching is called for here. It will be sufficient to state that, while not an atheist, he did repudiate and scoff at most of the tenets of the organized Christianity of his day. The Inquisition got hold of him at Venice in May 1592; and the following year he was transferred to Rome: it took the Holy Office there seven years before it could reach a decision. During this long period he was kept in confinement, and doubtless from time to time subjected to torture. Refusing to submit or repent, he eventually perished at the stake.

It was, of course, in keeping with the general views of the time, both Catholic and Protestant, that a man who so flagrantly and sweepingly rejected the doctrines of Christianity, after having been born and brought up as a Christian, should suffer death for his temerity. It was in particular the conviction of Catholic inquisitors that such a man, especially one who had been a Dominican friar and had apostatized, should be publicly burnt alive. Yet the idea of killing a man – and especially of killing him by such a method – when he has already suffered seven years' imprisonment, is so shocking to the modern sense of justice that Bruno's death has been called by one writer "a judicial murder", and a statue of him was erected in his honour at Rome in 1889. Ludwig von Pastor parries the criticism by referring to the brutal executions inflicted on Catholic priests condemned for treason by Elizabeth's government in England, to the irritation which Bruno's obstinacy (like Galileo's later) probably caused to his judges, and to the view which these latter would naturally take of their work as simply a painful but inescapable duty.[20] Dr. Walsh (p. 683) finds justification for the pope in the plea that Bruno "scoffed at all religion, the Jewish as well as the Christian revelation, and taught a philosophy of paganism that would, if accepted, have destroyed society".

---

19. Von Pastor (*Popes*, vol. xxiv [1933], pp. 200 ff.) gives particulars.
20. Von Pastor, *Popes*, vol. xxiv (1933), pp. 202-213, esp. p. 213 n.

Dr. Walsh would, however, have done well to remember that the destruction of society by Giordano Bruno was on the whole a not very threatening danger. The Church herself, or even Dr. Walsh's hero Philip, had inflicted far more serious damage on society than Bruno had. Von Pastor's pleas are more reasonable. The English method of executing men for high treason at this period was indeed horrible, including as it did evisceration before death had resulted from the hanging. Whether it would involve more actual pain than burning alive may well be doubted. Allowance must, of course, also be made for the good faith of the judges: they were acting according to their lights. But viewing their actions and principles *objectively*, what ought we to say (1) of Bruno's seven years' imprisonment, (2) of the infliction of the death-penalty for honestly-held, even if erroneous, opinions (as compared with religious proceedings like those of the Jesuits in England, inextricably bound up with the repeated efforts of a foreign power to invade one's country and to assassinate its sovereign), and (3) of burning a condemned man alive? Was it a good thing, or was it a bad thing, that a system and institution necessitating and sanctioning such proceedings should be opposed, and compelled to submit to drastic alteration in its methods?

Clement VIII's hope that the absolution of Henry would make it easier to get the Society of Jesus readmitted to France turned out to be justified. In 1603 the edict of readmission was published; but the king stipulated that all members of the Society in France must be Frenchmen. It is, however, clear that he was very far from carrying out the pope's ideal of a dutiful son of the Church: and possibly, had it not been for Clement's fear of Spanish ascendancy, the tension between France and Rome might have become serious. As we have seen, the pope found it very hard to stomach the Edict of Nantes and Henry's persistent failure to publish the Decrees of Trent. Henry, moreover, constantly resisted the papal pressure to make an alliance with Spain. He not only refused to help Austria against the Turks, but encouraged them to attack both Austria and Spain, thus frustrating one of Clement's great hopes. In 1603 the pope sent a nuncio to France with the object of confirming Henry in the Catholic faith (since he could hardly have received adequate instruction in it as yet), and of urging him to bestow less favour on the Huguenots and to deal them a blow now and then, to publish the Tridentine Decrees, and to compass the destruction of Geneva.[21] But Henry did little or nothing to fulfil these desires.

Clement's pontificate spanned the transition from Elizabethan to Jacobean England. After the ruin of the Armada, the Spanish plan for the forcible conquest of England received virtually no papal support. Both Sixtus V and Clement VIII decided to depend on spiritual weapons, such as were wielded by the devoted itinerant priests. An effort was made in 1601 to bring about some understanding between the English government and the Catholics. But on both sides the supreme rulers wrecked all hopes. Elizabeth refused all concessions, and the pope forbade all submission to her. The result was that in 1602 the queen issued a proclamation dismissing all Jesuits and secular priests from the realm. Some of the latter evaded exile by swearing to defend the queen against all enemies, notwithstanding any papal prohibition.

James I, before he had left Scotland, had engaged in friendly correspondence with Clement VIII; and this continued after he had become king of England. His wife, Anne of Denmark, was a convert to Catholicism; and the pope suggested to James that the Prince of Wales should be educated as a Catholic. James, despite his theological learning, was a man of unstable mind in religious matters, as we can see from his proceedings in the latter years of his reign. It was, therefore, quite natural that Clement should entertain hopes of the return of England to Catholicism through him. But James doubtless realized that any effort to give effect to these hopes would cost him his crown: that of itself would be quite sufficient to deter him from the attempt.

Clement VIII died on March 5, 1605.

The foregoing sketch of the Roman pontiffs who successively filled the papal throne during the time that Philip was king of Spain is intended, not to furnish a full history of his papal contemporaries, but to present a brief outline of the main events

---

21. Cf. Von Ranke, *Popes*, vol. iii, pp. 291-293.

of the period, with special reference to the relations between the Roman See and the Protestants of Europe, viewed from a standpoint not ordinarily familiar to English readers. The chapter will at least serve to portray the types of character usually presented by the occupants of the papal throne, and to illustrate the complicated way in which the cross-currents of European interest at this epoch (as mentioned in my opening paragraph, p. 134) affected the development of the struggle between the rival ecclesiologies. With the next chapter we must return to the intensive study of the struggle as it was waged in the Low Countries.

Chapter Eight

The Character of the Resistance to Philip in the Netherlands

Protestant students of the history of the sixteenth century, who are apt to wax warm over the intolerance practised by the Roman Church, will do well to realize that the issue – liberty versus persecution – is not such a simple one as might at first sight appear. The sources of complexity are many, and are of varying degrees of seriousness. There is, for instance, the enormous difference between the various possible methods of coercion. When you have altogether condemned and abandoned the use of the rack and the stake, you must not suppose that you have thereby condemned and abandoned persecution: for other and gentler methods of coercion remain available. The problem as to what courses of action Christians may rightly forbid and punish, by whatever coercive means the community continues to practise, still awaits solution – unless one takes the ultra-Tolstoyan view (which some of the Anabaptists did) that no such courses of action exist. Most serious-minded religious men believe that there are at least *some* religious and moral convictions which, however conscientiously held, are so evil and harmful that it is only right that they should be most strenuously opposed.

There is the further complicating element of politics, which may perhaps be viewed as a special aspect of this last-named problem. The general assumption in the sixteenth century, on the part of Catholics and Protestants alike, was that not more than one type of belief and worship could be allowed to flourish, at least publicly, in any particular state, without destroying its social stability and its internal peace (see above, p. 46). Such was the tacit presupposition lying behind the religious Peace of Augsburg concluded in 1555, whereby each German prince was to be allowed to settle whether Lutheranism or Roman Catholicism was to be the public religion of his principality – "cujus regio, ejus religio". Not only so, but the more purely political question of how far alien rule could be tolerated at all, entered in, especially in the Netherlands, to confuse the issue further. Yet another factor emerged in the course of the struggle – the question, namely, whether the demand for religious liberty for oneself logically implies the willingness to grant it to others, and, if it does, whether that liberty ought to be extended to those who are determined to use whatever power they possess to deprive of freedom those who differ from them.

In face of so formidable an array of intricate problems, some of which are still living issues even in our own day, we shall be well advised to take a fairly modest view of our right to make sweeping judgments on the question of toleration and the way to get it. Certainly we must at the moment forgo the attempt to dogmatize comprehensively and in detail regarding a particular historical struggle. As was pointed out near the commencement of this essay (see above, p. 2, n. 1), however much we may desire to identify ourselves with one of the two sides engaged in a great historical struggle, we nearly always feel constrained to sympathize, to some small extent at least, with the other. Yet no complexities in the story or the picture will suffice to shake our conviction that it is a bad custom to torture men or to bury or burn them alive, or to deny them the right to worship God and to shape their beliefs about Him in the way they feel best. So much at least we can say with confidence; and any movement tending to the adoption of that conviction can surely be approved, notwithstanding the fact that other motives than a pure love for God and one's fellows were intermingled with worthier aspirations in the minds of some of its champions, that consequently much injustice was committed by them in the course of the struggle, that even the protagonists of freedom understood only imperfectly the implicates of their own convictions, and that the liberty they won was to some extent misused after their victory. However, before we go any further in our attempt to arrive at a just judgment regarding the Netherlanders' resistance to Philip, perhaps we ought to attempt an examination of its varied characteristics.

There can, I submit, be no real doubt that the original and, throughout, the main motive behind the revolt of the Netherlands against Philip was the widespread disgust, not only on the part of the multiplying Protestants (as of course would be only natural), but on the part of the Catholic population also, at the cruelty and rigour with which the Spanish government endeavoured to suppress all dissent from the Roman Church. Motley argued that the cause of the revolt was simply the Inquisition:[1] and I submit that, roughly speaking, he was right. Since, however, this thesis has been challenged in recent years, and among the "newer trends" in the study of the subject is the idea that Motley's thesis has been exploded, that the main cause of the war was a national, cultural, and political resentment at foreign rule, the religious issue being by comparison subordinate, the subject demands a little special discussion.[2]

The main ground for the newer view is that the Protestants were numerically quite a small minority, whereas the Spanish domination was resented and resisted by Catholics, who naturally regarded Protestantism as grievous heresy.

Now I do not wish at all to deny or forget that sheer anti-foreign sentiment was a real force behind the revolt of the Netherlands against Spain: and I shall presently say something more about that. What I want to establish at the moment is that the *main* force behind it was resentment at religious persecution, and that this resentment was provoked by the ruthless cruelty with which that persecution was carried on. I adduce the following considerations in support of my contention.

(1) The country had been under foreign rule for many years before anything was heard of Protestantism: yet, except for the defection of Ghent (1539) and a few even less important incidents, nothing had been heard of any general agitation for political and cultural liberty, until Philip II made his strenuous endeavours to enforce the persecuting edicts. True, his father Charles had persecuted, and Philip's personal unpopularity certainly sharpened the tension: but, cruel as Charles's anti-heretical measures were, Philip's were more cruel still, because they were

---

1. Motley, *Dutch Republic* (ed. 1874), pp. 164 ff.
2. Dr. Geyl, for instance (in *Revolt*, etc., pp. 16, 75 top, 141, 150, 165-168, 170 f., 215 f., 232, 258, 267, etc.) is disposed to subordinate the religious issue to the cultural and anti-foreign; and he is cordially supported in this by *The Times Literary Supplement* for July 14, 1932, p. 509, and May 6, 1944, p. 226, as if the matter were a "chose jugée". Pirenne had also laid stress on the conflict between the "Burgundian" and the Spanish traditions as the *prime* cause of the revolt (*Belgique*, vol iii [1912], pp. 375 top, 378, 385, 420, 425, etc.): yet he also emphasizes Philip's obstinacy and energy in persecuting heresy as a powerful factor (see pp. 310, 377 f., 387, 390, 397, 415, 432, vol. iv [1911], pp. 138, 147, 202).

more thoroughly carried out. One would have thought that, had anti-foreign sentiment been the main cause of the revolt, it would have broken out earlier.

(2) The severity of the government's efforts to suppress the steadily spreading Reformation-doctrines would naturally and inevitably rouse very wide public discontent, and quite evidently did so. This discontent was not confined to the sufferers themselves and their co-religionists. We have actual evidence to the effect that Catholic magistrates strongly objected to torturing heretics brought before them, and that loyal Catholic nobles like Egmont were keenly opposed to Philip's oppressive measures.[3] No argument, therefore, founded on the numerical inferiority of the Protestants suffices to prove that persecution was not the main issue out of which the struggle arose. In any well-ordered community, the denial of elemental human rights to a minority and the exercise of atrocious cruelty towards them are quite sufficient to account for a violent outburst of public wrath. Catholic writers may, if they wish, point to what they consider the lax and Erasmian type of Catholicism prevalent in the Netherlands: but that strengthens the very point on which I am insisting, namely, that it was disgust at Philip's severity which primarily occasioned the revolt. Can it be maintained that the Netherlands would have revolted in any case, even if the Spanish government had been tolerant and humane?

(3) At every stage of the struggle in the Netherlands against Spain, from the very commencement onwards, the question of the abolition of the placards, the restraining of the Inquisition, and the freedom of conscience and of worship, were in the very forefront of the controversy. They are never for a moment out of sight, however demands for the dismissal of Spanish troops and officials may accompany them.

(4) The reason why the unanimity of the revolt broke up was not that certain folk withdrew their objection to the severities of the Spanish persecution, but that they withdrew their objection

---

3. Cf., e.g., G. Edmundson in *Camb. Mod. Hist.*, vol. iii (1904), p. 201, and *Encyc. Brit.*, vol. xix (1911), p. 417. b; also R.T. Davies, *Golden Century*, p. 154 (he accounts for the unpopularity of persecution by saying: "As yet the Catholic Netherlander had had but little experience of Calvinism with its fierce intolerance and destructive energy". The reply to this is, of course, that no intolerance could well have been fiercer and no energy more destructive than that with which Catholicism had met the peaceable rise of Protestantism: see below, pp. 178 f., 216 f.

to foreign rule. What made them withdraw it was primarily their Catholic disapproval of heresy, stimulated as this disapproval was by the intolerant conduct of the Calvinists themselves and by the threats and blandishments of Alexander Farnese. If the theory that the *main* cause of the struggle was anti-foreign sentiment be right, one would hardly have expected them to drop it so easily.

The priority of the toleration-issue, then, being duly insisted upon, we need not hesitate to recognize frankly the operation of other motives as helping to reinforce the spirit of rebellion. We need have the less hesitation in doing so, seeing that by far the most important of these secondary motives was one worthy on its own account of our respect and sympathy – I mean the Netherlanders' discontent with the foreign and despotic government of the Spaniard. Under the evil system of the Middle Ages, it was simply as the result of family-inheritance, marriage-alliances, and so forth, that Charles and Philip came to be regarded as the legal sovereigns of the country; and it was simply as an implicate of the autocratic character of medieval monarchy in general and of the Hapsburg-rule in particular, that the Netherlands found themselves under the heel of a foreign despot. No one for a long time thought of questioning the legitimacy of such a system of government: but after the foreign despots had for a considerable time been acting on the (doubtless quite honest) assumption that they were entitled to set aside the charters and liberties of their subjects, to keep hosts of Spanish soldiers quartered in the country, and to drain it of money for extraneous enterprises, men naturally began to wonder whether after all the system of government was as sacrosanct as they had previously thought. "'Very well!' 'go to!' I cannot go to, man; nor 'tis not very well: nay, I think it is scurvy, and begin to find myself fopped in it".

Natural, and indeed inevitable, as this resentment was, it forms the most important of those various cross-currents which complicate the struggle in the Netherlands as a contest on behalf of freedom from the Catholic yoke. For of course it was a resentment which Catholics might well feel, and did feel, almost as strongly as Protestants felt it. And while it is true that many

Catholics, nobles and burghers alike, were in favour of religious toleration, it is also true that to most of them Protestantism was extremely abhorrent – a feeling which the violence of some of the Calvinists (itself engendered by Catholic persecution) naturally tended to accentuate. As a result of the operation of those diverse conflicting interests already alluded to, not only is Catholic against Protestant; France also is against Spain, the emperor and/or the Spanish king against the pope, and the Christian against the Turk. That the same sets of men should as a result be found fighting now as allies, now as enemies, was neither wholly evil nor wholly good: it rendered impossible, not only the forcible suppression of Protestantism, but also an adequate measure of resistance to the Turk. But it is in every case a confusing factor; and in the microcosm of the Netherlands it serves to embarrass the issue, and both helped and hindered the attainment of a satisfying settlement.

While it must be frankly admitted that the demand to be free from a foreign yoke is very different from the demand to worship God as one thinks best, it is not for that reason an unworthy demand; nor is there any reason why an honourable man should not at one and the same time press both of them. Honest insistence on one does not imply that insistence on the other must be dishonest. To feel strongly that the Spanish rule was a gross injustice is not inconsistent with feeling strongly that the Holy Inquisition was the reverse of holy. The two motives are rightly distinguished, but must not be set over against one another as mutually exclusive: and where they were operative in the same bosom, they reinforce rather than discredit each other.

The same cannot indeed be so emphatically said of the factor which has next to be mentioned – I mean, the jealousy of the Netherland-nobles at their virtual exclusion from what they considered their fair share of responsibility for the government of the country. Philip made his half-sister Margaret, Duchess of Parma, regent; and her council was to consist of Granvelle (Cardinal-Archbishop of Arras), the Frisian Viglius, Berlaimont, the Prince of Orange, and the Count of Egmont. Of these, the last two found themselves hardly ever consulted; and Granvelle kept the main responsibility (under the regent and the king) in his hands. It may well have been the case that these inner councillors were really moderate and tolerant men: but they were the agents of the inexorable Philip, and thus constrained to pursue a policy which was calculated, not only to rouse national resentment, but also to offend the susceptibilities of the other nobles. Some of the nobility were heavily in debt, and hoped to rehabilitate their fortunes from the emoluments of office, the spoils of war, and the secularization of Church-lands. Mr. Trevor Davies lays great stress on the resulting discontent of the aristocrats, as if it were the chief factor in producing public discontent and ultimately revolt.[4]

The dissatisfaction of the nobility, then, must be frankly recognized as one vera causa, among others, of the revolt of the Netherlands. But it is one thing to admit this, and another to imagine either that their dissatisfaction was groundless, or that it was at all a *determining* factor in evoking rebellion. Let us suppose, for the sake of argument, that certain of the nobles were actuated by base and self-centred motives. But was there nothing in the placards, the Inquisition, the Spanish troops, the executions, to justify a general sense that the country was being misgoverned, and its prosperity ruined, and therefore a sense to that effect on the part of the nobles? These men rightly regarded themselves as charged with a certain responsibility for the public welfare; and their influence doubtless had some weight in rousing popular enthusiasm. But that was only because the rank and file were already feeling similarly. There is abundant evidence to show that the mainstay of the revolution was the burgher-class, whereas many of the nobility fought on the royal side. The imperfect system of government that eventuated as a result of the struggle might be described as a broadly-based and popular aristocracy.[5] This would indeed be a strange result if the first potent impulse had been given by a set of discontented and inebriated noblemen, whose main motive in stirring up trouble was to replenish their own depleted coffers.[6]

---

4. R.T. Davies, *Golden Century*, pp. 154 ("These causes of discontent would probably have had little visible effect but for the discontent of the nobility,..."), 155, 157, 158 ("... the greater nobles roused themselves to the utmost to stir up trouble among the lesser nobles and the middle class..."), 159.
5. See P.J. Blok, *Netherlands*, vol. iii (1900), pp. 377 – 392: also above, p. ix.
6. Cf. Pirenne, *Belgique*, vol. iii (1912), pp. 374, 420 f.

The attempt to discredit the opposition to Philip in the Netherlands by linking it up with the over-potent influence of a little group of scheming nobles is parallel to the equally erroneous attempt to account for the Protestantism of England in the same way. Thus, Dr. Walsh describes Philip, prior to his marriage with Mary of England, picturing himself "as King, hailed by the Catholic majority of Englishmen as savior of their country, and winning over or suppressing the little handful of upstarts who, for their own enrichment, had violently torn the country from the Catholic unity".[7] But make what allowance we will for the schemers, and for the willingness of many of the population to go either way,[8] it is unreasonable to put forward the organizing powers of Cecil as the explanation of the strength of Protestantism in England.

At a still greater remove from the centre of causality, but as playing some part in prolonging and embittering the struggle, was the commercial rivalry between the Dutch and the Spanish nations. In exploiting both the east and the west, the Spaniards were first in the field; and the pope had assumed the right of allotting all acquisitions within certain areas to the control of the kings of Spain and Portugal respectively.[9] When the Dutch also found themselves able to make voyages in these distant seas, they not unnaturally ignored the Spanish claim to possess them as a monopoly. Apart from the normal desire of gain, they were doubtless also eager to deprive Spain of the valuable sources of revenue for the support of her overlordship in Europe. Their insistence on the right to trade with the Indies, over against the stubborn Spanish denial of this

---

7. Walsh, *Philip II*, p. 124: cf. pp. 125 ("… the little group of anti-Catholic conspirators who had mastered the boy Edward…"), 211 ("… each of its [Protestantism's] victories was won by a small highly-organized and partly secret minority in the midst of a large but poorly-organized Catholic majority.… It was so now in England because the Catholics had no leadership comparable to the skilful and patient direction of Cecil"), 212, 735 b ("… a small group of church looters").
8. As was argued by Macaulay in his essay on "Burleigh and his Times" (two-thirds through). Yet cf. Hallam, *Const. Hist, of England* (ed. 1891), vol. i, p. 176 n. ("The whole tenor of historical documents in Elizabeth's reign proves that the Catholics soon became a minority, and still more among the common people than the gentry"), and Merriman, *The Emperor*, pp. 383 ff. ("… the Venetian ambassador [in England]… had reported in 1551, that 'the detestation of the Pope was now so confirmed that no one, either of the old or new religion, could bear to hear him mentioned', and there is no reason to believe that the situation was very different in 1553…").
9. See Mirbt, *Quellen*, etc. (ed. 1924), pp. 246-248, for Pope Alexander VI's bull on this subject (1493). Cf. Motley, *United Netherlands* (ed. 1875-76), vol. iv, pp. 98 f., 393.

The Character of the Resistance to Philip in the Netherlands 167

right was one of the causes which protracted the negotiations culminating in the truce of 1609.[10]

Such being the motives actuating discontent, what were the characteristic forms in which it found expression?

The reaction first entitled to be mentioned is that unresisting submission to suffering which recalls the touching records of early Christian martyrdom and the counsels of perfection in the Sermon on the Mount. It is easy to say that men and women sentenced by the government of their country to be burnt alive had no option but to submit: but we possess one or two detailed narratives, typical no doubt of many others, did we but possess them, describing a meek acceptance of death in a spirit of exemplary quietness and charity. The natural field for such nobility of conduct was, of course, the martyrdom of individual saints. The story of the Anabaptist refugee who sacrificed his safety in order to rescue his pursuer from drowning has already been mentioned on a previous page (see above, p. 98): but it deserves to be alluded to again in the present connexion. On a wider scale, the response of the afflicted was of a less ideal kind. Disapprobation made itself felt in every variety of verbal protest and the outpouring of popular feeling.[11] We get an example of the juxtaposition of the two types of conduct in the execution of a certain Fabricius at Antwerp in October 1564. Having deserted a monastery, become a Protestant, and married, he was betrayed by a woman who got evidence by pretending to accept his

---

10. It should be mentioned that the Spanish government assumed the right of executing out-of-hand any Protestant mariners or colonists who might fall into their hands within the area assigned to Spain. A horrid incident of this character occurred in 1565. Some French Huguenots had settled in Florida; and Philip sent Pedro Menéndez to deal with them as trespassers. He took their fort, and hanged the 130 men within. The rest of the settlers (about 140) surrendered to him, after endeavouring to stipulate that their lives should be spared, and being told that Menéndez would act as God had ordered. "Then", wrote Menéndez to Philip, "... they came to deliver up their arms. I had their hands tied behind them and had them stabbed to death... deeming that to punish them in this manner would be serving God, our Lord, and your Majesty. Hereafter they will leave us free to plant the Gospel and enlighten the natives..." Sixteen artisans and about fifty women and children were spared. Philip wrote to Menéndez his warm approval of the action he had taken (R. Putnam, *William the Silent*, etc. [1911], pp. 477 f.; Merriman, *Philip the Prudent*, pp. 162-176, 265-269, 395 f. ["... According to present-day standards, he (Menéndez) was wholly and unquestionably wrong; but in passing judgment on him and on his admiral it is but fair that we should bear in mind the theories and the principles of the times in which they lived"]).
11. "To suffer, however, in silence has at no time been a virtue with our protestant dissenters" (Hallam, *Const. Hist, of Eng.* [ed. 1891], vol. i, p. 200).

teaching. When condemned to the stake, he wrote to her assuring her of his forgiveness; but the crowd made a violent, though unsuccessful, attempt to rescue him from the scaffold.

It is noteworthy that an interval of about thirty-five years (1522-57) elapsed between the commencement of persecution and the public manifestation of discontent regarding it – on the part of others besides the Anabaptists; and a further interval of nine or ten years passed before active rebellion broke out. It was not for another fourteen years after that (1567-81) that Holland, Zealand, Brabant, Flanders, Utrecht, and Gelderland renounced their allegiance to the king of Spain. These figures help to prove – what has already been urged – that the movement, despite its passion, was not in essence and primarily a revolt against the sovereignty of Philip, but an insistence that he should respect the freedom and privileges of his subjects. Even the agitation about the retention of Spanish troops in the country and the exclusion of the nobility from a real share in government-affairs must not be construed as an effort to deprive Philip of his position as sovereign. This last-named effort developed only as a result of his persistent refusal to make any real concession to the grievances of his subjects.[12]

Perhaps the first quality which characterizes the revolt as a revolt is the extraordinary courage of it. When we compare the resources and military power of the one side with those of the other (reflected as it was in the almost uniform victory of the Spaniards in the field), we cannot but marvel at the courage of the men who dared to

> "Threaten the threatener, and outface the brow
> Of bragging horror",

and who, strangely unaided by their fellow-Protestants of Germany, and but grudgingly supported by Elizabeth, maintained the struggle for little less than fifty years, until in 1609 they were able to extort from their oppressors an unqualified acknowledgment of their independence. True, their cause was a two-fold

---

12. Pirenne (*Belgique*, vol. iii [1912], pp. 332, 425, 458) ascribes to Calvinism, as distinct from Lutheranism, an inherently aggressive and rebellious character, which he sees appearing in the Low Countries "à peu près en même temps que le règne de Philippe II". This representation makes, I feel, insufficient allowance for the provocative circumstances explained in the text above.

one – the hostility to Spain springing with some from a desire for religious freedom, with others from a desire for emancipation from the foreign yoke. True it is also that this duality enabled Alexander Farnese to divide their forces and, by playing on the Catholic prejudices of the south-eastern states, to withdraw them from union with their fellow-countrymen to the north-west. Moreover, even in the north-west it was inevitable that in the heat and desperate vicissitudes of the conflict the Catholics should here and there suffer oppression: but it is safe to say that, apart from one or two isolated episodes (to be spoken of presently), the lives of Catholics were not, among the free states, rendered unendurable, as were the lives of Protestants in the submissive south-east, where the best they could expect, as an alternative to going over to Rome, was a space of time to enable them to wind up their affairs and decamp. Subject to the complexities inseparable from this twofoldness of interest, the unity and constancy of the leading insurgents is as striking as their energy and pluck.[13]

What we have next to consider is the variety of forms taken by the violence of the resistance offered. Violence exercised on inanimate objects is ethically very different from the violent destruction of human life. A striking manifestation of the former occurred in August 1566, when there took place an extraordinary series of iconoclastic outbreaks, commencing at St. Omer, involving the destruction of all the art treasures in the great cathedral of Antwerp and several other churches in that city, and extending to numerous other towns in the Low Countries. The general testimony as to these acts of violence is that they were the work of comparatively small sections of the rabble, that crowds were present as more or less inactive spectators, and that hardly any efforts were made by the authorities to prevent or check the devastation. We are, however, told that there was no wilful destruction of life on the part of the rioters. It is, of course, impossible to prove, and very difficult to imagine, that no

---

13. Dr. Walsh says (*Philip II*, p. 183), with reference to the religious struggle in England: "The enemy's theories were legion, but his cohorts could stand together, organize, hate and strike with the canny cooperation of the children of this world". This is a serious inaccuracy as a description of the situation in England (see above, p. 166): it would be equally wide of the mark if applied to the Low Countries.

pilfering took place or that, in the frenzy of the hour, when priests, monks, and nuns were fleeing in panic, no individuals suffered violence, possibly even death: but the broad fact remains that the outbreaks were on the whole innocent at least of bloodshed.[14]

Even allowing for the fact that the actual work of wreckage was carried out by only a comparatively few persons, the episode must in general be viewed as a truly extraordinary outbreak of popular resentment (remarkable alike in its violence and in its self-restraint) against the heavy-handed oppression with which the rank and file of the population had for so long been treated. Whatever we may think of the rightness of armed resistance, and however much we may sympathize with the indignation of the populace against the Catholic Church, there can be no doubt that the outbreak was a sad error. It alienated those Catholics who sympathized with the Protestant victims of persecution; and it naturally rendered both the regent and the king more implacable than ever.

As we might expect, Catholic and catholicizing writers make the very most of it, speaking of it as if it were the work of Protestants generally, and using it to incriminate them as a class, exaggerating its evils, and extending the responsibility of it to the nobles, whose conduct however is inconsistent with their complicity, whatever sympathy some Protestants among them may have felt. Thus, Professor Poullet speaks of the rioters generally as "ces nobles apôtres de la tolérance, de la civilisation, du progrès et de la lumière,…": but he does not refer to the fact that there was no considerable destruction of life.[15] Mr. Trevor Davies (p. 160) says definitely, "Monks and nuns were maltreated or killed", and "The malcontent nobles everywhere were secret supporters of the destroyers". Dr. Walsh quotes a report to the effect that it was all "the work of a paid gang of wreckers";[16] "the chief motivating passion at work was a cold implacable hatred, not merely of priests, but of Christ and His

---

14. See the account in Pirenne, *Belgique*, vol. iii (1912), pp. 464-468.
15. Poullet, "De la répression", etc., pp. 932 f.: cf. pp. 157, 167 f.
16. Walsh, *Philip II*, p. 406: cf. p. 735 a ("… evidence that such vandalism [in England] was always the work of small but noisy bands of paid wreckers and propagandists, as in later Communist manifestations, as in the Huguenot cities, and in Antwerp in 1566").

Mother" (p. 406): he speaks, with apparent reference to August 1566, of "the dismal history of martyred priests and profaned temples" (p. 543), and tells us (p. 690) that Philip and his Council were convinced that the sacking of the Antwerp-churches was "no popular uprising in any sense, but had been skilfully engineered... by some international organization". Lastly, after describing the sacking of Antwerp by the Spanish soldiery in 1576, when, as he says, they "succeeded in butchering thousands and driving seven thousand others to death in flames or water. Some eighty splendid houses were burned", he adds, "Thus was the sacking of the fine old churches of Antwerp in 1566 avenged" (p. 562).

What, however, of the methods by which the armed struggle itself was carried on? Of the cruelty of the Spanish generals and soldiers enough has already been said in our fourth and fifth chapters. But how about the behaviour of their Netherland-enemies? It would not, indeed, be surprising, human nature being what it is, if – after years of severe oppression – some advantage were taken of a more favourable military situation to inflict savage reprisals on the oppressors and their supposed sympathizers. Such likelihood would be enhanced by the fact that "every political party, however honourable may be its objects and character, is liable to be disgraced by the association of such unscrupulous zealots".[17]

We naturally get illustrations of reprisals of this kind on the part of the Netherlanders in the course of the struggle with which we are here concerned. Thus in 1569, after Alva had for three years been shedding blood like water up and down the country, a small fleet nominally in the service of William as independent Prince of Orange, began to cruise up and down the Dutch coast, in order to fight and capture Spanish ships. Their success was considerable; and their numbers rapidly grew. Their leaders – William de la Mark and his colleagues – made landings from time to time, and committed acts of terrible barbarity on such Catholic priests, monks, and officials, as fell into their hands, and also on the crews of captured vessels. Being at Alva's request forbidden by Elizabeth to harbour in the English ports, they descended on

---

17. Hallam, *Const. Hist, of Eng.* (ed. 1891), vol. i, p. 208.

to the Dutch coast; and on April 1, 1572, they captured Brill, and committed cruel excesses there. A few months later, in connexion with another exploit, De la Mark tortured and hanged seventeen monks or friars on one day, July 9. He was reproached by the States of Holland for his cruelty.[18] But it was impossible, if resistance was to continue at all, to prevent the excesses of Philip and Alva from evoking occasional blameworthy and cruel reprisals on the part of the less temperate leaders of the revolt.

A few years later, in 1575, Diedrich Sonoy, governor of the northern portion of Holland, inflicted the most fiendish tortures on certain Catholics in the effort to identify and punish those guilty of plotting to facilitate a Spanish invasion. William of Orange did all he could to put an end to these enormities: but Sonoy was a difficult man to control. After Jauréguy's unsuccessful attempt on William's life in 1582, the estates were deterred from having two of his accomplices (Jauréguy himself having been killed on the spot) dragged to death by wild horses, only by the intercession of William himself. Such was the indignation and fury excited by Balthasar Gérard's successful attack on the Prince in 1584 that, besides being horribly tortured during his examination, he was executed by means of the most excruciating mutilations that could be devised.[19]

In the actual hostilities which continued off and on between Spain and the Netherlands, from 1567 to 1609, the operations of the latter in the earlier part of this period consisted mostly of the defence of besieged towns and the fighting of a few unsuccessful pitched battles – so that there was little opportunity, and therefore little temptation, for the rebels to manifest any unusual cruelty, though the bitterness and long continuance of the struggle might have rendered a certain amount of excess intelligible. Such atrocities as did occur were of a sporadic and exceptional kind. Of the barbarities committed by the Prince of Orange's own troops, against his will, in 1572 I shall speak later (see below, p. 195). Two Spanish soldiers were roasted alive by the townsmen of Neusz in July 1586; the five or six hundred men constituting the garrison of Axel were massacred by the English and Dutch about the same time; and the 1500

---

18. Poullet, *op. cit.,* p. 158.
19. They are specified in detail by Motley in *Dutch Republic* (ed. 1874), p. 896.

Irish kernes then attached to the English force committed wild excesses.

Two other categories of horrible incidents must be mentioned. One comprises the exceptional occasions on which Prince Maurice proceeded (or intended to proceed) to acts of severity by way of reprisal against the unseemly behaviour of the enemy. Thus in 1597, after the victory of Turnhout, he threatened to hang or drown 500 Spanish prisoners, unless within twenty days the reported order of the Cardinal Archduke Albert to the effect that no quarter was to be given to the soldiers of the Republic were disowned: fortunately the awaited denial arrived in time. Later the same year Maurice took Brevoort by storm, and burnt it. In 1603 the Archduke ordered twelve wounded soldiers en route to the hospital at Flushing, whom he had captured at sea, to be immediately hanged, on the ground that no laws of war were valid at sea. In revenge Maurice hanged in full view of the enemy's camp an equivalent number of Spanish prisoners chosen by lot, and threatened to hang in future two of his prisoners for every one executed by the Archduke.

The other category consists of acts of cruelty or excess committed by the Netherlanders at sea, where – as has just been intimated – no laws of humanity were thought by some to be valid. Possibly the fact that at sea danger from the elements was added to danger from the foe let loose among combatants afloat fiercer passions than among combatants ashore. However that may be, the Hollanders and Zealanders in 1592 killed every man on board twelve large Spanish vessels endeavouring to enter the mouth of the River Seine in order to relieve Rouen, which was undergoing siege at the hands of Henry of Navarre. In 1596 the English and the Dutch sacked and burnt Cadiz; but there was no massacre: on the contrary the women in the fortress were left entirely unmolested, and conveyance to a place of safety was specially provided for the nuns and the sick. In 1599 the Dutch attacked and pillaged the Canary Islands, inflicting much damage on the inhabitants; and they sacked and burnt towns and villages on the Isle of St. Thomas, near the equator. In 1605 the Dutch admiral Haultain deliberately caused to be tossed into the sea all the Spanish soldiers he had captured in overcoming a small flotilla of vessels bringing troops to Flanders, on the ground, apparently, that they were sailing in merchant-ships and not in war-vessels.[20] In 1607, after the great victory of the Dutch over the Spanish fleet off Gibraltar, a terrible massacre took place of the crews and soldiers on or from the conquered ships, the fierceness of the victors being inflamed by the death of their own admiral Heemskerk and by the discovery, on the Spanish admiral's ship, of royal instructions for the most inhuman persecution of the Netherlanders.[21]

On the other hand, the standing army organized and led by Prince Maurice was trained to exercise as much humanity and self-restraint as was compatible with the attainment of military success. There was no pillaging of the country-side, no sacking of captured towns, no massacring of their garrisons or inhabitants. Prisoners of war were not reduced to the status of chained galley-slaves, as was the custom with those captured by the Spaniards. During a victorious sea-fight off the coast of Flanders in 1602, the Dutch boats picked up such of the drowning Spanish crews as they were able. Most of the 1,500 Turkish galley-slaves captured when Maurice took Sluys in 1604 were sent back to their homes by the Dutch government. It is clear, therefore, that on balance there was a very considerable amelioration of the normal horrors of war on the part of the revolted Netherlanders, in contrast with what had been the customary Spanish practice.

But what of tolerance or intolerance when and where the military issue was not in question?

In November 1576, a few days after the Spanish troops had sacked Antwerp, and when Don John of Austria stood on the threshold of the country as the newly-appointed governor, there was signed and promulgated the so-called "Pacification of Ghent", a treaty between Holland and Zealand on the one hand, and the whole of the rest of the States on the other. Its main purpose was to unite the whole country in expelling the Spaniards from the Netherlands – in the name and on behalf of the nominal

---

20. See Motley's censure of this barbarity in *United Netherlands* (ed. 1875-76), vol. iv, p. 214: cf. p. 235.
21. Motley's description and censure – *United Netherlands* (ed. 1875-76), vol. iv, p. 304. Cf., for a similar incident on a smaller scale, p. 390, and in general, pp. 514 f.

sovereign, King Philip himself. When this should be done, the question of the religious settlement was to be taken in hand. In the meantime, Holland and Zealand were recognized as Protestant, but undertook to attempt no measures against Catholicism outside their own borders. The Catholic provinces were not required to allow the right of public worship to their Protestant citizens, but they agreed not to prohibit Protestant worship if it were carried on privately, the heresy-edicts being suspended. In February 1578 Amsterdam was induced, after troublesome hindrances, to join the Union, on the understanding that only Catholic public worship was to be allowed within the city, but the Protestants were to be free to carry on their worship outside the walls. This compromise, however, was overthrown by a Protestant revolution a few months later: by it public worship was at first denied to the Catholics, but shortly afterwards restored to them – according to the provisions of Ghent, though with diminished privileges.

The Pacification of Ghent, however, was not destined to last. In October 1578 Don John died; and Alexander Farnese succeeded him as governor. A consummately skilful diplomatist, he was able to induce one Catholic city after another to desert its uneasy alliance with the Protestant powers of Holland and Zealand, and be reconciled with King Philip, until the great "Pacification" was merely a thing of the past. Early in January 1579 a number of the mainly Catholic states, aggrieved by the foolish excesses and reprisals of the Calvinists within their borders, formed at Arras a league in defence of Catholicism and the Spanish domination. Then it was that the states of Holland, Zealand, Utrecht, Gelderland, and other provinces in the north replied by forming "the Union of Utrecht" for the purpose of maintaining their religious freedom and their independence of foreign control (though without as yet explicitly renouncing the sovereignty of Philip). Thus were founded "the United Provinces" which, with subsequent additions, constituted a new unit in the political concert of Europe.

With the detailed arrangements made between the contracting parties for the pursuance of their common objects we are not here concerned. What is, however, of importance is the thirteenth of the Articles of Union, which dealt with the question of religious worship. In substance, this article left each of the uniting states free to take its own line, *provided there was no curtailment of individual liberty, and no molestation of any man on account of his creed or worship.* The extent to which freedom of *public* worship was allowed to more than one type of faith was left to the discretion of each state. The dominant Protestantism of Holland and Zealand was tacitly recognized; and the freedom of a wholly or dominantly Catholic state to join the Union if it wished was explicitly provided for. No state was to interfere with another in the matter of its ecclesiastical regulations.

Such was the high ideal aimed at in 1579. But as the conflict proceeded, it was found impossible to adhere to it. It became increasingly the settled policy of the Union – led as it was by Holland and Zealand, and tending more and more to subordinate the local freedom of the states to the exigences of military unity – to forbid and suppress all public Catholic worship within its borders, to confiscate Catholic churches for Protestant use, and ultimately to take over for various charitable purposes other Catholic ecclesiastical buildings as well. Such (except for the immediate appropriation of ecclesiastical property) was the practice enforced also by Prince Maurice in the case of the towns he captured.

It should, however, be observed that nothing approaching a general persecution of Catholics was undertaken. No inquisition was made into the personal beliefs and practices of individuals, and no interference exercised in regard to domestic worship. Such acts of violence as occurred were involved in the local and individual excesses incidental to a fierce and prolonged conflict: they were not the deliberate acts of a persecuting government. After the foundation of the Republic, no death-sentence was ever formally passed or inflicted on any person on grounds of heresy. On special occasions further concessions were made to Catholics. Thus in 1582 public worship was allowed to them in the church of St. Michael at Antwerp, out of deference to the Duke of Anjou, in his new role as Duke of Brabant and "Prince and Lord" of the Netherlands. Round about 1597, partly in view of the shortage of Protestant ministers, Catholic priests found themselves in possession of a certain amount of public freedom in the northern provinces, though still, of course, needing to act with caution.[22] When Prince Maurice took Jülich in 1610 he made no change in the liberty of Roman Catholic worship.

It will be seen that, notwithstanding these sundry mitigations, very considerable restrictions were imposed on Roman Catholics in the United Provinces. This measure of suppression, if such it is to be called, is in Dr. Walsh's eyes nothing other than enmity to Christ and hatred for his Church. Speaking of its earlier phase, he says that Protestantism "sought something more than freedom; it sought nothing less (and this was more evident in Calvinism than in Lutheranism) than the utter destruction of the Catholic Church. Here was a hatred that began manifesting itself by the burning of churches and convents, the violation of nuns, the torture and execution of priests, the defiling of the Cross and the unspeakable desecration of the Blessed Sacrament. It was an old and international hatred. It was the hatred of the church-burning Donatists, the hatred of Islam, the hatred that had opposed Saint Paul in Rome and Saint James in Jerusalem, the hatred of Annas and the scribes and pharisees crying, 'Come down from the Cross, and we will believe!' There was nothing new about it except the form it took; but the preparation and organization were better, and the time was ripe…" (p. 243).

It is indeed difficult to understand how any person possessed of the most moderate knowledge of Charles V's placards, of Philip's governmental instructions, of Alva's executions, of the Spanish massacres generally, and of the characteristics of average Calvinistic piety, could allow himself to describe the struggle in these inaccurate terms. Such measure of antipathy against the Roman Church as did undoubtedly exist (though Dr. Walsh greatly exaggerates it) is to a large extent explicable from the resentment which the prolonged and unspeakable cruelties of the Church herself had aroused. I have the impression that Dr. Walsh, like other Catholic and pro-Catholic writers, hardly allows enough for the operation of this cause.[23] To it, just as much

---

22. Geyl, *Revolt*, etc., pp. 227, 229.
23. The cruelty meted out to Protestants in the sixteenth century is sometimes excused or condoned on the ground that the Church feared, and with good reason, that – unless somehow checked – Protestants would overthrow the Church of Rome by force. Now such a climax *was* probably from time to time envisaged by Protestant hot-heads in their preaching and pamphleteering. But

as to the "odium theologicum" which so easily besets zealous religious men in all ages, was owing that fierce repugnance to Catholicism which was manifested by the majority of sixteenth-century Protestants, and which, it must not be forgotten, was cordially reciprocated in the Catholic estimate of Protestantism. The treatment accorded by the Catholic states outside the Union of Utrecht to such few Protestants as were still to be found in their midst was no whit better, and in many respects far worse, than that meted out to Catholic residents in the United Provinces. The burying alive of Anna van den Hove at Brussels in 1597 (see above, p. 61) has no contemporary parallel within the borders of the United Provinces. In those Provinces, moreover, a Catholic minority did find it possible to survive: virtually no corresponding Protestant minority was allowed in the southern provinces that remained loyal to Spain.

But there was, unfortunately, more in it than either resentment or "odium theologicum". It was the fixed belief of all parties in that age, Catholic and Protestant alike, that the public exercise of more than one type of religious worship in a state could not be allowed without gravely imperilling that state's social order and well-being (see above, p. 46). Even so enlightened a Protestant as Hugo Grotius was of this opinion; and John of Oldenbarneveld claimed that at least state-control of ecclesiastical matters was an absolute necessity. Now no power had done more to rivet these convictions on the European mind than the Roman Church herself. For centuries she had taught mankind that the power of the sword could be rightly used to coerce and punish heresy. Of course, in doing this, she had not meant to allow to anyone but herself the right of defining heresy. But it was hardly to be expected that the first men to throw off the most vulnerable of her tenets, and presume to fashion their spiritual lives for themselves, would thereby free themselves at once from the age-long conviction that errorists must be made to suffer for their error. The principles which rule out persecution as a normal Christian operation were *inherent* in Protestantism from the first; but it was only natural – in view of the

---

there can never have been any serious likelihood of its realization. In any case, the vehemence out of which the idea sprang was the direct and inevitable reaction to the merciless aggression with which Rome had from the first treated Protestantism. On the other hand, it must be remembered that the Catholic hope of completely blotting out Protestantism was by no means confined to a few Romanist hotheads; it was the deliberate and avowed wish and plan of numerous Catholic politicians, ecclesiastics, sovereigns, and popes.

deeply-rooted Catholic precedent – that they should take time in becoming clear and explicit to the Protestant conscience. If in the sixteenth century reconciliation between the two great parties was impossible, the primary responsibility for that state of affairs unquestionably rests with the Roman Church.

If it were once admitted in the rebellious Dutch states that only one publicly-practised religion could be allowed, there was no question but that that religion must be Calvinism. For although many Roman Catholic Netherlanders had been strongly averse to the Spanish rule, the backbone of the revolt had been found in the zeal of the Calvinists. Not only so, but – as the event showed – the patriotism of the Catholics was not strong enough to enable them to work in double harness with the Protestant patriots, especially when they were exposed to the unrivalled diplomacy of Alexander Farnese;[24] nor unfortunately did the intolerant zeal of the Protestants themselves make the co-operation between the rival systems any easier.

While we may not exonerate the Protestant party from its share of responsibility for the failure of the joint attempt against Spain, it is only fair to recognize that, as the diplomatic successes of Farnese suffice to show, Catholicism was still a very real danger. The Roman Church had not for one moment abandoned its claim to call upon the secular ruler to coerce and punish all who were disobedient to her despotic authority. How then was it possible for the most fair-minded Protestant to regard his Catholic fellow-citizens, and especially Catholic ecclesiastics, as other than prospective supporters of a reintroduced Inquisition and a revived Spanish autocracy to uphold it? The danger was by no means an imaginary one, the papacy and the Catholic powers of Europe being then minded as they were; and the pro-Catholic insurrection at Utrecht in 1610 is a good illustration of it.

There were, however, in the Protestant ranks a few men farsighted and courageous enough to see that to vindicate the country's liberty from foreign control was a worthier use of force than to employ it for the purpose of molesting those of a different type of Christianity from one's own, and who thought it worth while to call upon their fellow-countrymen generally to

---

24. Geyl, *Revolt*, etc., pp. 165, 172-179, 228, 231.

act accordingly. Of these, William of Orange and John of Oldenbarneveld were the most eminent. Of course, it was said then, as it has been said by the unsympathetic since, that the real motive behind this plea for a larger tolerance was a fundamental unconcern for religious truth as such. And certainly, if one *is* inwardly unconcerned about religion, one will naturally be opposed to intolerance and persecution as inherently senseless. We shall have to discuss in the next chapter the basis for this charge as regards William of Orange: but for the moment it may suffice to observe that there would seem to be no necessary incompatibility between personal religious seriousness and zeal on the one hand, and on the other a rooted objection to the Inquisition and all its ways. But, as regards William of Orange and John of Oldenbarneveld, both men seriously lost popularity as a result of their known leanings towards a wider toleration than their fellow-countrymen were willing to sanction; and the latter of the two even owed his ultimate downfall largely to his difference from the majority on this issue. Despite their influence and skill, they were unable to command the national mind and so to prevent Parma from scoring many of his most notable successes on behalf of Philip.

During the few years preceding the conclusion of the Truce between the United Provinces and Spain in 1609, one of the most insistent demands made by the Spanish side was that liberty of public worship should be allowed to Catholics in the Provinces. The concession of it was uniformly and steadily refused, not only for the reasons set forth in the last few pages, but also because the demand for it was regarded as an unwarrantable interference with the sovereign rights of the Dutch States, and because Spain was wholly unwilling to grant any corresponding privilege to non-Catholic worshippers on Spanish soil. The deadlock prolonged the negotiations; but in the upshot, nothing was said in the terms of the Truce about the rights of Catholics in the States, the king of Spain simply expressing to the Dutch his desire that they would treat his co-religionists kindly.

The official ban on the public practice of Catholicism remained in force throughout the United Netherlands during the whole period of the Truce; that is to say, although Catholics were not molested or persecuted for their personal beliefs and domestic practices, they enjoyed no liberty of worship in public consecrated buildings. Unhappily, the possibility of a further advance in the practice of toleration during the period of the Truce was foreclosed by the outbreak of bitter strife between different sections of the Protestants. A new movement arose, associated with the name of Jacob Hermann or Armin (Arminius), which advocated a relaxation of the predestinarian rigour of traditional Calvinism. It has long since been recognized by virtually all that that rigour did need to be relaxed: and the venerable name of John Wesley, not to mention a host of pressing theological arguments, has sufficed to invest the name of Arminianism with no mean glory. But the effect of the rise of this movement on the adherents of the older Calvinism in the land of Arminianism's birth was to evoke the most violent and bitter animosity. The broadmindedness of Oldenbarneveld inclined him to sympathize with the newer school of thought, whereas Maurice of Nassau, Stadtholder and commander-in-chief, supported by the majority of the population, stood fixedly for the older doctrine. Owing to the intensity of feeling on the part of the strict Calvinists, the theological divergence could not be prevented from developing into civil strife. The most tragic upshot of the ensuing struggle was the illegal trial and execution of Oldenbarneveld at The Hague in May 1619. But in 1621 the renewal of the Spanish War – this time as part of the great European "Thirty-Years-War" – and in 1625 the death of Prince Maurice gave the United Provinces something else to think about. In order to obtain French help against the Emperor, Maurice's half-brother and successor Frederick Henry felt compelled to lend Richelieu a Dutch fleet for use against the Huguenots. The war ended victoriously for the Dutch in 1648: but by that time the question of the treatment of Catholics had ceased to be one of the major problems of public policy. In practice, the treatment became more lenient, even though the oppressive laws remained nominally in force. The last persecution directed by the Dutch government against the Catholics occurred in 1685. The anti-Catholic laws were not, however, finally withdrawn until the time of the French Revolution, when full liberty of public worship was accorded to all.

The great struggle waged by the Netherlanders against Spain, looked at as a whole, has no doubt its seamy side. In the course of a conflict lasting over forty years, there was time and occasion for many acts of personal and communal injustice, cruelty, greed, and lust, masquerading as religious zeal. It is not likely that the Netherlands wholly escaped that orgy of excess, which is known to have been one of the results of the abolition of the rule of Rome in large parts of Germany. That a considerable element of intolerance and even persecution was involved in the Protestant insurrection we have already seen. It is not pleasant to note that William of Orange confidentially begged the Sultan in 1569 to declare war on Philip,[25] and at a later stage (1577-78) was aided diplomatically by the Porte. At the siege of Leyden (1574), the Zealanders had worn crescents in their caps to show that they hated the pope more than they did the Turks; and when the country was flooded, the Sea-Beggars descended on the Spanish besieging army, shouting "Sooner Turks than Papists!"[26] These titanic historical conflicts, in which the intensest passions collide and strive for mastery, are not carried through save with many manifestations of human faultiness –

> "With thousand shocks that come and go,
>   With agonies, with energies,
>   With overthrowings, and with cries,
> And undulations to and fro".

But the recognition of this fact does not necessarily prevent us from recording a fairly definite vote of confidence on one side as against the other. That question, however, brings us face to face with the. main issue with which this book is concerned; and I must hold over the discussion of it until I reach my last chapter.

---

25. M. Schloessinger in *Jewish Encyc.*, vol. ix (1905), p. 173 b; Walsh, *Philip II*, p. 411.
26. Is this the sort of thing that Dr. Walsh has in mind when he speaks of "the Protestants on the north and their spiritual brothers the Mohammedans on the south and east" (p. 703)?

Chapter Nine

The Personal Character of William of Orange

John, Count of Nassau-Dillenburg (an important principality on the east of the Rhine, in the latitude of Bonn and Coblenz), died in 1516, and left two sons – Henry and William. To Henry there fell his possessions in the Netherlands, to William those in Germany.

Henry married in 1515 Claude, the sister of Philibert, Prince of Orange-Chalons. Orange was a small independent principality on the lower Rhone, to which the house of Châlons had succeeded in 1393. Philibert was greatly esteemed as a soldier and statesman by Charles V, who gave him considerable estates in the Netherlands. He died without children in 1530; and René, the son of his sister Claude and her husband Henry of Nassau, succeeded to his Orange-principality and his other possessions.

Henry's brother William married as his second wife Juliana of Stolberg, and had by her five sons and seven daughters. The eldest son William (the "William the Silent" or "William of Orange" of history) was born at Dillenburg on April 25, 1533. He was baptized with Catholic rites: but shortly after his birth, his father went over to a moderate and tolerant Lutheranism; and with him the whole family became Protestant.

In 1544, when "William the Silent" was eleven, his cousin René was killed at the siege of St. Dizier, fighting for the Emperor. He left no children; but he named this William as heir to the independent sovereignty of Orange and to his very extensive possessions in the Netherlands and elsewhere. The Emperor, however, refused to allow William to enter on his inheritance unless he could be brought up at Brussels as a Catholic. He was accordingly educated there at the court of Charles, who made a great favourite of him. He surrendered his prospective inheritance in Nassau to his brother John, but kept the title of "Prince of Orange-Nassau". In 1550 the Emperor secured for him the hand of Anne of Egmont, heiress of the Count of Buren. This marriage, which took place in July 1551, together with his already extensive territorial possessions, rendered him enormously wealthy.

I have given these particulars regarding William's antecedents and early life, because it is needful for any proper understanding of his position that we should know who he was and whence he came: but I must resist the temptation to follow up this introduction with a sketch of his most interesting career, and must turn rather to a discussion of his character, in conformity with the main purpose of my book.

William of Orange was far and away the most important individual among the enemies of Philip in the Low Countries. He was the heart and soul of the resistance offered to the Spanish king, who eventually thought it worth his while to place him under a ban and to offer a reward to any one who should succeed in murdering him. William was the idol of his people, and wielded an enormous influence over them. As one of the very few who advocated the largest possible toleration between Catholics and Protestants, he was ahead of his time and has earned the esteem of posterity. How needful therefore for those concerned in minimizing the importance of the religious issue to reduce the regard usually paid to him, and for those concerned in rehabilitating the Catholic case, to make the very most of such blemishes as they can find in his character.

Dr. Pieter Geyl finds fault with Motley for treating the death of William as a pivotal point in the story of the rebellion, and with the Rev. G. Edmundson for entitling his chapter in *The Cambridge Modern History* on the first stage of the revolt, "William the Silent".[1] Dr. Geyl's reviewer in *The Times Literary Supplement* for July 14, 1932 (p. 509), notes with apparent approval that, although Motley took the murder of William as the terminus ad quem for his first great work on *The Rise of the Dutch Republic*, Dr. Geyl does not even end a chapter with it. But (1) Dr. Geyl shows himself throughout his work somewhat disposed to minimize the religious factor in comparison with the military factor and such geographical and economic conditions as affected the military issue; and (2) later in his work he pays a tardy tribute to William of Orange's importance as leader

---

1. Geyl, *Revolt*, etc., pp. 16 f. The chapter (vii) in *Camb. Mod. Hist.*, vol iii (1904), begins with 1568, and is therefore not quite exactly described as dealing with "the first stage of the revolt".

of the revolt and to the grandeur of his resistance.[2] Dr. Walsh tries to belittle Orange's achievement. "The small state of Holland, with a slight Protestant majority, was the net result of a generation of striving by William of Orange" (p. 619).

Catholic and catholicizing writers do not usually, however, make the foolish mistake of pretending that William of Orange was not a character of absolutely first-rate importance in the story. They prefer to endeavour to discredit his cause by blackening his character. Only so can they shield Philip a little from the disgrace of having purposely compassed William's death by means of a base act of wilful murder, and of having richly rewarded the murderer's kin.[3]

Some of the charges made against William are either couched in terms too general to need any reply, or else refer to vague qualities like loquacity, cunning, etc., which are either not serious defects, or else reflect on the bare fact that he had the audacity to oppose Philip.

Thus, Mr. Trevor Davies (p. 155) and Dr. Walsh (pp. 167, 228) both complain of his loquacity. The former also speaks of him as "that crafty prince" (p. 184), "that agile political gymnast" (p. 206), and an "unscrupulous enemy" (p. 150). "This coarse and brutal materialist", he complains (p. 156), "has often been transformed by religious and political partisanship into an angel of light…" Dr. Walsh is a trifle less severe. He pays tribute to William's patience, persistence, and courage (pp. 586, 617); and he never calls him coarse, brutal, or materialistic. On the contrary, he goes so far as to say that "the truth about his character is probably halfway between the idealization of the Motley and Prescott school and the extremely low opinion entertained of him in Spain" (p. 227). Yet he has many very unfavourable judgments to pass on him. He speaks of William's "avenging rancor" (p. 483), and of his "effrontery" in giving commissions to sea-captains in the name of King Philip to act against Philip's own government (p. 537).

---

2. Geyl, *Revolt*, etc., p. 120: cf. pp. 154 ff.
3. Mr. Trevor Davies, though recording (*Golden Century*, p. 207) the assassination of William, does not, I think, mention Philip's ban against him, or his offer of a large reward to the assassin. Dr. Walsh (*Philip II*, p. 617) justifies the deed as one would justify the slaughter of a mad dog.

He groups together "Cecil, William of Orange, and the whole network of Jewish bankers and spies" (p. 615). But his main general accusations are levelled at the Prince's cunning. The Emperor Charles, he says (p. 167), was on this ground warned against him, but to no purpose. He calls him "the astute William of Orange, in whom the Emperor's sister had so early discovered a fox" (p. 343), "this Machiavellian politician" (p. 564), and "that wily gentleman" who virtually dictated a reply from the States-General to Don John "in exceedingly insolent terms" (pp. 568 f.). Don John, he says (p. 564: cf. p. 586), "had to deal essentially with one of the most astute and unscrupulous politicians of that wicked century. Motley has no difficulty in condoning the lies and deceptions of Philip's arch-enemy on the plea that he lived in the treacherous age of Philip II. It does not seem to have occurred to him to apologize for the less frequent and more excusable deception of Philip on the ground that he lived in the treacherous age of William of Orange".

Something will have to be said presently (see pp. 196 ff.) about this allegation of mendacity and insincerity on William's part: but for the rest, it is not to charges of this general nature, however strongly worded, that a direct reply can or need be made. It is only when we get to the more specific accusations that it seems both possible and needful to discuss them seriously. In doing this, I shall make no attempt to prove that William of Orange invariably acted with perfect Christian judgment. But I shall, as justice and charity alike require, try to assess the goodness or otherwise of his actions and his aims, so far as we can know them, to claim for him (as I have done for Philip) the benefit of the doubt on issues that are bound to be uncertain or obscure, and to advance mitigating considerations where his actions lie open to adverse criticism.

It is not easy to know where to begin: but one of the most obvious censures cast on him is that he was disloyal to his lawful sovereign, who had bestowed favours upon him, and to whom he had sworn fealty. Thus, Von Pastor writes, "Such was the man who, though he was the vassal and councillor of state of Philip II., used all his abilities to thwart the policy, both at home and abroad, of his king..."[4] Dr. Walsh speaks of his

---

4. Von Pastor, *Popes*, vol. xviii (1929), p. 77.

"treachery", "his deliberate and carefully concealed betrayal at a time when he was accepting favours from the King for himself and his brother, and when Philip was making every concession to keep him loyal" (p. 411). "He was traitor to Philip, to whom he had sworn allegiance,…" (p. 412: cf., more at length, p. 473). "… he had professed loyalty to Philip II, as his liege lord and the author of his greatness, even after he had introduced a secret organization of alien allegiance to shatter the unity on which the Spanish authority rested" (p. 617). Mr. Trevor Davies conjectures (p. 155) "that he intended rebellion from the very beginning", i.e., from 1559.

Let us set aside for one moment the question of "cracking the strong warrant of an oath", and let us acknowledge that loyal obedience to a constituted authority is both a normal and a strong obligation. We still have the right to press the question, Is this an *unconditional* obligation – one to which no conceivable circumstances, no imaginable misrule on the part of the authority, can ever constitute a justifiable exception? Clearly the answer to that question is in the negative, as Peter and the Apostles saw when they affirmed, "We ought to obey God rather than men". Granted that such occasions have often been imagined to exist when there was no real ground for them, the solid fact remains that the obligation of civil obedience, though great, is *not* unconditional. Before therefore William can be condemned for treachery to his lawful sovereign, we shall have to ask whether there was a sufficient case for his rebellion or not. If the foregoing pages of this book, or any accurate summary of the facts, do not suffice to satisfy the reader that under Philip's rule such a case not only existed, but shouted aloud for action, probably nothing that can now be said will avail to convince him. Only, as focusing the issue, let us take a look at two items in the background against which the "treachery" of the Prince of Orange has to be viewed.

Firstly, what is the basis for Mr. Trevor Davies's conjecture (p. 155) that he intended rebellion from the first? It is the narrative William himself gives in his *Apology* of 1581 to the effect that, when he was in Paris in 1559 as one of the hostages for the observance of the Treaty of Cateau-Cambresis, he was informed by the French king, Henry II, that it was the wish and intention both of himself and of Philip II to bring about in their respective dominions a gigantic massacre of the heretics. William was astute enough to refrain at the moment from any overt expression of dissent or disapproval (his self-control on this occasion being said by some to be the origin of his title "Le Taciturne"):[5] but he tells us that he then and there formed the resolution to drive "this vermin of Spaniards" out of the Netherlands. Mr. Trevor Davies discreetly refrains from saying what "the plans" were which William detected in Paris, and in a footnote says: "Like so many statements in the *Apology*, the story is quite possibly a mere invention of the author". But he adds in the text (p. 155), "His statement probably has this amount of truth in it, that he intended rebellion from the very beginning,..." That is to say, what William says possibly to his own discredit is probably true; but what he says to the discredit of the sovereigns of France and Spain is "quite possibly" not true. I must protest against this one-sided use of the evidence, as special pleading. If anything, we may more easily suppose that, in his *Apology*, William somewhat ante-dated his own fixed opposition to the presence of Spaniards in the Netherlands, than that he misrepresented what Henry II had said to him. Why should not what he reports about the French king be true? It exactly fits his temper and policy as one of the bitterest Catholic persecutors of the century. It anticipates by only thirteen years what actually happened in France – the massacre of St. Bartholomew, an event which made even the solemn Philip rejoice, drew down upon Catherine de' Medici the congratulations of most of the Catholic princes in Europe, and caused the pope to sing Te-Deums, celebrate masses, and strike medals. There is nothing in the least unlikely about William's story: and if it be true, was there not then as strong a case as a righteous man – even a righteous Catholic – could want for opposition to his legal sovereign?

---

5. It has long been recognized that this customary epithet is not only quite unsuitable to the character of the genial and talkative prince, but that its application to him rests on a philological misunderstanding. Either the Inquisitor Titelman or Cardinal Granvelle described him as "sly" (in Dutch "sluwe"). This term was erroneously latinized as "taciturnus": but it was not apparently till the nineteenth century that it was applied to the prince in a *complimentary* sense, and was referred to the incident narrated in the text. Miss Wedgwood (*William the Silent*, p. 31), while agreeing that it is a misnomer, adds: "Yet it was not without truth, even in its mistranslated form, for these were the years of suppressed and divided feelings".

Secondly, Dr. Walsh describes (p. 420), with a sneer at William of Orange's wealth, a fiery and rebellious speech, in which he called for armed resistance to the Spanish yoke. But what was the occasion of this speech? The occasion was the arrival of news that the Duke of Alva had reached Italy, en route for the Netherlands with a powerful army. Was not the approach of a ruthless soldier known to be charged with the task of destroying the liberties of the country by the power of the sword, justifiable ground for a rebellious speech?

William's critics wisely refrain from making too special a point of the breach of his oath of allegiance to Philip. It comes in mainly as a make-weight in Dr. Walsh's more general denunciations. Waiving the problem as to whether, in view of Matt. 5: 33-37 and James 5: 12, it is ever right for the Christian to swear an oath about anything, we must observe that oath-keeping, like promise-keeping, and like the general obligation to obey the laws of the state, is – as we had occasion to observe above (see pp. 73 f.) – not unconditional: and if the sufferings of William's fellow-countrymen under Philip's rule were such as to justify him in resisting that rule, they justified him in breaking any promise he had given not to resist it. I realize that, formally, the same excuse might be pleaded in defence of Philip's own repeated violation of his oath to respect the charters and liberties of his Flemish and Dutch subjects (see above, p. 85). My answer would be that there are oath-breakings and oath-breakings: and I invite the reader to decide for himself whether an oath to obey a monarch who, having promised to respect his subjects' liberties, proceeds to exercise a bloody tyranny over them is as binding in conscience as the monarch's own oath to respect those liberties.

Although the undeniable horrors of Spanish rule amply suffice to explain why any political leader with a spark of justice and humanity should strive to alter it, the critics of William of Orange insist on turning their eyes away from the obvious, in order that they may concentrate their gaze on another explanation of their own devising. They will have it that his motive was personal ambition and self-glorification. Margaret of Parma secretly told Philip that that was her opinion. Von Pastor, while recognizing some of William's great qualities, says of him:

"... full of ambition, this coldly calculating man had a keen eye for anything that could advance or interfere with his aims".[6] Mr. Trevor Davies (pp. 156 f.): "Behind his fine words about patriotism, liberty and resistance to tyranny – the regular stock-in-trade of the rapacious nobility of the time – is the desire to carve out an independent principality for himself in the Netherlands". Dr. Walsh (p. 567): "... it was not peace or conciliation that William sought, nor even the prosperity of those provinces..., but a kingdom for himself or for a figurehead whom he could control in the interests of that international anti-Christian conspiracy in which he evidently was a person of some importance".

Such charges can, of course, always be brought with a certain amount of apparent plausibility against any man who assumes political leadership in any irregular way. They were made century after century against Oliver Cromwell (whom even so judicious an historian as Henry Hallam thought of as an ambitious hypocrite[7]), until Carlyle's publication of his *Letters and Speeches* showed conclusively that they were baseless. What evidence is there for the truth of charges of this sort in the case of William of Orange? Does the fact that fine words about liberty and resistance to tyranny were the stock-in-trade of certain rapacious nobles constitute evidence against him? Was there no tyranny? What of the placards and of Alva? It is perverse to assume that, just because a man undertakes leadership in a revolt, he must needs be animated solely, mainly, or even partly, by personal ambition. Things being as they were, it could be said of William of Orange with better title than it was said of the Archbishop of York under Henry IV that he

> *"Turns insurrection to religion:*
> *Supposed sincere and holy in his thoughts,*
> *He's followed both with body and with mind;...*
> *Derives from heaven his quarrel and his cause;*
> *Tells them he doth bestride a bleeding land,*
> *Gasping for life under great Bolingbroke;*
> *And more and less do flock to follow him".*

As for his alleged desire to carve out an independent principality

---

6. Von Pastor, *Popes*, vol. xviii (1929), p. 75.
7. Hallam, *Middle Ages*, vol. i, p. 29, *Const. Hist, of Eng.* (ed. 1891), vol. ii, p. 265.

or kingdom for himself, all the facts regarding his personal conduct during the revolt tell against it. For eight years after Philip's departure from the country (1559-67), the population was being steadily goaded into seething disaffection by the application of Philip's oppressive measures. It is quite inaccurate to put the unrest down to the ambitions of discontented noblemen in general, or of Orange in particular. It was the rank and file of the people who were at issue with their rulers. So far from fomenting the disorder, William, at the entreaty of the Regent, repeatedly used his influence to appease it (see below, p. 194). Such opposition as he offered took the form of perfectly constitutional protests. It was only on the eve of Alva's entry into the country that he advocated recourse to armed resistance.[8] Withdrawing for a time to Germany, he was early in 1568 proclaimed an outlaw, unless he would submit to be tried by Alva's Council of Tumults, i.e., unless he would submit to certain death. He replied publicly denying the competence of the tribunal, putting the blame for all the troubles on the king's advisers, and claiming that he had served his sovereign to the best of his power. The campaigns which he and his brother led into the Netherlands in 1568 and 1572 ended in failure. In 1569, in his capacity as an independent sovereign, he issued commissions to eighteen vessels to attack the Spaniards in the narrow seas. After his second defeat in 1572, he made his roundabout way with a few followers to Holland. There, largely as a result of the victories of the "Sea-beggars", the revolt against Spain had already in his absence reached full flood; and city after city was pledging its allegiance to him as Stadtholder of Holland, Zealand, Friesland, and Utrecht. He had been invested with that office by Philip in 1559; and though he had resigned it

---

8. Miss Wedgwood (*William the Silent*, pp. 29, 40, 77, 78, 104) has rightly laid stress on the genuine loyalty felt by William to be owing to Philip as the legal ruler of the country (cf. R. Putnam, *William the Silent*, etc. [ed. 1898], vol. ii, p. 423: "while he was still holding Philip's seals he certainly did try his best to carry out that monarch's will,..."). Miss Putnam is inclined to think that the idea of armed resistance first occurred to him in 1565 (*op. cit.*, vol. i, pp. 181, 232): Motley and Miss Wedgwood (pp. 62, 84, 90) think not earlier than 1566. But whatever the precise date may have been, the resistance undoubtedly rested on a well-grounded conviction of the impracticability and injustice of Philip's government. The legal fiction by which the revolt against the king's officers was carried on in Philip's own name was, of course, construed by the king himself as outrageous treason: but it doubtless represented an honest attempt on William's part to solve the dilemma between treason against Philip and treason against the Netherlands (cf. Wedgwood, *William the Silent*, pp. 128, 218).

before leaving the country in 1567, and Philip had appointed a successor, William – by the vote of the local Estates – calmly resumed his previously-held office. No doubt the act was technically illegal and essentially rebellious,[9] just as the claim to be acting on Philip's behalf was a legal fiction. But it served the purpose, in a desperately anomalous situation, of casting at least a show of legal justification over what the prince felt to be the unquestionable duty of resisting the Duke of Alva. It does not suffice to prove that William's course was morally wrong; still less does it prove that he desired to carve out an independent principality for himself.

Henceforth, to the end of the story, we find him rather shrinking from and declining the powers and offices offered to him than seeking to aggrandize himself. Dictatorial powers were proposed for him in Holland, and were a little later actually conferred; and the resources he demanded for the maintenance of the struggle were granted. In 1575 Holland and Zealand were formally united, and supreme authority over them was conferred on the Prince of Orange. He was to wield all the powers which Philip himself had wielded as Count of Holland. In 1576, under "The Pacification of Ghent", he was declared to be Admiral-general of Holland and Zealand, and tacitly recognized as leader of the whole confederacy; and the previous confiscation of his property was rescinded. In 1577 he was elected to, and reluctantly accepted, the office of "Ruward" (virtually equivalent to that of Stadtholder) of Brabant.[10] Instead of thrusting himself forward into the supreme place, he pursues the policy of entrusting that to others – who, as things worked out, proved themselves unable to fill it. Thus we find him acting as second-in-command to the young Archduke Matthias, still under the nominal authority of Philip. Subsequently, after the arrival of Alexander Farnese, William negotiated for the conferment of the nominal leadership of the country (other than Holland and Zealand) on the French Duke of Anjou. When in 1579 the Pacification of Ghent had broken down, and the northern provinces formed the Union of Utrecht on a mainly Protestant basis (see above, p. 175), William of Orange, so far from grasping at this new chance of

---

9. As Miss Putnam (*William the Silent*, etc. [1911], pp. 233 f., 473) observes.
10. Cf. Geyl, *Revolt*, etc., pp. 154-159.

sovereignty, actually refrained for several months from signing the treaty of Union, as he still clung to the hope of a larger confederacy on a more inclusive basis. Again, had he been playing for his own hand, as his critics suggest, he could have had a little later the same year (1579), through the mediation of the king's emissaries at Cologne, pardon, wealth, honours, and estates in ample measure, on the single condition of quitting the Netherlands. All these splendid offers he refused, as he had already refused similar offers from Requesens (1574) and Don John (1577), determined as he was not to separate his fortunes from those of the cause he had espoused.

In the spring of 1580 Holland, Zealand, and Utrecht secretly decided that for the future they would not even nominally recognize Philip as sovereign; and they offered the supreme sovereignty, with the title "Count of Holland" to the Prince of Orange for as long as the war should last. The Prince, however, would not consent; and the matter remained for a time a secret.[11] In July 1581, however, under further pressure, he accepted the supreme authority over Holland and Zealand, including the provisional and temporary tenure of the title "Count of Holland". This step confirmed him in the exercise of the powers he already possessed. The limitation of his authority to the period of the war was shortly afterwards secretly cancelled. Before that happened, and only two days after Orange's investiture, the provinces of Holland, Zealand, Utrecht, Gelderland, Brabant, and Flanders, by a public Act of Abjuration at The Hague, solemnly renounced their allegiance to Philip.

Arrangements had already been made with the Duke of Anjou to accept the sovereignty of the United Provinces, with the exception of Holland and Zealand, which refused to recognize any ruler but William of Orange. Anjou was installed in office in February 1582; and in August of the same year the prince consented to accept the proffered sovereignty of Holland and Zealand without limitation of time, together with the permanent and hereditary honour of Count of Holland. Some time elapsed, however, before the formalities connected with this last honour

---

11. Dr. Walsh's words (*Philip II*, p. 618: italics mine), "*By the Union of Utrecht* he [William] caused that province to join with Holland and Zealand in deposing Philip as their sovereign", are incorrect.

could be completed. On the disgrace of Anjou (1583), Orange found himself virtual master of the anti-Spanish provinces: he was urged to become Duke of Brabant, and accept the leadership himself. Yet still he declined, strangely hoping that even yet use might be made of the French Duke. Whatever this last-named hope may signify as to his sagacity, it is at least hard to reconcile with the theory that his real wish all the time was "to carve out an independent principality for himself".[12]

He never lived to become actual hereditary Count of Holland and Zealand. The necessary documents were apparently ready in December 1583; but the formal investiture had not taken place when in July 1584 he was shot dead by Philip's hired assassin.

Over and above the purely political aspect of his behaviour during the revolt, there are one or two other aspects of it which have relevance here. Though possessed originally of enormous wealth, he not only forfeited much of it through having to flee the country, but he reduced himself to poverty by devoting his possessions to the payment of the troops which he led into the Netherlands against Alva. When he came, with a very small force, into Holland towards the end of 1572, he was virtually a pauper. He was thenceforth largely dependent on the subsistence with which Holland supplied him. He refused on several occasions to accept the lavish bribes offered to him by Philip's representatives on the condition of his leaving the country. Towards the close of his days he lived mostly at Delft in a modest dwelling and in the humble garb of a burgher, with no such luxury as usually accompanies wealth, rank, and high office. He died almost penniless.

To his financial disinterestedness we have to add the devotion of his extraordinary powers of persuasion, at the request of Philip's regent, to the task of pacifying and appeasing popular discontent during the days before the rebellion actually broke out (1566-67). In addition to this, there is his enormous popularity,

---

12. G. Edmundson in *Camb. Mod. Hist.*, vol. iii (1904), p. 257: "Had Orange been willing to accept for himself the dukedom of Brabant and other sovereignties offered to him, and essayed to stir up a national resistance without the damaging assistance of the French, he might perhaps have longer held back the advancing Spanish tide. But he himself judged otherwise. On the ground that he would not accept any dignity unless he possessed the means to uphold it, he refused for some time to place any of the proffered coronets upon his head". Cf. also Geyl, *Revolt*, etc., p. 189.

which, despite the naturally pro-Spanish tendencies of Catholics after his public avowal of Calvinism in 1573, and despite the inability of most of his Calvinistic supporters to sympathize with his desire to tolerate Catholics and to support the Duke of Anjou, remained a factor of prime importance in the country's history until his death.[13]

So far as William's personal conduct and influence went, the great struggle he carried on was carried on with comparative humaneness. Many incidents attest his normal kindheartedness and his aversion to the infliction of suffering. As a young man he spent a lot of his own money in maintaining the welfare of his tenants and paying the Emperor's troops. He found time, while mourning the death of his first wife (1558), to beg Philip to reprieve a soldier who had killed a man in a brawl. When he was at Paris in 1559, he interceded with the French king to release from sentence of execution and even imprisonment a rascal who had been stealing his (William's) table-silver. In 1571 he pardoned John Rubens (the painter's father) for committing adultery with his wife Anne of Saxony, and refused to exercise his legal right of taking his life, "in accordance" (as the repentant Anne put it) "with his innate goodness". When he drove into Utrecht in 1577, a little girl of nine fell in front of his horses and was killed: he sprang out, and himself carried the dead child in to her parents, and endeavoured to console them.

It was, however, impossible for him to make sure that all those associated with him in the contest with Spain would act humanely. Thus, the cruelties exercised by De la Mark and the other "Beggars of the Sea" were practised in defiance of all his efforts to keep them in order: eventually De la Mark and the worst of his lieutenants were thrown into prison for disobedience to orders. William did his best to prevent barbarities being committed by his own hired troops which he led into the Low Countries in 1572.[14] He peremptorily commanded the brutal tortures inflicted on suspected Catholics by Sonoy in 1575 to be stopped. He strove to restrain the excesses of the Calvinists at Ghent in 1577. At Antwerp in 1580 he refused to take any

---
13. Cf. C.V. Wedgwood, *William the Silent*, pp. 203 f.
14. Dr. Walsh (*Philip II*, p. 537) speaks of William "sacking the towns on the plain of Gueldre", but not his proclamation commanding his troops to respect the rights of all individuals, whether Catholic or Protestant.

punitive action against a fanatic, who publicly accused him of selling the Netherlands to France. When the Duke of Anjou treacherously attempted to seize Antwerp in 1583, William stopped the cannonade against the French as soon as he could.

Did he ever enter into a plan for an assassination? The charge has been made, especially with reference to Don John:[15] but it is doubtful if it rests on any better authority than the allegations of his Spanish enemies. Mr. George Edmundson and others categorically deny it.[16]

When the first actual attempt on his own life was made in 1582 – in conformity with the wish expressed by Philip in his ban – and Jauréguy shot him through the mouth, William immediately exclaimed, "Do not kill him. I pardon him my death". He prevailed on the Estates not to use torture in executing the accomplices of the would-be assassin, and even professed his willingness to pardon them. The pistol with which he was finally shot dead in 1584 was purchased by his murderer with money given to him by the prince in charity.

All this does not read very like the record of a "coarse and brutal materialist", whose main concern was "to carve out an independent principality for himself in the Netherlands". Of course, it is always open to a writer to put the worst possible construction, if he wishes, on the actions of a man of whom he writes. But that is not the way genuine history is written. As with Cromwell, so with Orange: one can support the charge of personal ambition only by assuming hypocrisy and insincerity at every turn of the story – an assumption entirely unjustified, because it is purely imaginary and is discredited by the facts.

Granted that William of Orange was, as we have argued at length, justified in organizing armed resistance to Philip, the charges that he was untruthful and insincere in his negotiations, and employed spies, find their own answer.[17] It would be bordering

---

15. Walsh, *Philip II*, pp. 567 f., 583, 593.
16. Cf. Edmundson in *Camb. Mod. Hist.*, vol. iii (1904), pp. 238 f. ("despite so much provocation to retaliate, there is not a shred of testimony to show that he ever stooped to employ against his adversaries the same base and cowardly weapons which so frequently threatened his own life"); F. Harrison, *William the Silent*, p. 158.
17. Cf. Walsh, *Philip II*, p. 227 (quoting the Spanish historian Cabrera: "generally he was unfaithful, untruthful, a flatterer, a dissembler and a hypocrite"), p. 229 (similar), p. 564 (quoted above, p. 186).

on the childish to make William's employment of spies a ground of moral reproach,[18] seeing that to this day most of the civilized governments in the world regularly make use of such secret agents even in time of peace. As for the charge in its more general form, it is not for apologists of Philip II, who interwove in his dispatches so much needless deceit and so many injunctions to others to practise deceit (see above, pp. 125-132), to blame William of Orange for not being more straightforward. Dr. Walsh (p. 564) speaks of Philip's deceptions as being "less frequent and more excusable" than William's. I cannot but regard Philip's as far less excusable, and should certainly judge them to have been more frequent – though a precise count is of course impossible. The only moral standard according to which William of Orange could be criticized for being deceitful would be a standard which unconditionally condemned all resistance to an established government, whatever it did, and all use of arms. Mr. George Edmundson says: "If Orange's methods do not always commend themselves for straightforwardness, if he met duplicity with duplicity, and cunningness with greater cunning, it must be remembered that he was reduced at times to almost desperate straits, and that those with whom he had to deal were absolutely unscrupulous".[19]

Moreover, as we shall have occasion to observe in other connexions presently, it is needful, when studying the character of this man, to make allowance for the fact that between the earlier and later stages of his career he passed through a very radical change. After having been in his early manhood a libertine, he finished as an heroic patriot. The change did not take place in the twinkling of an eye; but it corresponds roughly to his change from Catholicism to Calvinism. It was in 1573 that he publicly avowed his adhesion to the Calvinistic communion, though the process must have been going on several years before that. Von Pastor adduces to William's discredit the deception he practised in connexion with his marriage to the Protestant Anne, daughter of Maurice, Elector of Saxony, in

---

18. Cf. R. Putnam, *William the Silent*, etc. (ed. 1898), vol. ii, p. 426; R.T. Davies, *Golden Century*, p. 155 bott. The fact is generally accepted, though, curiously enough, Miss Putnam herself, earlier in her work (vol. i, p. 205), says that "it is difficult to trace this statement to its origin in contemporaneous authorities."
19. G. Edmundson in *Camb. Mod. Hist.*, vol. iii (1904), p. 238.

1561; his assurance to Pope Pius IV the same year that he wished as a good Catholic to extirpate heresy in his principality of Orange; his repetition of this intention to Pius V in 1566; and his confidential avowal to William of Hesse a little later that he had always "held and professed" the Confession of Augsburg.[20] In admitting an element of untruthfulness in his conduct in these connexions, we may observe that they all belong to the period before the prince had completed his thirty-fourth year, and before the revolt in the Netherlands had broken out. Besides which, some allowance must be made for the fact that a swing-over from one religious attachment to another, however honest, is always a gradual, difficult, and. elusive process, in which it is hard to seem consistent in the eyes of others. Nor is it fair to forget how William of Orange's difficulties were multiplied by the unprecedented and complicated position in which his relations to the king of Spain and other parties placed him.

Dr. Walsh (pp. 564-567) is particularly severe in his criticism of the prince's negotiations with Don John of Austria. What happened was this. A day or two after Don John arrived in disguise at Luxemburg, "the Pacification of Ghent" was – as a consequence of the outrageous sack of Antwerp by the Spaniards – concluded between William, Holland, and Zealand on the one hand, and the Catholic states of the south on the other. All parties agreed to expel the Spaniards; but the king's authority was acknowledged, and the supremacy of the Catholic religion was to be maintained in places where it was already dominant, the religious question generally being left to be settled by the States-General when the military struggle was over. Meanwhile,

---

20. Von Pastor, *Popes*, vol. xviii (1929), pp. 76 f. It seems certain that William was not perfectly candid in what he said regarding his real intentions for the territory of Orange: see R. Putnam, *William the Silent*, etc. (ed. 1898), vol. i, pp. 144, 369-371, vol. ii, pp. 450 f., *William the Silent*, etc. (1911), p. 126; F. Harrison, *William the Silent*, pp. 39 f.; C.V. Wedgwood, *William the Silent*, p. 55.

The question of his straightforwardness in the matter of Anne of Saxony is more complicated. He promised Philip and other leading Catholics that she should live "catholically", by which he doubtless meant that she should comply outwardly with the requirements of Catholic ritual. He refused, on the other hand, to give to the Protestant authorities more than general verbal assurances of right conduct or to sign any specific undertaking about her religious observances. There is no doubt that he acted with a degree of diplomatic caution and skill that could not perhaps be described as wholly ingenuous: on the other hand, he probably felt that he was not really responsible to others for his matrimonial plans, and was therefore entitled to use with them language which, though it could not be described as actually false, was undoubtedly ambiguous and evasive. Cf. Pirenne, *Belgique*, vol. iii (1912), p. 417.

the persecuting edicts and the activities of the Inquisition were suspended: and there was to be no persecution of private Protestant worship in the Catholic states. William was to remain in full possession of his powers, as representing the king, in Holland and Zealand. The States-General then commenced negotiations with Don John. Early in January 1577 the Pacification of Ghent was popularly confirmed throughout the country by what was known as "the Union of Brussels". In the negotiations with Don John, the States' deputies absolutely insisted on his acceptance of the principles of the Pacification of Ghent: and eventually, on being assured that it contained nothing that was detrimental to the king's authority and to the supremacy of Roman Catholicism, he consented to agree to it.[21]

Dr. Walsh says that "the insincerity of Orange in putting forth this proposal is admitted by historians as well disposed towards him as Motley…" (p. 564). It is true that Orange had lent his support to the Union of Brussels, as the confirmation of the Pacification of Ghent. Motley says indeed that he was disconcerted by Don John's unexpected acceptance of it: but I cannot find that he charges William with insincerity.[22] We must remember that William was not entirely a free agent in the matter, that the negotiations with Don John were not in his hands, and that he expressed to the States-General his disappointment and displeasure when the new governor accepted the terms in his "Perpetual Edict" (February 1577). William certainly did his best to wreck the settlement, for he strongly suspected the good faith both of Don John and of King Philip, who confirmed the "Edict" a few days after his half-brother had signed it. This suspicion of William's, so far from being insincere or unnecessary, was thoroughly justified by past experience (see above, pp. 78 f.) – a fact for which Dr. Walsh makes no allowance. There can be no doubt that Don John's willingness to make concessions, and Philip's willingness to confirm them, were simply temporary expedients, adopted pending a better opportunity for crushing resistance.

Summing up, it may fairly be argued that, apart from a few

---

21. Not "promptly", as Dr. Walsh says (*Philip II*, p. 564), but only after prolonged haggling.
22. Motley, *Dutch Republic* (ed. 1874), p. 666a.

acts of diplomatic deceit and evasion belonging to the earlier stages of William's career, he was not more deceitful than the great struggle on which he had embarked might honestly have appeared to him to require.

To many it is bound to seem a great stain on the prince's reputation that on two occasions at least (1569 and 1577-78) he sought for help against Spain from the Sultan of Turkey (see above, p. 182). To a Catholic author like Dr. Walsh this act is nothing but a "cold-blooded selling-out of the cause of Christendom to the enemies of Christ" (p. 411). "He was traitor to Philip, to whom he had sworn allegiance, and traitor to the whole Christian world" (p. 412). When, however, we make the effort – as in justice we ought to make it – to put ourselves in the place of the prince and his supporters, launched as they were, with their slender resources, on a life-and-death struggle with the strongest and cruellest power in Europe, we shall readily understand, even if we cannot wholly approve, their readiness to receive help from the Sultan, notwithstanding his heathenism, and notwithstanding the Christian pretensions of Spain.[23]

It has been made a complaint against William of Orange that he was savagely and scurrilously bitter in the struggle, the glaring example of this defect being the *Apologia* for himself, which he published in 1581. Mr. Trevor Davies says (pp. 198 f.; cf. p. 118) that into it "he eagerly raked every possible scrap of garbage", and that he exploited to the uttermost the suspicious character of Philip's connexion with the death of his son Carlos (pp. 151 f.: see in the present work, above, pp. 112 f.). Dr. Walsh (p. 618) speaks of William's "savage *Apologia* of July, 1581, in which he accused the King of Spain of all manner of crimes, including incest and adultery and the murder of Don Carlos and Queen Isabel" (cf. pp. 451, 459). "William of Orange declared in his bitter *Apology* that Philip had married [Dona Isabel de Osorio] secretly even before his marriage with Maria of

---

23. It is perhaps worth mentioning in this connexion that Philip himself incurred the displeasure of the popes for his lukewarmness against the Turks, and for his undue eagerness to negotiate with the Sultan for peace after Lepanto (Merriman, *Philip the Prudent*, p. 59: cf. pp. 154 f.).

Portugal" (p. 115: see above, p. 115). Dr. Walsh also states that William invented the story of a love-affair between Don Carlos and his step-mother (pp. 424 f.).

Now we are under no obligation to accept as Gospel-truth every accusation which William made against Philip, or indeed to exculpate him from the reproach of indulging in bitter invective. But while some of his charges are improbable, I am not aware that there is one which he may not, with some show of plausibility, have honestly believed to be true. Moreover, it has to be remembered (1) that the very publicity given to the *Apologia* (which was put into French, Dutch, and Latin, and sent to all the courts of Europe) was up to a point a guarantee that it would contain nothing too palpably untrue: and (2) that the duty of speaking of a real enemy with gentleness and courtesy was in that period very imperfectly understood. What, however, makes complaints about the *Apologia* being "bitter", "savage", and so on, look really a little silly, is the very relevant fact that, a few months before its publication, Philip had denounced William of Orange to the world as a miscreant, traitor, and enemy of his country and of the human race, and had offered a reward of 25,000 crowns in gold or land and a patent of nobility to any one who would murder him. A certain amount of violent language on William's part when replying is perhaps pardonable under such provocation.

We have now to consider the question of the character of William of Orange's religion, the motive (whether disinterested or otherwise) of his public conversion to Calvinism in 1573, and the real reason of his having been, throughout the whole of his public life, an advocate of religious toleration.

In the eyes of his adverse critics, he figures as an essentially irreligious man. Von Pastor, for instance, says of him: "Being filled with purely worldly ideas, he entirely ignored the supernatural; it is certain that very little remained in his mind of the Lutheran training which he received until his eleventh year. When, at that age, he became a Catholic in order to receive the rich inheritance of his cousin René, he was given an education in accordance with the views of Erasmus. It is no wonder then that he fell into the state of indifference that was prevalent among the aristocracy of the Netherlands...."[24] "He seems, from the beginning", writes Mr. Trevor Davies (p. 156), "to have been completely indifferent to religion".[25] Dr. Walsh (p. 229) will not allow that he was a good Catholic. To such critics his public conversion to Calvinism seems a purely political manoeuvre, designed to secure for himself a larger measure of support from the Calvinists as the stronger and more vigorous element in the anti-Spanish movement. So Von Pastor again: "Since the Calvinists were Orange's strongest supporters, he formally joined their church in October, 1573..."[26] Also Dr. Walsh (p. 167): "Now seemingly a Catholic, he had been a Protestant, and would be again when it suited his purposes".[27] Even Mr. George Edmundson, a great admirer of William of Orange, and believing him to have been more sincerely religious than either Elizabeth or Henry IV, thinks his transition to the Protestant camp was mainly motivated by political and patriotic (as distinct from religious) considerations.[28]

Now it is admittedly a ticklish undertaking to be sure of oneself in regard to one's real motives in certain situations. Still more difficult is it to speak confidently about the motives of others, especially of those who lived long ago. But as regards William of Orange, this at least must be said. There is a very discernible difference in the man's behaviour and speech during the earlier years of his manhood as compared with those of the later (see above, pp. 197 f.). The charge of being religiously superficial or indifferent has probably a measure of justice in it, so far as his early manhood is concerned. But judging from the evidence, we gather that, from about 1560 onwards, a change set in, leading to the final emergence of a deep and serious religious faith. "During his exile in 1568", writes T.M. Lindsay, "he had made a daily study of the Holy Scriptures, and, whatever the

---
24. Von Pastor, *Popes*, vol. xviii (1929), p. 75.
25. Pirenne inclines to the view that William had a statesman's indifference to purely religious issues (*Belgique*, vol. iii, [1912], pp. 405, 449, 462, vol. iv [1911], pp. 27, 120).
26. Von Pastor, *Popes*, vol. xx (1930), p. 2.
27. Note how in this passage, as Von Pastor in the first passage quoted above, Dr. Walsh insinuates that William's conversion to Catholicism at the age of eleven constituted on his part a self-interested change of front. Yet surely at that age a boy can hardly be held responsible for the decisions of his elders. Similarly with regard to the particular (Erasmian?) type of Catholicism in which he is asserted to have been educated.
28. G. Edmundson in *Camb. Mod. Hist.*, vol. iii (1904), pp. 237 f.

exact shade of his theological opinions, had become a deeply religious man, animated with the lofty idea that God had called him to do a great work for Him and for His persecuted people. His private letters, meant for no eyes but those of his wife or of his most familiar friends, are full of passages expressing a quiet faith in God and in the leadings of His Providence".[29]

One can, in fact, maintain that the prince was religiously indifferent during, say, the last eighteen years of his life only by assuming that he was a consummate and deliberate hypocrite – an assumption which is not only needlessly ungenerous, but is also inconsistent with the serious and self-sacrificing character of his conduct as a whole. I venture to think that a truer version of the facts can be offered.

That in his earlier manhood he was something of a worldling (in the evil sense) cannot, I think, be denied. Our Catholic friends ought, however, to be willing to admit that such worldliness is not necessarily incompatible with a genuine religious instinct. There is certainly nothing improbable about the belief that even in his youthful years, William's Catholicism meant more to him than a mere pretence.

What makes it easier to believe that his religion, even at this early stage, meant something to him, is the well-attested fact of his habitual kindness and of his aversion from all deliberate infliction of suffering. We have evidence to show that this phase of his character was visible from early manhood. He was deeply revolted by the thought or prospect of human beings suffering torture or violent death. This, as we know, was the main consideration behind his opposition to the persecuting

---

29. T.M. Lindsay, *The Reformation*, vol. ii, p. 269. Similarly, G. Edmundson in *Encyc. Brit.*, vol. xxviii (1911), p. 672 b, and in *Camb. Mod. Hist.*, vol. iii (1904), pp. 222 f. (too long to quote in full, but very clear and emphatic: e.g., William wrote to his wife: "I am determined to place myself in the hands of the Almighty, that He may guide me, where it shall be His good pleasure, since I see well that I must needs pass this life in misery and travail, with which I am quite contented, for I know that I have deserved far greater chastisement; I pray Him only graciously to enable me to bear everything patiently, as I have done up to the present". "His correspondence", adds Mr. Edmundson, "is full of similar passages"), p. 236 (in 1573: "The very staunchest of the patriots began to despair; but the spirit which breathes through all William's utterances at this time is that of absolute trust in God, and submission to His will. When his followers urged that the cause was hopeless without an alliance with some great potentate, he nobly replied, 'When I took in hand to defend these oppressed Christians I made an alliance with the mightiest of all Potentates – the God of Hosts, who is able to save us if He choose'").

policy of the Spanish government, as later to the persecuting tendencies of his fellow-Calvinists. Now it is easy enough for Catholics to take it for granted that his opposition to persecution arose directly from his religious indifference. My answer would be that, since the tree is to be known by its fruit, an aversion to cruelty is entitled to be regarded as arising from a Christian spirit, and points in the direction of a real piety rather than away from it.

There is, however, another factor to be considered. A distinction must be recognized as existing between real piety (in the sense of trust in God as revealed in Christ, and a desire to serve Him) and any particular doctrinal, ritualistic, or ecclesiological embodiment of such piety. Doubtless such a distinction is hard for many to admit: but most civilized Christians of to-day, whatever their type and connexion, realize *in practice* that it has to be allowed for. However important we may feel our own doctrinal or ecclesiastical convictions to be, we know that inward loyalty to God is more important still. And if it be wrong, as it obviously is, to try to coerce a man by penalties to be inwardly loyal to God, it must be still more wrong to afflict him with torments for the sake of certain doctrinal and ecclesiastical tenets. William of Orange's personal religion seems to me to have been of the sort which, being based upon a deep inward piety, sat loose to the fixed requirements made by any particular religious organization. If that were so, I submit that he was right as against those of his contemporaries, whether Catholic or Protestant, who differed from him.

We cannot, of course, trace the stages of the change from the kindhearted, pleasure-loving, and conventional type of Catholicism which characterized his earlier manhood, over to that equally kind, but devout and tolerant Calvinism of his later years.[30] But it is easy to see that the transition must have been gradual, and such as to lay him easily open to hasty charges (on the part of the unsympathetic) of duplicity and inconsistency. As for his conversion in 1573, I am not concerned to deny that it simplified his task politically, and that that may have been a

---

30. I cannot think that the subtitle of Miss Ruth Putnam's valuable two-volume work on *William the Silent* (first published in 1895), viz., *The Moderate Man of the Sixteenth Century*, quite does justice to him.

factor in bringing him to it. At the same time he may well have felt that, despite its tendency to intolerance, Calvinism had in it on the whole fewer hindrances than Catholicism had, to what was religiously and morally most precious to his own soul.

In the immediately foregoing paragraphs, we have to some extent anticipated what needs to be said about William's policy of toleration. Let us, however, first briefly survey the actual facts. We begin with recalling the revulsion which he says he felt when in 1559 he first heard of the plans in the minds of Henry II and Philip II for a general extermination of the Protestants (see above, pp. 187 f.). In 1564, 1565, and 1566, he openly and repeatedly protested against the persecuting measures of the government. Frequent allusion has been made to his steady advocacy of toleration from the time when in 1572 he wielded some authority in the country; and there is no need to repeat the details. In commissioning Sonoy to be Lieutenant-Governor of North Holland, or Waterland, he bade him see that the Word of God was preached, without however allowing any hindrance to the Roman Catholics in the exercise of their religion. When in 1575 he accepted the government of Holland and Zealand, the clause requiring him, not only to protect the exercise of the evangelical Reformed faith, but also to suppress the exercise of the Roman religion, was on his insistence altered to one requiring him to suppress the exercise of any religion "at variance with the Gospel". Even so, the reference was only to public worship; and search into the personal creed of any individual was not to be permitted. It is clear that, if he had had a free hand, complete religious toleration would have prevailed throughout all the provinces. The allusions we sometimes find in criticisms of him to his persecuting Anabaptists, Jesuits, and others, must be discounted as having reference either to his youthful days, or to fear of social disturbance, or to practices of his followers whom he could only imperfectly control.[31] It was

---

31. It seems that William's attitude towards the Anabaptists did undergo some change – but this would be accounted for by the fact that, while normally peaceable, they had in 1534-35 occasioned very serious disturbances, and it was naturally feared for a long while afterwards that they might at any time do so again. Mr. E. Armstrong (*Charles V* [ed. 1910], vol. ii, p. 347) says: "William of Orange himself, in Philip's reign, while advocating tolerance for Lutherans and Calvinists, favoured the suppression of Anabaptists, on the grounds, firstly, that it was possible, and

only his inability to secure the agreement of his supporters generally on this issue that made the full adoption of a policy of toleration throughout the Low Countries impossible, and thus prevented – to the prince's profound disappointment – the permanent union of all the provinces against Spain (see above, pp. 174-176).

Such, broadly, were the facts. To-day no one questions for a moment that the policy which William of Orange advocated is the right way to treat religious and ecclesiastical differences, and that the policy is perfectly compatible with the advocate thereof being himself a religiously sincere and zealous man. But because, forsooth, the adoption of this policy happened also to be favourable to the common effort against the Spaniards, William's critics will not allow him to have been tolerant from the best motives. His toleration, they insist, must – in the light of his earlier levity – have been based on purely political motives, the prince himself being religiously indifferent. Thus, Von Pastor says: "Since the Calvinists were Orange's strongest supporters, he formally joined their church in October, 1573, but, *for political reasons*, he was still unwilling to consent to the immediate suppression of Catholic worship, and at first would only countenance a division of the churches and of ecclesiastical property between the Protestants and the Catholics..."[32] And Mr. Trevor Davies (p. 156): "... he stood almost alone on the side of religious toleration in an age that refused it. In reality his tolerance was not due to any moral or intellectual superiority to his age, but to his need of certain allies within and without the Netherlands who held widely divergent religious views. His aim was toleration for nobles and city councils on the *cujus regio ejus religio* principle that obtained in the Empire. To see him as a paladin of political or religious equality for the proletariat is grotesquely to misunderstand both William and his age".[33]

---

secondly, that they were socially dangerous". Similarly Walsh, *Philip II*, pp. 345 f., 353 (referring to the period 1562-63). It was in 1566 that William suggested to the Regent that the Anabaptists might be expelled from the country (Pirenne, *Belgique*, vol. iii [1912], p. 360). In 1577-78 we find him strenuously opposing, and indeed forbidding any persecution of Anabaptists in the territories under his control.

32. Von Pastor, *Popes*, vol. xx (1930), p. 2: italics mine.
33. Cf. also the depreciatory remark in R.T. Davies, *Golden Century*, pp. 134 f.n., on the toleration of "William the Silent, who was compelled by circumstances to

To Mr. Trevor Davies's criticism I would reply, firstly, that I know of no one who claims William as a paladin of *political* equality for the proletariat: he was concerned with the more immediate problem of excluding the foreign persecutors from the country. Nevertheless, his immense popularity is not without significance as to what the proletariat thought of him. Secondly, the *cujus regio* reference is, so far as I know, true only of the scheme outlined in the Pacification of Ghent, as the best thing to which *all* the states could be induced for the moment to agree: moreover, even so, it was unlike the similar principle inaugurated in Germany by the Peace of Augsburg in 1555, which provided no toleration for any but Catholics and Lutherans: all that was conceded to Catholics in a Lutheran state was the option of either being converted to Lutheranism, or departing; Lutherans in a Catholic state were faced with a similar choice of alternatives. Under the Pacification of Ghent, on the contrary, the persecuting placards and edicts on the subject of heresy were suspended. The worst that religious minorities would suffer on these terms would be the prohibition of public worship. Whatever his reasons may have been, William's own objective was undoubtedly the establishment of complete toleration, including liberty of public worship, for all Christian communities, so long as they were not morally scandalous, politically dangerous, or enemies of the public peace. Mr. Trevor Davies therefore seems doubly mistaken and – if William's motives were due (as I hold they were) to his being morally superior to his fellow-Protestants – trebly so.

I contend for his moral superiority on the ground (1) that he shrank from the inhuman cruelties incidental to sixteenth-century persecution (see above, pp. 203 f.), and (2) that he regarded the ecclesiastical, doctrinal, and ritualistic sides of a man's religion as a matter in which his own conscience ought to be left free, since he is entitled to judge for himself. The prince was confident that if any set or group of men were gravely wrong in their beliefs, these beliefs would in course of time be caused to fade away by the diligence and learning of those who believed the

---

attempt to find some *modus vivendi* for the many conflicting religious bodies in the Netherlands". Even Mr. George Edmundson is disposed, to my surprise, to regard Orange's advocacy of toleration as due more to statesmanship than to religious conviction (*Camb. Mod. Hist.*, vol. iii. [1904], pp. 238, 646 ["... due not so much to religious conviction, as to a statesmanlike desire for toleration in matters of faith,..."]).

truth. There is clear evidence that such were his views; and I submit that therein his moral judgment and even his religious discernment were superior to those who differed from him. The assumption that they rested on an indifference to truly religious interests is gratuitous, and in my judgment false to the evidence.

I have, however, no wish to deny that toleration was also politically expedient for him and his fellow-countrymen, that he knew it to be so, and that this knowledge added weight to his convictions as an advocate of toleration. But a man is not justly open to adverse criticism because in a complex situation he sees more than one good reason for a certain course; nor is it fair to assume that, if one of the reasons is less profoundly religious than the other, that reason must necessarily have been his main or only one. There is nothing improbable in even a good Catholic morally revolting against the hideous butcheries necessitated by Philip's idea of how heresy should be treated: and it is significant that William of Orange adhered to his personal views, even though, despite their general wisdom, they made his path as a politician in certain directions harder.

There remain one or two other matters in regard to which William's character has been criticized, and which therefore call for brief discussion. There is the important department of life associated with the physical appetites. It is on record that he maintained so magnificent a household as to involve himself in debt. "His kitchen was regarded as the greatest school of gastronomy in the world – so much so that few German princes of consequence did not possess at least one cook who had served an apprenticeship in his kitchen".[34] This, however, was incidental to his princely inheritance and to his early associations with the life of the court. Later on, as we have seen, he reduced himself to poverty for the sake of his cause. Apparently in his last years he returned at times to a more lavish style of living – for a minister at Leyden rebuked from the pulpit the extravagance of his table. But this probably referred to some special state-occasion: it is well known that his normal style of living was exceedingly modest and inexpensive.

It would probably be unwise on the part of a would be

---

34. R.T. Davies, *Golden Century*, p. 156: cf. Walsh, *Philip II*, pp. 227 f.

apologist for William of Orange to attempt to prove that he was a total abstainer! The northern races of Europe have always been addicted to heavy drinking. The Dutch were notorious for it: but – according to a certain eminent contemporary of the prince – they were surpassed by the English. "… in England,… indeed", so Shakespeare makes Iago say, "they are most potent in drinking: your Dane, your German, and your swag-bellied Hollander – Drink, ho! – are nothing to your English".[35] If William of Orange was a heavy drinker, as in his early manhood he probably was,[36] it was a weakness which he shared not only with his heretical friends, but also with most of his loyal Roman Catholic fellow-countrymen, as well as with some eminent Britons of the period. We do not need to admire him for it: but it is clear that it did not gravely impair his capacity for work or the clarity of his judgment.

In regard to his relations with women, we are to some extent at least dependent on conjecture. It is certain that the custom and example of his fellow-courtiers would not be very uplifting. But how far, if at all, he was in his early manhood corrupted by them is not known. When he was only just over eighteen he was, by the Emperor's friendly contrivance, married to Anne of Egmont, daughter and heiress of the Count of Buren (see above, p. 183), who bore him two children. To judge from their correspondence, they were happy together; and there is no evidence that he was ever unfaithful to her.[37] But that at this period his views on sexual morality were not rigid is made clear by the report that, at the Diet of princes at Frankfort in February-March 1558, he stated at a drinking-party that in his view adultery was no sin. From that Diet he returned to see his wife die (March 24). In the course of the next year or two he lived from time to time with mistresses. One of these, Eva Elincx, bore him in September 1559 a son, Justin of Nassau, who lived to distinguish himself as governor of Breda and admiral of Zealand: after his birth his mother married respectably.

William's second marriage turned out very unhappily both

---

35. Cf. Mistress Page's reference to Falstaff in *Merry Wives* as "this Flemish drunkard".
36. Von Pastor says (*Popes*, vol. xviii [1929], p. 75): "He was so addicted to the national vice of drunkenness as to endanger his vigorous constitution".
37. C.V. Wedgwood, *William the Silent*, pp. 17 f.

for himself and his wife. He married at Leipzig in August 1561 Anne, the daughter of the celebrated Maurice, Elector of Saxony, who had died in 1553, and grand-daughter through her mother of Philip, the celebrated Protestant Landgrave of Hesse. She was a tolerably good-looking girl of seventeen, living under the guardianship of her uncle Augustus, Elector of Saxony; and she brought her husband a fairly handsome dowry. She was, however, slightly lame and had a curvature of the spine and, besides that, a strong will and a violent temper.[38] It is impossible to say how far William's personal affections were engaged; but it is not unreasonable to suppose that the bride's rank and dowry had much to do with his choice.[39] Of her children one son (the famous Stadtholder Maurice) and two daughters survived her. The couple were not permanently happy.[40] With the passage of the years, Anne's latent mental derangement became more and more noticeable in the violence and unseemliness of her conduct. The prince bore it all as patiently as he could: but matters reached a climax when in 1567 he departed with her from the Netherlands to Nassau. It was a time when he was heavily weighed down with political discouragement, and stood in special need of wifely consolation. Eventually she absconded from her husband's home to Cologne, where in 1571 she committed adultery with John Rubens (see above, p. 195); and William privately divorced her. At last she was handed over in despair to the care of her family in Saxony: after six years' confinement she died hopelessly insane.

In 1575, two years before Anne of Saxony's death, William of Orange, now an avowed Calvinist, married Charlotte de Bourbon, daughter of the Duke of Montpensier, and an ex-nun. A phrase in one of his letters to his brother John, who disapproved of the new match, indicates that William professed to have remained continent since he had parted from Anne. He had

---

38. Mr. Trevor Davies's description of her as "a deformed and half-mad dwarf" (*Golden Century*, p. 156) is an exaggeration if taken to refer to the time of her marriage. On the deceptions William is supposed to have practised in connexion with the match, see above, pp. 197 f.
39. Mr. R.T. Davies (*loc. cit.*) writes as if the money were his only object: per contra, Motley, *Dutch Republic* (ed. 1874), p. 152.
40. Dr. Walsh (*Philip II*, p. 346) says that both husband and wife "were notoriously unfaithful". I do not know on what evidence this allegation rests, or precisely to what period it refers.

satisfied himself, both in conscience and by the formal declaration of his spiritual advisers, as to his freedom from responsibility for Anne.[41] Charlotte's freedom from responsibility as regards her conventual vows, which had been forced upon her before the canonical age, were clear to them both. The parties consulted their personal inclinations, and what they understood to be their duty: and the marriage was a happy one. The prince was able to enjoy a domestic peace and comfort which he had not experienced for many years. Yet the match gave great offence, especially to the Catholics, for whom the marriage of an ex-nun was always as smoke in the nostrils. According to Dr. Walsh (p. 568), in 1577 William was guilty of "flaunting" his third wife at Antwerp, though he does not tell us the particular forms which this objectionable method of behaviour took. The good woman bore her husband several daughters. She died in May 1582, partly in consequence of the strain occasioned to her by the unsuccessful attempt on her husband's life the previous March.

In April 1583 he married his fourth and last wife, Louise de Coligny, daughter of the famous Huguenot admiral. She bore him one son, the Stadholder Frederick Henry, and survived him for many years.

It is clear from this record that William of Orange's character, as reflected in his relations with women, as in other personal respects, was not beyond criticism. He was obviously of a somewhat amorous and uxorious temperament, depending much on the response he found to his personal affections. The main defects, however, seem to be traceable to that earlier period of his manhood, when he was still subject to the unregenerate ethos of the nobility and royalty of his day, and before the advance of years and closer attention to his adopted country's needs had matured his character into that sober and upright dignity which marked it throughout the later years of his life. Admirers of Orange are under no necessity of denying that in his earlier manhood he lived loosely; but they are entitled to protest when these excesses are adduced without reference to the far-reaching change of mind and character through which he

---

41. Mr. Trevor Davies (*Golden Century*, p. 156) says of William and Anne: "Years later he obtained the consent of Protestant ministers to put her away in order to make a third marriage". In view of the dates and of Anne's behaviour, this statement is misleading, and unjust to the prince.

passed in his middle years. Recognizing that his first marriage was made for him by the Emperor, and that his second was probably motivated at least in part by the desire for its financial and political advantages, we can see nothing to cavil at in his third and fourth, while the extra-marital excesses of 1558 and the following years were of the kind that stain, in differing measure, the youth of all-too-many of the race, of many who are exposed to less temptation than he was, and of many who never in their later years rise above them as did he.

William of Orange did not possess the gifts and virtues of a great soldier. Though not deficient in personal courage – for over and over again his life was in imminent danger – he had little skill as a military commander: and that fact, coupled with the slenderness of his resources, lent to his generalship a certain appearance of hesitation and timidity. The marvel is that, with so little in the way of armed force, as against the magnificent efficiency of the great Spanish army, he was able to accomplish so much as he did in defiance of it.

I have tried to delineate the character of William of Orange objectively and without bias, and to keep in mind the fact that, whatever my personal sympathies might be, my task was one of description (even if it inevitably included some comment on the moral value and otherwise of his conduct) rather than one of final judgment on him as a man. Perhaps the result has been to show the task to have been beyond my powers. It is certainly not easy to limit praise and blame to a man's deeds (and intentions, so far as these can be known) and not either to applaud or condemn the man himself. Possibly there is a subtle, if healthy, bias in the human mind, which bids us applaud the man whensoever his record is pleasing, but to refrain from condemning him when the record is the opposite. The aim, however, of the foregoing sketch of the prince's character is mainly to rebut those depreciations of him which certain recent writers have expressed, and to put in their true perspective the qualities and characteristics which marked him as the leader and champion of a great national movement of liberation. Looked at in the large and with at least that minimum degree of sympathy which it is not more than decent to start with, the prince's figure surely cannot fail to command respect. There must be few characterizations of him less just than that of Mr. Trevor Davies – "this coarse and brutal materialist". His true place, on the contrary, in so far as we are entitled to assign it, is among the heroes, who, notwithstanding certain undeniable defects of character, enthrone themselves in the heart of humanity, by dint of the far-seeing, long-sustained, and self-denying service which they render to their afflicted fellow-men.

Chapter Ten

Conclusion

It now remains to gather together the threads of the foregoing discussion, and to attempt some kind of synthesis of the findings to which I have from time to time felt the facts to point. I feel compelled at least to admit that the contrast between the two main parties engaged in the struggle is less of a contrast between dead black and pure white than has sometimes been imagined. Certain modifications assuredly need to be made in our previously customary judgments, if we are to arrive at a true and balanced verdict: and throughout the writing of the book, it has been my wish and endeavour to make all reasonable allowance for them. Yet when all is said, I cannot escape the conviction that the struggle between Philip of Spain and the Netherlands was at bottom a struggle over the following three issues:

(1) that between virtual (or shall we say, potential) democracy and irresponsible monarchical despotism;
(2) that between religious freedom and intolerance; and
(3) that between humaneness and savage cruelty.

I am fully aware that a good deal needs to be said in order to justify this way of putting it. I do not wish to claim that either Philip himself or those who loyally collaborated with him were dishonest or insincere men: they were for the most part following out what they had been brought up to believe was right and needful, and they were prepared to suffer on its behalf. On the other hand, the Protestant side lies open to some fairly severe criticisms.

It is, for instance, quite true to say that in the sixteenth century there was hardly any more idea of toleration in Protestantism than there was in Catholicism.[1] What was yet more remarkable, and what occasioned William of Orange such distress, was that the German Lutherans, mainly, no doubt, because of their antipathy to Calvinism, felt no call to lend the Netherlanders

---

1. Cf. H.C. Lea in *Amer. Hist. Review*, vol. ix, p. 240 (January 1904): those who demanded religious freedom wanted freedom only in order to coerce the consciences of others. He quotes a number of instances.

an ounce of help against the great and menacing foe of both of them – the Church of Rome. "Neither prince nor peasant", writes Motley, "stirred in behalf of the struggling Christians in the United Provinces, battling, year after year, knee-deep in blood, amid blazing cities and inundated fields, breast to breast with the yellow-jerkined pikemen of Spain and Italy, with the axe and the faggot and the rack of the Holy Inquisition distinctly visible behind them".[2] Nor must we forget that the Reformation, within the borders of Germany itself, set up a long-drawn-out spell of most tragic confusion, moral as well as social, and that it was only after a considerable interval of painful unsettlement that any permanent fruits on a large scale were seen.[3] When the Thirty Years War (1618-48) had finished with Germany, not only was the country itself laid in ruins, but the population that emerged was less religious than that with which the Reformation had begun. In the Netherlands, the people who had fought so gallantly for liberty were far from being consistently loyal to the ideals of tolerance and charity upheld by the Prince of Orange. As so often happens, these ideals became "soiled with ignoble use". Starting by being fiercely intolerant to Roman Catholics, they went on to being almost equally bitter towards those of their number who, as Arminians, had retreated somewhat from the rigid predestinationism of John Calvin. One of the ugly crimes resulting from this controversy was the decapitation in 1619, on a charge of treason, and with the full consent of Maurice, the Prince of Orange's son, of John of Oldenbarneveld – the prince's former friend and ally, who had spent his long life in the service of Dutch independence. It has more than once been pleaded in mitigation of the charge of cruelty exercised by Philip in rigorously suppressing all religious dissent in Spain, that he was wisely and (on a long view) humanely endeavouring to preserve his dominions from the horrors that devastated Germany, France, and the rebellious Netherlands.[4] An extension of the same argument points to the various calamities which have beset humanity (particularly in Europe) from 1648 down to our own day, and declares them to be the natural

---

2. Motley, *United Netherlands* (ed. 1875 – 76), vol. i, p. 33.
3. Cf. Butterfield, *The Whig Interpretation*, etc., pp. 87 – 89.
4. E.g., H.C. Lea in *Amer. Hist. Review*, vol. ix, pp. 241 f. (January 1904).

ulterior consequences of throwing off the yoke of the Church of Rome. Dr. Walsh quotes approvingly (pp. 250, 737) the words of Pope Pius IX's encyclical letter of 1849, when he wrote: "The beginnings of all the evils, whereby we are so greatly afflicted, are to be sought in the losses which have now for a long time been inflicted on the Catholic religion and Church, but which were so especially in the age of the Protestants". Dr. Walsh explicitly includes "Communism and its attendant miseries" among the evils he refers to.

Something at least can, indeed, be said by way of reply to these criticisms.

On the point that Philip's opponents, though claiming freedom, were claiming it only for themselves, and were no more tolerant to others than he was, it is pertinent to reply: (1) that, even allowing for numerical and durational differences, Protestant persecutions, however bad, were far less extensive and cruel than were the Catholic; (2) that, as I have argued above (pp. 178 f.), the example and practice of Rome throughout several centuries preceding the Reformation had thoroughly indoctrinated Christian Europe with the idea of the rightness of treating heterodoxy with persecution; and Protestants at first naturally did not see that the essence of their revolt from Rome implied the duty of toleration; (3) that nevertheless they, unlike the Catholics, early had in their ranks great leaders of thought like Sebastian Castellio, William of Orange, and Oliver Cromwell, who realized the iniquity of persecution and the value of toleration, and whose lead was eventually followed – and that willingly – by Protestantism as a whole.[5]

As for the value of persecution in keeping Spain and Italy free from the horrors of religious war – the lesson tells more heavily against the Romanists than against their opponents. For not only was the all-pervading spirit of cruel intolerance due to the strongly intrenched Roman precedent, but the occurrence of religious wars was primarily owing to Roman aggression. Let the persecuted be sufficiently numerous and well-organized and, human nature being what it is, some of them will inevitably

---

5. I have discussed this comparative estimate more fully in Chapter II of my *Roman Catholicism and Freedom*, pp. 36 – 49. Torture was abolished in Prussia in 1740, and, in the ensuing decades, throughout Germany. The last witch to be burnt in Germany suffered in 1775. Both reforms were the fruit of the now despised "Aufklärung".

resist. When that happens, those who formerly were able to go to their persecuting work with rack, gallows, and the stake are now naturally constrained to fly to arms. The main responsibility for the devastation resulting from the religious wars in Germany, France, and the Netherlands, is therefore to be laid at the door, not of the Reformation, but of Romanism.[6]

In regard to the regnant evils of modern Europe, as typified in the ideals of the "Axis", it is to be observed that these evils have been as manifest in Catholic Italy and Spain as they have in partially Protestant Germany or in heathen Japan. Let it be gladly admitted that in Germany at least the Roman Church offered – along with the Protestants of the Confessional Church – a noble resistance to the worst demands of Nazism. But when we take account of all that has happened during the past twenty-five years, not only in Hitler's Germany, but also in Mussolini's Italy, Franco's Spain, and Lenin's Russia, it must surely be obvious that this attempt to ascribe all Europe's major evils to the Reformation is far too simple a solution to fit the facts, that neither is Protestantism the cause of the world's great troubles, nor is a dominant Catholicism any adequate safeguard against them.

It seems to me, therefore, that even when we make full allowance for the lofty motives and sincerity of Philip and his associates, and for the undoubted shortsightedness and other limitations of the Protestants of his day, we are confirmed in our initial claim that the struggle between them was in essence a struggle against irresponsible autocracy, religious persecution, and inhuman cruelty. Only gradually perhaps did the positive ideals, which had to replace these evil things, come to be envisaged clearly and in their true bearing: but I fail to see how it can be denied that those were the essential issues of the conflict.

And when we put ourselves realistically in the position of the typical, honestly convinced Protestant, who found himself a subject of Philip II and witnessed the proceedings of Philip's authorized agents – or, still more, when we impartially survey from a distance the ethos of each of the two main parties, as shown in their characteristic methods of fighting, and in the contributions to human liberty, progress, and welfare latent respectively within them – can we hesitate to declare that, as

---

6. Cf. my Roman Catholicism and Freedom, pp. 43 f.

between the two, it was the Dutch rebels who had right on their side?[7] The enthusiastic sympathy which their cause evoked in the breasts of the Englishmen of that day – however little the caution of Queen Elizabeth allowed it to find expression in the foreign policy of her government – points to something more than a common jealousy of Spain or a political or commercial rivalry with her: it points to a nation-wide sense that the Netherlanders were struggling to free themselves from such a nightmare of suffering and tyranny as they themselves had been freed from only by the timely death of Bloody Mary. Can any one seriously maintain that, if Philip's scheme for dominating the whole of western Europe in the interests of the Hapsburg monarchy and the Roman Church had succeeded, if his great Armada had been victorious in 1588, and the Holy Inquisition had thereby been given a free hand in the Low Countries and in Great Britain, if Dutch independence had been drowned in blood and the Huguenots of France killed off or expelled, regardless of personal suffering, the world would now be a better place, the sum of human misery smaller, the moral achievements and true godliness of mankind greater? Hypothetical questions of this sort are admittedly not easy to answer.[8] The convinced Romanist will, of course, say "Yes"; and even an Anglican like Mr. Trevor Davies looks favourably on Philip's statesmanship for his "half-success of keeping France Catholic and of retaining the southern Netherlands".[9] The relevant facts, however, so far as I know them, dispose me to agree with the feelings of a certain Catholic acquaintance of mine, who frankly admitted to me in conversation that he believed Mother Church to be all the better for a little opposition, and that of all places where he would hate to live Spain and Italy came first.

---

7. Mr. Butterfield (*The Whig Interpretation*, etc., p. 49) parries the argument that Luther "worked for purposes greater than those of which he was conscious", by observing that the same is true of his enemies. But is it? It can, I think, be shown that the abandonment of cruel religious persecution was at least *implicit* in Lutheranism, however long the fact took to become consciously recognized. But what great new advance in the morals of mankind was implicit in the Romanism that opposed him, Romanism not having even yet in our own day freed itself from the reproach of intolerance and persecution (see my *Roman Catholicism and Freedom*, pp. 50-92)?

8. In this paragraph of the text, I have purposely left out of account the possibilities open to a non-injurious opposition such as would harmonize with Christian pacifism. For a brief discussion of the conditions of the efficacy of such opposition, see below, pp. 220 – 223.

9. R.T. Davies, *Golden Century*, p. 226: see above, p. 38.

Of those ideas of democracy, toleration, and personal liberty which are associated with liberal Protestantism the recent war has given us an opportunity and an invitation to re-examine our judgment. That perhaps is one of the indirect compensatory blessings strangely involved in what we cannot but regard in the main as a major world-tragedy. We shall not for some time to come, I imagine, hear in our midst any more of the silly talk we sometimes heard in the years immediately following 1933, about the Germans happening to prefer a different system of government from our own, about a great nation carrying out a fresh experiment in the art of politics, and so on, and so forth. Now that the true character of Nazi-despotism in all its naked and hideous brutality has been unmistakably seen, we shall probably be a little more willing than we were in the pre-War years to appreciate the blessings of religious and political freedom, the abolition of torture and other forms of wanton cruelty, and the enthronement of a standard of humaneness and of respect for personal life. Earlier attainments of this kind, which during these last years we have seen so savagely outraged, were in point of fact won for us mainly by those imperfect yet stubborn champions who rose against Rome and Spain in the sixteenth century. I am prepared to make Professor Butterfield a present of all that can reasonably be urged about the complexity of the story, the limited vision of the Protestant leaders, the contributions made by the Roman Church itself, and so on. It remains, however, in my judgment clear that the great principles of democracy, toleration, and humaneness, which in recent years have been so spurned in this region and in that, grew out of Protestantism in a way that we have no reason to believe they would ever have grown out of Catholicism. So let a man reflect that it was for these very principles that – with whatever partiality of vision and imperfection of method – the war of independence in the Netherlands was waged. It is mainly by reference to that basic fact that such moral judgment as we can pass on the doings of Philip of Spain and the Netherlands will need to be framed.[10]

---

10. Mr. W.F. Rea begins his article entitled "A Good Word for the Inquisition" in *The Month*, vol. clxxvii, pp. 32 ff. (January-February 1942), with a reference to the modern custom of likening authoritarian Fascism and Nazism to authoritarian Catholicism. But although he doubtless means to disallow the comparison, I cannot see that he says anything to disqualify the argument advanced in the text.

"With whatever imperfection of method". In endeavouring to pass any sort of judgment of the kind referred to, we cannot altogether avoid considering whether armed revolt, however nobly carried on, can have the *unqualified* approval and applause of Christian men. For the religion of Christian men has as one of its basic and indubitable ethical principles, "Render to no man evil for evil: ... but *overcome evil with good*". It may indeed be said that this particular principle was laid down at a time when, in contrast to the sixteenth century, the Christian had no direct political responsibility, but could confine himself to private or semi-private relationships, and that therefore Christian idealism did not inculcate this particular principle when those primitive conditions no longer prevailed. But surely some deeper and fuller reason is required to justify so complete a reversal of a characteristic feature of Christian living, than the simple fact that the individual has passed from private to public activity. The duty of meeting this demand is especially incumbent upon us when we bear in mind (1) that the so-called non-resistance teaching of Jesus originally had reference, in all probability, to the relations between his fellow-Jews and their *national enemies;*[11] (2) that the *positive efficacy* of "overcoming evil with good" has been repeatedly demonstrated in experience, as for instance, among others, by the pre-Constantinian Church, the Anabaptist groups in the sixteenth century, and the Quakers in the seventeenth; (3) that the virtual certainty of violent death for some, and the possibility of total defeat for all, are conditions regarding which gentle rebels are in no worse a plight than are violent rebels; and (4) that armed strife, however apparently justified and however successful, never seems able to effect a real and permanent healing.

It is interesting to observe, as regards the struggle in the Netherlands, that the only group who, though as strongly opposed to Rome and Spain as the Calvinists were, refused on principle to bear arms against them, were the Anabaptists. Anabaptist groups existed here and there over almost the whole of Europe: they were almost to a man strongly pacifist in their ethic; and though cruelly and violently persecuted by virtually

---

11. The grounds for this judgment are stated in detail in my *Historic Mission of Jesus* (1941), pp. 171 f.

all governments (William of Orange's being among the exceptions), and consequently numbering many martyrs in their ranks, they managed somehow to survive. Their view of the wrongness of the use of arms was rejected as palpably mistaken by everyone outside their own ranks. A half-conscious leaning towards this view, however, was visible at one juncture in the mind of Philip Marnix, Seigneur de St. Aldegonde, who in 1573 wrote to William of Orange thus, after having long been a prisoner of the Spaniards: "For my part, since I see that religion by which we trust wholly to God's Word, is so hated and cried down that it is impossible for it to find any repose in this world without crosses and persecutions,… I think it would be far better to forsake all conveniences of fatherland, all this world's goods, and live in a strange country, possessing one's soul in patience, than to go on in a continued war, which can result in nothing but impiety and miseries, and provoke divine wrath.… Consider, too, that Alva is retiring, and that there is hope that the king may exercise his natural clemency. If he does not, at least a rigorous government would be more endurable than the burdens of this war, if it last much longer…"[12] In his reply, William of Orange – notwithstanding his general belief that religious error did not need to be corrected by force, but would in time disappear through the diligent teaching of the truth – made it clear that he could see nothing better in St. Aldegonde's appeal than an inaccurate political forecast. He felt sure, as the vast majority of his contemporaries felt, and as the vast majority of the readers of this book will no doubt feel, that, if Spain were not resisted by force of arms, the independence of the Netherlands and such Protestantism as went with it would have been crushed out of existence without hope of revival. From such a conviction, the natural inference is that abstention from the use of arms must be, at least in this and similar cases, a misinterpretation of the Christian ethic.

So strong indeed does the case for armed revolt appear in such circumstances to be, that not only did no alternative ever suggest itself to the majority of Christian minds at that time, but many even to-day will still regard the customary conclusion as the

---

12. R. Putnam, *William the Silent*, etc. (ed. 1898), vol. ii, pp. 52-54, *William the Silent*, etc. (1911), pp. 251 f.

perfectly obvious one. I am fully alive to the force and pressure of the arguments behind this view, especially on the score of practical effectiveness; and I do not want to suggest that the problem is a simple one. The bare fact that many equally sincere and equally intelligent modern Christians are found differing from one another on the main issue is itself a proof that it is not simple. For myself I can only say that, while prolonged reflection on the pros and cons constrains me to stand on the pacifist side, I feel bound to make room, in my judgment of the case as a whole, for the *relative* element in all human ethical choices. What I mean is that the rightness and efficacy of the pacifist choice is relative to (that means, dependent upon) a clear acceptance on the part of the pacifist concerned of a certain interpretation (exegetical and practical) of our Saviour's meaning, and can have no validity or authority without such acceptance. From this it follows that, for those who cannot help understanding His meaning and purpose differently, the non-pacifist choice is the right one. This apparent dualism does not imply a denial of the existence of an absolute right: it simply means that, in our present state of partial vision, we believe that God's Will (when put in terms of human duty) may on certain controversial issues be something different for different men, without necessitating disrespect or censure between man and man.

I do not pretend that such an application of the idea of ethical relativity frees us from all the difficulty inherent in the problem: and I have fully discussed elsewhere the various issues it involves.[13] That must be my apology for not doing more at the moment to justify an opinion which I fear some readers may regard as inherently absurd, but which – in a consideration of moral judgments regarding the revolt of the Netherlands against Philip of Spain – cannot be altogether denied expression and consideration. Meantime the appeal to relativity has the advantage of enabling the pacifist, without inconsistency, and without needing to refuse his share of the risk of suffering and martyrdom, to accord a measure of genuine approval and sympathy to men of his own or any other period who, faced with terrific evils, feel that they must oppose them even to the point of shedding blood, and that they can do so without disloyalty to Christ. Paul's

---

13. In Christian Pacifism Re-examined (Oxford, 1940).

question, "Who art thou that judgest the servant of another?", applies to both sides: and so does Paul's answer, "To his own Lord he standeth or falleth". And God doubtless has ways of utilizing the unselfish labour of *all* who endeavour to give Him the best service within their power, of whatsoever kind it be.

For these reasons I feel the less hesitation in offering as a conclusion to this whole inquiry the view that, while it is our business, not to sit in judgment on the inmost character either of Philip II or of any of his contemporaries, but to confine ourselves to describing and assessing their outward deeds and their practical purposes and intentions, we cannot but pronounce the cause of Philip to have been reactionary and evil, and his methods morally loathsome. The cause of his rebellious subjects in the Netherlands, on the other hand, apart from the elements of vindictiveness and narrowness which marred it, we hold to have been righteous and fraught with good for mankind, and the behaviour and ideals of William of Orange to have been exceedingly noble, and as such deserving of the praise and gratitude of posterity.

The "divine right of kings" – the absolute and irresponsible authority of him who, by inheritance, marriage, conquest, or treaty, has become the sovereign ruler of a piece of territory – was in the sixteenth century taken for granted. There was something to be said for it, as we have seen above (pp. 64 f.); and we are not in a position to blame any man who, having been born and educated in that belief, endeavoured to act on it according to his lights. But clearly it was a belief that had to go: and if we need any convincing of the evils inseparable from it, a study of the career of Charles I of England, or of either of the two great dictators of our own time, should suffice. So much being clear to us, it is worth observing that the successful revolt of the Netherlands was one of the first conspicuous historical nails in the coffin of that picturesque medieval illusion.

Again, the idea of religious freedom was foreign to the mind of the sixteenth century. One of the generally acknowledged prerogatives of the Roman Church was to dictate to every baptized individual (whether baptized willingly or forcibly) what he was to believe and how he was to worship. So deeply had

Romanism stamped into the human mind this idea of religious intolerance that even Lutherans and Calvinists for a long time persecuted, not indeed as cruelly, but as complacently as Rome had done. Who can blame them for not seeing the full truth all at once? Yet the obligation to be tolerant was implicit in the Reformers' position; and even in the mere struggle for existence the Protestants were, if to a large extent unconsciously, laying the foundations of the freedom that was yet to be. If any man be disposed to point to the irreligion and other evils of to-day as the natural result of the rejection of the Roman yoke, let me ask him whether he regards modern Spain and modern Italy (where that yoke has *not* been rejected) as paradises unplagued by the evils of the modern world, and whether he would seriously prefer to see installed in power, in place of that religious freedom which is one of the most valuable assets of modern civilization, the coercive and persecuting authority of a single religious organization, even if it were the one to which he himself owes allegiance? In destroying the domination of the Roman Church in their provinces, the rebels of the Netherlands were at least laying the foundation of what we now know to be the only wise attitude to the religious dissenter, though it was but few besides their great leader who discerned at the time the full implication of the stand they made.[14]

And lastly, that comparatively modern virtue – humaneness in dealing with an opponent – is here seen coming gradually and painfully to birth. In the Middle Ages, people were not so squeamish as we are to-day. The wilful infliction of extreme physical anguish (by means of torture, burning alive, and so on) was taken for granted as a normal part of the necessarily coercive and punitive functions of government. In the great struggle

---

14. Cf. R.B. Merriman, *The Emperor*, p. 403: "... there can be no question that religious toleration is one of the greatest blessings which the progress of the last four centuries has conferred upon mankind. That Protestantism does not mean toleration, the history of those four centuries has abundantly proved; but it was at least through the persistency of Protestantism's efforts to win for itself the right to exist, that men first came to realize the horrors and the futility of religious persecution. And Spain's inherited religious role... committed her in advance to that very policy of persecution and intolerance which the more... enlightened nations to the north of her were gradually to abandon in the succeeding years..." The statement that "Protestantism does not mean toleration" I regard as incorrect, and inconsistent with what follows: but for the rest I agree. Cf. Merriman's allusion in *Philip the Prudent* (p. 676) to "the nascent conception of religious toleration".

between Spain and the Netherlands in the sixteenth century, the gradual dawn of a new ethic of Christian mercy is discernible. If any of my esteemed readers is disposed to be sceptical about this "moral judgment" of mine, may I ask him to tell me, or preferably to tell himself, whether in the first place it was a good thing or a bad thing that such customary indifference as then prevailed to the physical agony of the supposed wrongdoer should be discredited and abolished? I cannot believe that, with the abominations and atrocities of Nazism before his eyes, the supposed critical reader will find the answer difficult. Now which side was it, in the great struggle we have been studying, in whose behaviour there can be seen some promise of better and humaner things? The change, let it be granted, is slow; and deeds of cruelty continue to be done on both sides. But how does Prince Maurice's treatment of a captured city compare with that normally meted out by one of Philip's generals? How does the usual Dutch treatment of Catholics, taken at its worst, compare with the policy adopted by the Duke of Alva or by the Inquisition towards Protestants? Who was it who exerted himself to curb the excesses of impulsive allies like the Sea-Beggars and Dirk Sonoy – as earlier of his own unruly troops? And what, pray, was the name of that so-called "coarse and brutal materialist" we seem to have heard of, who, when shot through both cheeks, immediately forgave the assassin and begged the bystanders in vain not to slay him, and who, while he lay at death's door, wrote and entreated the judges not to put the wretched man's accomplices to death by torture?

Chronological Table

The following table contains only such entries as are deemed relevant to the purpose of assisting the reader to keep his hand on the thread of the story with which this book deals.

Philip II of Spain, son of the Emperor Charles V, and William of Nassau, Prince of Orange, are designated "Philip" and "William" respectively.

Events of which I have not discovered the exact date are recorded *first* under the year to which they belong. I cannot vouch for events that occurred in the same month being in every case entered in the correct order of time.

1527. Three Anabaptists slowly roasted to death at The Hague.
Charles V's German troops sack Rome (May).
Philip born at Valladolid (May).

1528. Charles V issues an edict against unlicensed books in the Netherlands (Jan.).
France and England declare war on Charles (Jan.).
Overyssel submits to Charles (March).
Charles accepted as lord by Utrecht (Oct.).

1529. At the imperial Diet of Speier the reforming minority submit their "protest" on behalf of their freedom of conscience (hence the name "Protestant") (April).
Charles concludes Treaty of Barcelona with Pope Clement VII (June).
Charles concludes Peace of Cambray ("Paix des Dames") with France: he gains Flanders and Artois, and recognition of his rule in Italy (Aug.).
Charles threatens death-penalty for failure to surrender Lutheran books in the Netherlands (Oct.).
Abortive colloquy between Luther and Zwingli at Marburg over the Lord's Supper (Oct.).

1530. Ten Anabaptists executed by Charles's order at The Hague.
Pope Clement VII crowns Charles Emperor at Bologna (Feb.).
The German Lutherans submit their "Augsburg Confession" to the imperial Diet at Augsburg (June).
Philibert, last surviving male of the house of Orange-Châlons, killed in battle near Florence: René, son of his sister Claude and her husband Henry of Nassau, becomes his heir (Aug.). See under July 1544.
Death of Charles's aunt Margaret, regent of the Netherlands (Nov.).
Charles issues severe edict forbidding the printing of unlicensed books in the Netherlands (Dec.).

1531. Charles proclaims his sister Mary, ex-Queen of Hungary, as regent of the Netherlands (Oct.).

Chronological Table

	Zwingli killed at the battle of Kappel in Switzerland (Oct.).
	Papal bull inaugurates the Inquisition in Portugal (Dec.).
1532.	Three Anabaptists roasted to death at Haarlem; and the wife of one of them drowned.
	Charles forbids the harbouring of Anabaptists in the Netherlands (Feb.).
1533.	The regent Mary advises Charles that heretics should be severely punished, but so that the provinces should not be depopulated.
	Henry VIII privately married to Anne Boleyn (Jan.).
	Cranmer made Archbishop of Canterbury (March).
	William born at Dillenburg, Nassau (April).
	Pope Clement VII excommunicates Henry VIII, if he does not take Catherine of Aragon back (July).
	Birth of Elizabeth, daughter of Henry VIII and Anne Boleyn (Sept.).
	Catherine de' Medici married at Marseilles to Francis I's son Henry (afterwards King Henry II of France) (Oct.).
1534.	Anabaptist revolt in Münster.
	Utrecht united with Holland.
	Over 100 Anabaptists martyred in the Netherlands (April-May).
	Clement VII succeeded as pope by Paul III (Sept.-Oct.).
	Act of Supremacy declares Henry VIII to be Head of the Church of England (Nov.).
1535.	Charles issues another severe edict against the Anabaptists in the Netherlands.
	Many Anabaptists martyred in Holland and Friesland (Jan.-Feb.).
	Münster taken by German Catholic troops: the Anabaptist leaders savagely punished (June).
	Charles takes Tunis: it is horribly sacked (July).
1536.	Calvin's *Institutio Christianæ Religionis* first published, with a dedication to Francis I (March).
	Regent Mary obtains money from States-General for Charles's war against France (June).
	Erasmus dies at Basle. Calvin settles at Geneva (July).
1537.	Pope Paul III appoints two new Inquisitors for the Netherlands.
1538.	Charles secures control of Gelderland.
	James V of Scotland marries Mary of Guise.
1539.	Ghent revolts against Charles's taxation.
	Charles departs from Spain for the Netherlands, leaving Philip as governor of Spain (Dec.).
1540.	Charles punishes Ghent (Feb.-May).
	Charles issues another edict against heretics in the Netherlands (Sept.).
	Pope Paul III by the bull *Regimini* establishes the Society of Jesus (Sept.).
	Charles confers the nominal duchy of Milan on Philip, to hold as a fief of the Empire (Oct.).

1541. Abortive conference between Protestants and liberal Catholics at Ratisbon (April to June).
1542. Caraffa gets from Pope Paul III a bull, *Licet ab initio*, reviving the Roman Inquisition in Italy (July).
Mary Stuart (later Queen of Scots) born to James V. Death of James V (Dec.).
1543. Charles virtually severs Netherlands (now wholly his, except Liége) from Empire, and attaches it to Spain.
Philip at Salamanca (aet. 16+) marries, as his first wife, his cousin Maria Manuela of Portugal (Nov.).
1544. In Charles's siege of St. Dizier, René, Prince of Orange-Châlons and son and heir of the late Henry of Nassau (see under Aug. 1530), is killed, after making William his sole heir (July).
Charles signs Peace of Crespy with France (Sept.).
William (aet. 11+) brought by his father from Dillenburg to Brussels, to be educated as a Catholic at Charles's court (Sept.-Oct.).
Charles issues another edict against unlicensed books in the Netherlands, with severer penalties (Dec.).
1545. Massacre of the Waldenses in Provence (April).
Maria Manuela bears Don Carlos to Philip, and dies (July).
Birth of Alexander Farnese (Aug.).
General Church-Council opened at Trent (Dec.).
1546. The Inquisition renews its activity in Spain.
Death of Martin Luther (Feb.).
Charles confirms the bestowal of the nominal duchy of Milan on Philip (July).
Papal troops join Charles in his war against the Protestants of Germany (Aug.).
1547. Ex-Franciscan Lutheran, Baldo Lupetino, sentenced at Venice to be beheaded and burnt "to the honour and glory of Jesus Christ".
Pope Paul III withdraws his troops from the Emperor (Jan.).
Henry VIII succeeded by his son Edward VI as King of England (Jan.).
Don John of Austria, illegitimate son of Charles V, born at Ratisbon (Feb.).
Pope transfers Council of Trent to Bologna: vexation of Charles (March).
Francis I succeeded by his son Henry II as King of France (March).
Charles decisively defeats German Lutherans at Mühlberg (April).
Council of Trent prorogued (till 1551) (June).
1548. Jan Millar, Flemish Protestant, burnt alive after auto-de-fé at Lima in Peru.
The Netherlands virtually separated from the Empire (May).
Charles promulgates the "Augsburg Interim" (a modified and ambiguous Catholicism) as a law of the Empire (May-June).
Mary, princess of Scotland, sent to France (July-Aug.).

	Philip (aet. 21+) leaves Spain for a progress through Italy and Germany (Oct.).
1549.	Philip makes his state-entry into Brussels (April).
	Death of Pope Paul III (Nov.).
	Philip swears to observe all the ancient rights and privileges of the Netherland-states: consolidation of the Hapsburg rule in the Netherlands (Nov.).
	Charles again confirms nominal duchy of Milan on Philip, but continues to administer it himself till 1554 as a fief of the Empire (Dec.).
1550.	Julius III becomes pope (Feb.).
	Charles issues a severe placard against heresy in the Netherlands (April).
	Charles modifies his placard of April as a result of remonstrances: tension in the Netherlands over the feared introduction of the Spanish Inquisition (Sept. and Nov.).
1551.	At the Diet of Augsburg, Hapsburgs agree that Ferdinand should succeed Charles as emperor, Philip should succeed Ferdinand, Maximilian (Ferdinand's son) should administer the empire in Philip's name, and succeed him as emperor. The German princes refuse to agree (March).
	Council of Trent reopens (May).
	Philip leaves Germany for Spain (May), and reaches Barcelona (July).
	William is married to Anne, daughter and heiress of Count of Buren (July).
	Henry II of France declares war on Charles: William receives his first military appointment (Sept.).
	Maurice, Elector of Saxony, deserts Charles, and allies with Henry II of France and the German Protestant princes.
1552.	Campaigning on the border between France and Netherlands.
	Council of Trent suspended (April).
	Maurice compels Charles to flee from Innsbruck over Brenner Pass (May). Ferdinand, on Charles's behalf, concludes with German Protestants the Convention of Passau. End of Philip's hopes of becoming emperor (Aug.).
1553.	Regent Mary sends Inquisitors against the Anabaptists in northern Netherlands.
	Guise defeats Charles's army before Metz: Charles raises the siege, and goes to the Netherlands (Jan.).
	Charles takes Therouanne and Hesdin from French (June-July).
	Edward VI succeeded on the English throne by Mary Tudor ("Bloody Mary") (July).
	Maurice, Elector of Saxony, killed in battle; succeeded by his brother Augustus (July).
	Pope Julius III appoints Cardinal Reginald Pole papal legate in England (Aug.).

	Noailles (French ambassador) raises hatred against Philip in England (Sept.).
	Charles successfully defends Cambray against French (Sept.).
	Calvin gets anti-trinitarian Michael Servetus burnt at Geneva (Oct.).
1554.	Marriage-treaty concluded between Philip and Mary Tudor: London in a panic (Jan.).
	Mary of Guise becomes regent of Scotland (April).
	Philip and Mary married at Winchester: Charles makes Philip king of Naples and Jerusalem, and entrusts him with the actual government of Milan (July).
	Reginald Pole received by Philip and Mary at Whitehall: in Parliament he gives the country formal absolution (Nov.).
	Charles gives the Duke of Alva full powers in Italy (Nov.).
1555.	Charles modifies the legal penalties for heresy in the Netherlands (Jan.).
	Julius III succeeded as pope by Marcellus, and he by Paul IV (Caraffa) (March-May).
	Death of Juana, daughter of Ferdinand and Isabella, and mother of Charles V (aet. 75 +) (April).
	Philip leaves England for the Netherlands (August).
	Ferdinand, on behalf of Charles, concludes the Peace of Augsburg with the German Lutherans on the principle of "cujus regio, ejus religio" (Sept.-Oct.).
	Charles at Brussels abdicates his sovereignty over the Netherlands in favour of Philip. End of Mary of Austria's regency. Philip again swears to maintain local privileges (Oct.).
	Philip renews his instructions to the Inquisitors, and confirms the placard of September 1550 (Nov.).
	William writes to Philip about the excesses of the Spanish troops (Dec.).
	Secret treaty between Pope Paul IV and France (Dec.).
1556.	Charles resigns the government of Spain, Sicily, and the Indies to Philip (Jan.).
	Hollow truce of Vaucelles between France and Spain (Feb.).
	States-General demur to Philip's demand for money (March).
	Don Carlos proclaims Philip king of Spain, etc., at Valladolid (March).
	Philip modifies severity of persecution in the Netherlands (April).
	Death of Ignatius Loyola (July).
	Charles at Brussels abdicates the government of the Empire in favour of his brother Ferdinand (Aug.).
	Alva defeats the pope's troops in southern Italy (Sept.).
	Charles leaves the Netherlands for Spain (September).
	The Duke of Guise crosses the Alps to help the pope (Dec.).
1557.	Coligny sacks Lens. Henry II declares war on Philip (Jan.).
	Charles retires into monastery of St. Juste in Estremadura (Feb.).

Chronological Table 231

Philip visits England. Guise reaches Rome (March).
Pope's troops again defeated by Spaniards in Italy (April).
England declares war on France (June).
Philip finally leaves England (July).
Egmont, with Philip's army, totally defeats French at St. Quentin, and sacks the town (Aug.).
Alva is formally reconciled with Pope Paul IV at Rome (Sept.).
States-General present fifty-two grievances regarding the administration (Dec.).

1558. The Duke of Guise captures Calais for France (Jan.).
William at the Diet at Frankfort: he speaks inadvisedly about adultery (Feb.-March).
Death of William's first wife, Anne, heiress of Count of Buren (March).
Francis the Dauphin marries Mary of Scotland (April).
Egmont, with English aid, defeats the French at Gravelines (June).
Death of Charles V (Sept.).
Peace-preliminaries between Philip and France (Oct.).
Mary Tudor succeeded by Elizabeth as Queen of England (Nov.).

1559. Act of Supremacy: Elizabeth to be "supreme governor" of the Church of England. Act of Uniformity: exclusive use of Book of Common Prayer enjoined (Jan.).
Pope Paul IV issues bull *Cum ex apostolatus officio*, claiming authority over secular princes (Feb.).
Peace of Cateau-Cambresis between France and Spain signed. Italy secured to Spain. William for a time at Paris as hostage (April).
Auto-de-fé at Valladolid (May or June).
Philip married by proxy at Paris to Elizabeth (aet. 14), daughter of Catherine de' Medici – his third wife (June).
Henry II succeeded as king of France by his son Francis II, husband of Mary of Scodand. The Guises paramount (July).
Papal bull sanctions seventeen new bishoprics in the Netherlands (Aug.).
States-General at Ghent ask Philip for dismissal of Spanish troops. Philip leaves Netherlands for Spain, after appointing his sister Margaret, Duchess of Parma, governor, and William stadtholder of Holland, Zealand, and Utrecht. Margaret instructed to enforce the regulations against heresy (Aug.).
Paul IV succeeded as pope by Pius IV (Aug.-Dec.).
Philip arrives in Spain, and holds auto-de-fe at Seville. William's illegitimate son Justin born (Sept.).
William's father dies, aged seventy-two: William's brother John succeeds to the government of Nassau, William however becoming titular Count of Nassau. Auto-de-fe at Valladolid (Oct.).

1560. Philip meets his wife, Elizabeth of France, at Guadalajara.
Death of Melanchthon, aged sixty-three; he is buried near Luther at Wittemberg (April).

Granvelle made Archbishop of Mechlin (May).
The Edict of Romorantin grants French Huguenots a little relief (May).
Death of Mary of Guise (June).
Francis II is succeeded as king of France by his brother Charles IX (Dec.).
William visits Dresden to court Anne of Saxony (Dec.).

1561. The Spanish troops sent out of the Netherlands by the regent and Granvelle (Jan.).
Granvelle is made a cardinal (Feb.).
Egmont and William protest to Philip about their exclusion from important debates in the regent's council (July).
Mary Queen of Scots (aet. 19) lands in Scotland (Aug.).
William marries Anne of Saxony at Leipzig (Aug.).
Protestant outbreak at Valenciennes put down by troops (Oct.).
William assures the pope that he has ordered the extinction of heresy in the principality of Orange (Nov.).

1562. Council of Trent reopened (Jan.).
Massacre of Huguenots by Guise at Vassy: outbreak of the religious wars in France (March).
Persecution of Protestants at Valenciennes (April-May).
William, Egmont, and other prominent Netherlanders demur to help being sent from Netherlands to aid French Catholics (Aug.).
Montigny visits Spain to lay before Philip the nobles' grievances against Granvelle (autumn).

1563. The Protestant Johann Weyer of Cleves writes against witchburning.
Edict of Amboise, allowing relief to Huguenots, ends the first French religious war (March).
William, Egmont, and Hoorn write a formal protest to Philip, resigning all share in the government (March).
They petition Philip for the dismissal of Granvelle from the Netherlands. Alva advises Philip to use severity and deceit (July).
240 English seamen captured at Gibraltar: only eighty survive the subsequent investigation (Nov.).
Conclusion of the Council of Trent (Dec.).

1564. Pope Pius IV confirms Canons and Decrees of Trent (Jan.).
Granvelle leaves the Netherlands by Philip's secret advice (Mar.).
Death of John Calvin at Geneva (May).
Ferdinand I succeeded as emperor by his son Maximilian II (July).
Philip instructs regent to enforce the Decrees of Trent in the Netherlands (Aug.).
Riot at Antwerp over the execution of the Protestant Fabricius (Oct.).
Pope's bull Injunctum nobis embodies the Professio Fidei Tridentinœ (otherwise known as The Creed of Pius IV) (Nov.).
William protests in full assembly of the Council of State against Philip's refusal to allow religious liberty in the Netherlands (Dec.).

Chronological Table 233

1565. Egmont's futile visit to Spain to obtain relief from the persecuting edicts (Jan.-April).
Conference at Bayonne between (1) Alva and Queen Elizabeth of Spain, and (2) her mother Catherine de' Medici: possible discussion of plans for the suppression of heresy in French and Spanish dominions (June-July).
Mary Queen of Scots marries Darnley (July).
Turks driven from Malta by the Spaniards (Sept.).
Philip writes to regent of the Netherlands from Segovia, insisting on severer measures against heretics (Oct.).
Alexander Farnese (son of the regent) married at Brussels (Nov.).
Louis of Nassau (William's brother) and other nobles sign "The Compromise of Nobles" at Spa, protesting against the inquisitorial measures of the government (Dec.).
Death of Pope Pius IV (Dec.).

1566. Pius V (later "St. Pius") becomes pope (Jan.).
Publication of Catechismus Concilii Tridentini.
A group of nobles (excluding William and Egmont) present to the regent at Brussels a formal "Request", deploring the Inquisition and the placards. They take the title of "Les Gueux" ("the Beggars") (April).
The regent issues her so-called "Edict of Moderation" (May).
Free field-preaching rife in the Netherlands (summer).
Montigny goes to Spain again to plead with Philip (May-June).
The regent vainly forbids the field-preaching. William at Antwerp endeavours to calm disorders (July).
Philip consents insincerely to grant toleration in the Netherlands (Aug.).
Iconoclastic riots in the churches of Antwerp and elsewhere (Aug. late).
William at Dendermonde fails to induce Egmont and Hoorn to join him in concerting measures of resistance (Oct.).
Philip gives Alva his first commission against the Netherlanders (Dec.).

1566/7. Cruel legislation in Spain against the Moriscos.

1567. Philip's second and more rigorous commission to Alva (Jan.).
William returns to Antwerp, still temporizing (Feb.).
Murder of Mary's husband Darnley (Feb.).
William declines to take the new oath of allegiance demanded by the regent Margaret for Philip. A Calvinist force cut to pieces outside Antwerp (March).
Death of Philip, landgrave of Hesse (March).
Suppression of Protestants at Valenciennes (April).
William goes from Antwerp via Breda to Dillenburg. Alva leaves Madrid for Italy (April).
Mary Queen of Scots discredits herself by marrying Bothwell (May).
Alva leaves Italy for the Netherlands (June).

William at Dillenburg studies Scripture with a Protestant tutor (summer).

Alva reaches the Netherlands and enters Brussels. Montigny is imprisoned at Segovia (Aug.).

Alva arrests Egmont, Hoorn, and others. He establishes "The Council of Troubles" (Sept.).

Outbreak of the second religious war in France (Sept.).

Margaret, Duchess of Parma, resigns the governorship of the Netherlands to Alva (Oct.).

Anne of Saxony bears William a son, Maurice, at Dillenburg: he is christened with Lutheran rites (Nov.).

Margaret of Parma leaves the Netherlands (Dec.).

1567/8. Numerous executions for "heresy" and "treason" throughout the Netherlands.

1568. William summoned to appear at Brussels before Alva's Council, on pain of outlawry. Executions at Valenciennes (Jan.).

Philip puts Don Carlos under restraint (Jan.)

William's son Philip William (aet. 13) induced by Alva to go to Spain (Feb.).

Peace of Longjumeau (renewing terms of Amboise) ends the second French religious war (March).

William publishes from Dillenburg his "Justification", still professing loyalty to Philip.

Mary Queen of Scots takes refuge in England (May).

William's brother Louis defeats Spaniards at Heiliger Lee in the far north: his brother Adolf killed (May).

Egmont and Hoorn executed, after eighteen others, at Brussels (June).

Alva defeats Louis at Jemmingen, and after ravaging as far as Groningen, returns to Utrecht (July).

Death of Philip's son, Don Carlos (July).

William declares war on Alva (Aug.).

Death of Elizabeth, Philip's third wife (Oct.).

William invades Brabant but, being outmanœuvred by Alva, withdraws to Picardy (Oct.-Nov.).

Philip receives emperor's protest (brought by Archduke Charles) against Alva's severities. Elizabeth seizes Spanish treasure en route to Alva (Dec.).

1569. Philip repudiates the emperor's protest (Jan.).

Alva advises Philip against a breach with Elizabeth (Feb.).

Archduke Charles leaves Madrid with Philip's offer to marry the emperor's daughter (March).

French Huguenots, aided by Louis of Nassau, defeated at Jarnac. Conde killed (March).

Alva broaches heavy taxation-schemes in the Netherlands (spring and summer).

William returns in disguise to Germany: he commissions eighteen vessels to attack the Spaniards at sea (autumn).

Huguenots, led by Coligny and aided by Louis of Nassau, defeated at Moncontour (Oct.).

Unsuccessful Catholic rising in the north of England, instigated by Pope Pius V (Sept.-Dec.).

Philip sends Alva an edict of amnesty for the Netherlands (Nov.).

1569/70. War against the Moriscos in southern Spain: Don John completes their suppression.

1570. Pope Pius V issues a bull, *Regnans in excelsis*, excommunicating and deposing Elizabeth, and forbidding her subjects to obey her (Feb.).

Montigny, now in prison at Segovia, sentenced to death by Alva at Brussels (March).

Four Protestant pastors burnt at The Hague (May).

The Pope's bull fastened to the Bishop of London's door (May).

Alva proclaims Philip's futile amnesty at Antwerp (July).

Peace of St. Germain (favourable to Huguenots) ends third French religious war (Aug.).

Montigny secretly strangled in prison at Simancas (Oct.).

Philip at Segovia marries Anne of Austria, his fourth wife (Nov.).

William's agent captures the stronghold of Loevestein (Dec.).

1571. John Rubens, painter's father, confesses adultery with William's wife, Anne of Saxony (March).

Cecil discovers the Ridolfi Plot (May).

Louis of Nassau appeals for aid to King Charles IX of France (July).

Don John of Austria totally defeats the Turkish fleet at Lepanto (Oct.).

William appoints William de Lumey, Baron de la Mark, admiral of the "Sea-Beggars".

Diplomatic breach between Spain and England: Alva sends two Italians to England to murder Elizabeth (Dec.).

1572. With Philip's approval, Alva tries to enforce his taxation-scheme, but is soon obliged to grant relief (Feb.).

The "Sea-Beggars" seize Brill, and hoist William's standard: other towns follow (April).

Pius V succeeded as Pope by Gregory XIII (May).

Louis of Nassau seizes Mons, and is besieged there by Alva's son, Don Frederick (May-June).

Duke of Norfolk executed for complicity in Ridolfi plot (June).

Alva suspends further parts of his taxation-scheme (June).

William acclaimed as stadtholder of Holland, Zealand, and Utrecht: he crosses the Meuse at Roermond (July).

Widespread massacres of Huguenots in France, beginning on St. Bartholomew's Day, August 24 (Aug.-Oct.).

William, after traversing Brabant, is surprised near Mons, and his army dispersed. Mons capitulates; Louis released (Sept.).

William makes his roundabout way to Holland (Oct.-Nov.).
Mechlin and Zutphen taken by Spaniards: inhabitants massacred (Oct.-Nov.).
Death of John Knox (Nov.).
Naarden surrenders to Spaniards: inhabitants massacred. Executions begin at Mons. Spaniards besiege Haarlem (Dec.).

1573. Convention of Nimwegen between Alva and England (March).
Haarlem surrenders: garrison and many citizens massacred. Holland rejects amnesty offered by Alva in Philip's name (July).
Peace of Rochelle (favourable to Huguenots) ends the fourth French religious war (July).
Don Frederick besieges Alkmaar. Cessation of executions at Mons (Aug.).
Alva recalled at his own request (Sept.).
Don Frederick raises siege of Alkmaar. William at Dort publicly declares himself a Calvinist. Leyden besieged by Spaniards. De la Mark imprisoned for cruelty and disobedience (Oct.).
French and English Protestants burnt after an auto-de-fe at Lima in Peru (Nov.).
Requesens arrives at Brussels. Alva and Don Frederick leave the Netherlands (Nov.-Dec.).

1574. The "Sea-Beggars" defeat the Spanish fleet off coast of Zealand (Jan.).
The Spanish garrison at Middelburg surrenders to William (Feb.).
Philip sends Requesens permission to proclaim a general pardon (March).
English and French Protestants burnt after an auto-de-fe at Mexico (March).
Louis and his brother Henry of Nassau defeated at Mookerheid and killed (April). The Spanish troops mutiny.
Charles IX succeeded as king of France by his brother Henry III (May).
Requesens offers a pardon to those willing to submit (June).
Leyden relieved (Oct.).
William given supreme power in Holland and Zealand (Nov.).

1575. Protestant university of Leyden inaugurated in Philip's name (Feb.).
Futile peace-negotiations carried on at Breda, at the emperor's suggestion (March-July).
William at Dort marries his third wife, Charlotte de Bourbon (June).
Cruelty of Sonoy to Catholics in north Holland (June-July).
William becomes joint ruler of Holland and Zealand, promising to suppress all religion "at variance with the Gospel" (July).
Spaniards storm Oudewater, and massacre the garrison and many inhabitants (Aug.).
Philip suspends payment of interest on his debts (Sept.).
Spaniards take Bommenede, and massacre the inhabitants (Oct.).
Anne of Saxony incarcerated at Dresden (Dec.).

Chronological Table

1576. Death of Requesens (March).
"Union of Delft" confirms union of Holland and Zeeland, and gives William powers of "Count": religion as settled in July 1575 (April).
Henry III's brother Francis, Duke of Anjou, secures the "Peace of Monsieur" for Huguenots, ending the fifth French religious war. The Catholic "League" comes into operation. Abortive suggestion that Anjou should become Count of Holland and Zeeland (April-May).
Zierickzee surrenders on terms: Spanish troops mutiny at not being allowed to pillage it, and seize Alost (June-July).
Anti-Spanish Catholics get control of Brussels (Sept.).
Maximilian II succeeded as emperor by his son Rudolf II (Oct.).
Spanish mutineers seize Maestricht, and massacre the German garrison and many inhabitants (Oct.).
Wanton sack of Antwerp by Spanish troops: 8,000 slaughtered. *All* the provinces agree to "The Pacification of Ghent", uniting to expel Spaniards and leaving religious settlement over. Don John arrives in the Netherlands as governor. The States-General decide to send a deputation to Anjou (Nov.).
Henry III compelled by the Guises to declare his adhesion to the League (Dec.).

1577. Pacification of Ghent confirmed by the "Union of Brussels" (Jan.).
Don John signs the "Perpetual Edict", making concessions to the States-General; and Philip later confirms it (Feb.).
Failure of attempt to bribe William into compliance (March).
Spanish troops leave Netherlands by land (March-April).
Don John enters Brussels (May).
After long negotiations with William and the States-General, Don John seizes fortress of Namur (July).
Peace of Bergerac ends the sixth French religious war (Sept.).
William by invitation goes to Antwerp and Brussels: zenith of his popularity (Sept.).
Breda taken from the Spaniards. William's brother John arrives in Netherlands to co-operate. The States-General at Brussels depose Don John, and reaffirm the Union of Brussels. William receives the emperor's brother, Archduke Matthias, on his arrival at Antwerp on the secret invitation of the Catholics of Brussels. William elected Ruward of Brabant (Oct.).
Protestants in south commence reprisals against Catholics (Oct.).
Death of Anne of Saxony, mad (Dec.).
William at Ghent, endeavouring to curb Protestant excesses (Dec.-Jan.).

1578. Elizabeth agrees to mediate between the States and Don John. Matthias is installed as governor at Brussels, William being his lieutenant-general. Alexander Farnese helps Don John to defeat States-General's army at Gemblours (Jan.).
Amsterdam joins the Confederated States (Feb.).

John of Nassau becomes stadtholder of Gelderland (March).

Don John of Austria gains Tirlement, Louvain, etc. (spring).

The States-General, under William's guidance, makes a prospective compact with Anjou, who had appeared at Mons: he to provide an army, and become "Defender of the Liberty of the Netherlands" (Aug.).

Death of Don John (aet. 33). Alexander Farnese, prince of Parma, succeeds him. Pro-Spanish "Malcontents" active in the southern states (Oct.).

Anjou, having failed to take Mons, returns to France (Dec.).

1579. Provinces of Hainault, Douay, Lille, and Artois, frightened by Protestant disorders at Ghent, form the "League of Arras", to defend Catholicism and return (on terms) to Philip. Provinces of Holland, Zealand, Utrecht, Gelderland, Groningen, etc., form the "Union of Utrecht" (under leadership of John of Nassau) to resist Philip and maintain Protestantism (Jan.).

After several more cities have joined the Union, William signs its terms. Several Walloon provinces make treaty with Farnese (May).

Peace-negotiations at Cologne, attended by everybody, but end in failure. William refuses to be bribed (Aug.-Nov.).

Farnese takes Maestricht, and commits cruel slaughter, especially of the women-defenders (June).

Antwerp joins the Union of Utrecht (July).

Granvelle suggests to Philip that he should offer a reward for the assassination of William (Nov.).

1580. William and Matthias journey via Breda to The Hague (Jan.-Feb.).

Farnese wins Groningen through treachery (Feb.).

Holland, Zealand, and Utrecht secretly decide to abjure Philip. William refuses their offer to put him in Philip's place (March).

John of Nassau resigns stadtholdership of Gelderland and returns to Dillenburg (May-Aug.).

Philip's ban, offering a reward for William's assassination, and dated Maestricht, March 15, is published in the Netherlands (June).

Jesuit missionaries, Campion and Parsons, arrive in England (June).

Alva conquers Portugal for Philip (Aug.).

The States-General make a treaty with Anjou at Tours (Aug.-Sept.).

Death of Philip's fourth wife, Anne of Austria, at Badajoz (Oct.).

Spanish force surrenders to English at Smerwick in Ireland, and is massacred (Nov.).

Peace of Fleix ends the seventh French religious war (Nov.).

William reads his *Apologia* before the States-General at Delft, and gets their permission to publish it (Dec.).

1581. States-General's treaty with Anjou ratified at Bordeaux (Jan.).

William sends a copy of his *Apologia* to every court in Europe (Feb.).

Philip received as king by the Cortes of Portugal at Thamar, later to be crowned at Lisbon (April).

Farnese recovers and pillages Breda (June).
Public Catholic worship suspended in the United Provinces (summer).
The United Provinces at The Hague abjure allegiance to Philip; William is given supreme control of Holland and Zealand during the war (July).
Anjou enters the Netherlands, and then visits England, courting Elizabeth (Aug.-Oct.).
Archduke Matthias, having earlier resigned, leaves the Netherlands (Oct.).
Farnese gains Tournai for Philip (Nov.).

1582. Anjou arrives at Antwerp from England, and is installed as Duke of Brabant (Feb.-March).
Jaureguy makes an unsuccessful attempt on William's life: the French wrongly suspected of complicity (March).
Death of Catherine de Bourbon, William's third wife (May).
Farnese takes Oudenarde for Philip (July).
Anjou formally accepted at Bruges as Count of Flanders (July).
William at Bruges consents to accept the countship of Holland and Zealand without time-limit (Aug.).
Farnese takes Steenwyk for Philip (late autumn).
Death of the Duke of Alva at Lisbon (Dec.).

1583. Anjou makes an abortive attempt to seize Antwerp; and then retires to Dendermonde (Jan.).
William refuses the dukedom of Brabant, and prevails on the States to make a new provisional agreement with Anjou (March).
William marries Louise, daughter of Coligny – his fourth wife (April).
Anjou finally leaves the Netherlands (June).
William, unpopular in Antwerp, leaves it finally for Holland (July).
Farnese gains Diest, Dunkerque, Nieuport, Zutphen, etc., for Philip (summer and autumn).
Throgmorton's plot for the assassination of Elizabeth discovered. Treasonable correspondence between Farnese and the stadtholder of Gelderland discovered (Nov.).
William agrees to become hereditary Count of Holland, Zealand, and Utrecht (Dec.).

1584. Elizabeth dismisses the Spanish ambassador Mendoza (Jan.).
Ypres won by the Spaniards (April).
Bruges surrenders to Farnese. Ghent breaks off negotiations with him (May).
Death of Anjou. The Protestant Henry, king of Navarre, becomes heir to French throne (June).
William assassinated at Delft by Balthasar Gérard: States-General decide to continue the war (July).
Farnese gains Ghent (Sept.), and begins the siege of Antwerp.
Philip allies himself by the Treaty of Joinville with the Guises (Dec.).

1585. Abortive embassy from Netherlands to Henry III, offering him the sovereignty and asking for help (Jan.-March).
Farnese closes the mouth of the Scheldt against Antwerp (Feb.).
Brussels surrenders to Farnese (March).
Gregory XIII succeeded as pope by Sixtus V (April).
Philip proposes to Sixtus V an invasion for the conversion of England (June).
Henry III capitulates to the Guises in the Treaty of Nemours (July).
Antwerp surrenders to Farnese, after a long siege (Aug.).
Henry of Navarre excommunicated by Sixtus V, and excluded for ever from the French throne. He takes arms: commencement of the "War of the three Henries" (Sept.).
Maurice, son of William, made stadtholder, captain-general, admiral, etc. (aet. 18) (Nov.).
After long negotiations between the provinces and Elizabeth, the Earl of Leicester lands with 7,000 men at Flushing, and later proceeds to The Hague. The Queen's support parsimonious (Dec.).

1586. By the death of his father, Farnese becomes Duke of Parma.
Leicester accepts the offer of the governorship of the States, to Elizabeth's vexation (Jan.-Feb.).
John of Oldenbarneveld becomes advocate of Holland (March).
Parma wins Grave and Venloo (June-July).
Maurice and Sir Philip Sidney take Axel (July).
The Spaniards take Neusz and massacre the garrison and 4,000 inhabitants (July). Leicester reduces Doesburg (Aug.).
Cardinal Granvelle dies in Spain (Sept.).
Sir Philip Sidney mortally wounded at Zutphen (Sept.).
Sir Francis Drake visits the Netherlands to concert measures against Spain (late autumn).
Leicester leaves Flushing for England (Nov. or Dec.).
Pope Sixtus V agrees under conditions to contribute to the cost of the Spanish Armada (Dec.).

1587. Execution of Mary Queen of Scots. Pope Sixtus V recognizes Philip as heir to the throne of England (Feb.).
Drake destroys shipping and stores in harbours of Cadiz and Lisbon (April).
Leicester arrives at Flushing. Oldenbarneveld opposed to him (July).
Parma takes Sluys (Aug.).
Henry of Navarre defeats Henry III's army at Coutras (Oct.).
Leicester finally leaves the Netherlands for England (Dec.).

1588. Death of Santa Cruz (in charge of the Armada) (Feb.).
Parma's deceitful parleying with English envoys at Ghent and Ostend (March).
Medina Sidonia receives at Lisbon the great standard for the Armada (April).

The Armada leaves the River Tagus, but has to take refuge at Corunna (May-June).

Henry III compelled by the Guises to leave Paris: two Protestant girls burnt in Paris (July).

The Armada sails from Corunna, is worsted in conflicts with the English fleet up the Channel, is driven from Calais by means of fire-ships, and retreats round Scotland and Ireland to Spain (July-Sept.).

Parma compelled to raise the siege of Bergen-op-Zoom (Nov.).

Henry III contrives the murder of Henry, Duke of Guise, and his Cardinal-brother (Dec.).

1589. Death of Catherine de' Medici (aet. 69) (Jan.).

Patent of nobility conferred on the brothers and sisters of Gérard, William's murderer (March).

Henry of Navarre appeals as a patriot to the French nation (March).

Gertruydenberg betrayed to Parma (April).

Henry III allies with Henry of Navarre at Plessis-les-Tours (April).

English-Dutch raid on the Spanish and Portuguese coast (April-July).

Henry III conditionally excommunicated by the pope (May).

Henry III – the last of the Valois – assassinated. Henry of Navarre proclaimed king as Henry IV (Aug.).

Henry IV defeats Mayenne at Arques (Sept.).

Pope Sixtus V offers to co-operate with Philip to keep France Catholic (Dec.).

1590. Sixtus V receives French Catholic peers graciously (Jan.).

Henry IV defeats the Leaguers' army and the Spaniards at Ivry, and lays siege to Paris (March-April).

Parma enters France, takes Lagny, and massacres the garrison. Henry IV abandons siege of Paris (Aug.).

Sixtus V resents attempt of Philip to intimidate him against Henry IV: he dies, and is succeeded as pope by Urban VII (Aug.).

Parma enters Paris (Sept.).

Urban VII succeeded as pope by Gregory XIV, who favours Spain (Sept.-Dec.).

Parma takes Corbeil, and massacres the garrison (Oct.).

Parma returns to Flanders (Nov.).

1591. Henry IV allies with the United Provinces (Jan.-May).

Maurice retakes Zutphen and Deventer (May-June).

Parma invades France again (Sept.).

Maurice retakes Hulst and Nimwegen (Oct.).

Gregory XIV succeeded as pope by Innocent IX (Oct.).

Henry IV lays siege to Rouen (Nov.).

Philip orders the death of the Justicia of Aragon (Dec.).

Death of Pope Innocent IX (Dec.).

1592. Philip insists that his subjects in the Netherlands must conform to his own religion (Jan.).

Clement VIII becomes pope – a less violent partisan of Spain (Jan.).

The Dutch destroy a Spanish squadron on its way to relieve Rouen (April).

Parma compels Henry IV to raise the siege of Rouen, and enters it in triumph (April).

Maurice takes Steenwyk and Coeworden (July and Sept.).

Final suppression of Aragonese liberties through the Inquisition (Oct.).

Parma dies at Arras (Dec.).

1593. Mansfeld (Parma's successor) takes Noyon (March).

Maurice retakes Gertruydenberg (June).

Henry IV reconciled with Roman Church (subject to the pope's sanction), and hears mass at St. Denis (July).

Pope Clement VIII receives Henry IV's envoy, the Due de Nevers, but still refuses Henry absolution (Nov.).

1594. Archduke Ernest (brother of the Emperor Rudolph) comes to Brussels as governor of the Spanish States (early).

Henry IV crowned king at Chartres (Feb.).

Henry IV enters Paris: the Spanish garrison leaves (March).

Maurice retakes Groningen (July).

Jean Chastel, pupil of Jesuits, makes an attempt on Henry IV's life. The Jesuits expelled from France (Nov.).

1595. Henry IV declares war on Spain (Jan.).

Death of Archduke Ernest at Brussels (Feb.).

The Spaniards take Dourlens, and massacre garrison and nearly all the inhabitants (July).

Drake sails on his last voyage against the Spanish possessions (Aug.).

Clement VIII formally grants absolution to Henry IV (Sept.).

The Spaniards take Cambray from Henry IV (Oct.).

1596. Death of Sir Francis Drake off Porto Bello in West Indies (Jan.).

Archduke Albert (formerly cardinal) enters Brussels (accompanied by William's eldest son, Philip William) as governor of the Netherlands (Feb.).

The Spaniards retake Calais (April).

England allies with France against Spain (May).

The English fleet under Howard and Essex sack and burn Cadiz (July).

The Spaniards take Hulst from the rebellious Provinces (Aug.).

The Spanish fleet, en route for England, shattered off Cape Finisterre. The States join England and France in a league against Spain (Oct.).

Philip suspends the payment of his debts (Dec.).

1597. Maurice defeats the Spanish army at Turnhout (Jan.).

The Spaniards seize Amiens (March).

The last two attempts of Philip to invade England (July and later).

Anna van den Hove, of Antwerp, buried alive at Brussels for heresy (summer).

Maurice captures Alphen, Brevoort, and other places (Aug.-Oct).

Henry IV recovers Amiens (Sept.).

1598. The Dutch ambassadors implore Henry IV not to make peace with Spain (Feb.-April).

Henry IV signs the Edict of Nantes, granting a liberal measure of toleration to the Huguenots (April).

Peace of Vervins concluded between Henry IV and Spain (May).

Philip transfers the Netherlands to his daughter Isabella and her prospective husband, the Archduke Albert (May).

Elizabeth finally agrees to remain in alliance with the Dutch States (Aug.).

Death of Philip II: Philip III succeeds (Sept.).

Archduke Albert at Ferrara marries by proxy Philip's daughter Isabella (Nov.). Wedding-ceremonies took place at Valencia in April 1599.

Index

The main guide to the subjects dealt with in this volume is the Table of Contents at the beginning. The following Index includes only such relevant items as cannot be properly tabulated there: it also excludes most of the headings, which would require *either* a batch of bare page-numbers, *or else* a swarm of explanatory verbal details.

One of its chief purposes is (as stated in the Preface) to direct the reader to those places where bibliographical details of works frequently quoted in more-or-less obscure abbreviated forms are given. No attempt however has been made to index the references completely.

The contents of the Chronological Table are indexed under *years*, listed after a dash.

Page- or year-numbers are bracketed where the item indexed is alluded to in the text, rather than specified by name.

Abyssinia, 22, 23
Acton, Lord, 3-7, 78 n.1
Adolf of Nassau – 1568
Adrian VI, Pope, 70
Albert, Archduke, 87, 91 f., 173 – 1596, 1598
Albigenses, 139
Aleander, 70
Alexander the Great, 2
Alexander VI, Borgia, Pope, 14, 25
Alkmaar, 99, 100 – 1573
Alost – 1576
Alphen – 1597
Alva, Duke of, 25, 57, 61, 67, 77 n.1, 78-80, 83-85, 89, 93-111, 123, 125, 129, 134 f., 142 f., 171 f., 177, 189-192, 194, 221, 225 – 1554, 1556 f., 1563, 1566-1573, 1580, 1582
Amador de los Rios, 27
Amboise, 25, 45 – 1563
American Historical Review, 4 n.3, 117 n.1, etc.
Amiens – 1597
Amsterdam, 70, 92, 175 – 1578
Anabaptism, ists, 70 75, 86, 98, 107 f., 159, 167 f., 205 f., 220 f. – 1527, 1530, 1532, 1534 f., 1553
Anjou, Francis Duke of, 97 n., 176, 192-196 – 1576, 1578, 1580-1584

Anna van den Hove, 61, 83, 178 – 1597
Anne of Austria, 80, 86, 116 – 1569 f., 1580
Anne of Denmark, 157
Anne of Egmont, 183, 209, (212) – 1551, 1558
Anne of Saxony, 195, 197, 198 n.1, 210-212 – 1560 f., 1567, 1571, 1575, 1577
Antichrist, 32, 55
Antwerp, 42, 70, 79, 82, 89-92, 98, 106, 167, 169-171, 174, 176, 196, 198 – 1564, 1566f., 1570, 1576 f., 1579, 1582 f., 1585, 1597
Apology of William of Orange, 116, 200 f. – 1580 f.
Aquinas, Thos., 50 n.1
Aragon, 51, 56 n.1, 91, 118 n., 123 f. – 1591 f.
Armada, The Spanish, 33, 109, 112, 114, 129, 131, 149, 157, 218 – 1586, 1588
Arminius, -ianism, 181, 215
Armstrong, E., *The Emperor Charles V* (ed. 1910), 2 vols., 42 n.1, 46 n.1, etc.
Arques, 150 – 1589
Arras, League of, 82, 175 – 1579
Artois, 1529, 1579
Aufklärung, 50 n.1, 216 n.1
Augsburg, 67, 76, 134, 159, 198, 207 – 1530, 1548, 1551, 1555

Index

Augustinian Monks, 70
Augustus, Elector of Saxony, 210 – 1553
Austria, 45, 156
Auto-de-Fé, 49, etc.
Avignon, 145
Axel, 172 – 1586
"Axis" – 217

Babington Plot, 124
Badajoz – 1580
Ballard, John, 147 n.1
Barcelona, 58 – 1529, 1551
Baroque Art, 20, 22
Basle – 1536
Bayonne, 77 n.1, 93 n.3 – 1565
Belloc, H., 24 f., 35
Benedict XV, Pope, 20
Berg, 91
Bergen-op-Zoom – 1588
Bergerac – 1577
Berghen, Marquis of, 128
Berlaimont, 101, 164
Bernini, 20
Bible, 135. *See also* Vulgate.
Binchy, Prof., 22 f.
Black, J.B., *The Reign of Elizabeth*, 46 n.1, 77 n.1, etc.
Blok, P.J., *History of the People of the Netherlands* (Eng. trans.), 68 n.1, 72 n.3, 103 n.1, etc.
Boleyn, Anne – 1533
Bologna, 32 – 1530, 1547
Bommenede, 89, 109 – 1575
Bor, 79 n.1
Bordeaux – 1581
Borgia-Popes, 3, 14, 25
Borromeo, Cardinal, 136
Bothwell, 141 – 1567
Bourne, Cardinal, 20
Brabant, 82, 97, 100, 168, 176, 192-194, 198 – 1572, 1577, 1582 f.
Brébeuf, Jean de, 21
Breda, 81, 209 – 1567, 1575, 1577, 1580 f.
Brevoort, 173 – 1597
Bridge, G.F., 2 n.1
Brill, 98, 104, 143, 171 – 1572
Brodrick, Jas., 28 f.
Bruges, 92 – 1582, 1584
Bruno, Giordano, 155 f.
Brussels, 61, 70, 78 n.1, 80, 83, 95, 97 f., 129, 178, 183, 199 – 1544, 1549, 1555 f., 1566-1568, 1570, 1573, 1576-1578, 1585, 1594-1597
Bryce, Jas., 43 n.3
Bull-fighting, 42
Buoncompagno, Giacomo, 144
Burghley. *See* Cecil.
Burgundy, Duke of, 120
Bury, J.B., 7
Butterfield, H., 5-8, etc.

Cabrera, 34, 77 n.1, 105 f., 109, 196 n.3
Cadiz, 173 – 1587, 1596
Cadoux, C.J., *Roman Catholicism and Freedom*, 19 n.1, 23 n.1, etc.; *Catholicism and Christianity*, 79 n.1, 145
Caesar, Julius, 8
Calais – 1558, 1588, 1596
Caligula, 14
Calvin, -ism, -ists, 45, 72, 75, 79, 81, 92, 107 f., 162-164, 168, 175, 177, 179, 181, 195, 197, 201, 204-206, 210, 214, 220, 224 – 1536, 1553, 1564, 1567, 1573, (1579)
Cambray – 1529, 1553, 1595
Campion, Edmund, 146 n.1 – 1580
Canary Islands, 173
Caraffa, Cardinal, nephew of Pope Paul IV, 134-136, 139
Carlos, Don, 48, 112 f., 116, 122, 128, 132, 200 f. – 1545, 1556, 1568
Carlyle, Thos., 190
Carnesecchi, Pietro, 143
Carranza, 46
Castellio, Sebastian, 52, 216
Castille, 118, 132 n.1
Cateau-Cambrésis, 37, (76), 187 – 1559
Catechism of Council of Trent, 138 – 1566
Catherine, daughter of Philip II, 113
Catherine de' Medici, 44 f., 76 n.2, 77 n.1, 93 n.3, 119, 144 f., 149, 188 – 1533, 1559, 1565, (1572), 1589
Catherine of Aragon, 20 – 1533
Cauzons, De, 74 n.4
Cecil, William, 32 n.1, 35, 121 n.2, 124, 131, 136 f., 166, 186 – 1571
Cenci, 154 f.
Chapman, Geo., 47 n.2, 146 n.
Charles the Bold, 65
Charles I, King of England, 24, (38), (65 n.1), (157), 223

Charles V, King of Spain and Emperor, 11 n.1, 28, 37, 39 f., 44-48, 50, 64, 66, 67, 69-75, 84, 93, 105, 115, 123 n.1, 132, 133 n.1, 134, 161, 163, 177, 183, 185 – 1527-1558
Charles IX, King of France, 45, 144 f. – 1560, 1571, (1572), 1574
Charlotte de Bourbon, 210 – 212 – 1575, 1582
Chartres, 153
Chastel, Jean, 154 – 1594
Chingis Khan, 14
Cicero, 9 f.n.1
Claverhouse, John Graham of, 14, 20, 30
Clement VII, Pope, 20, 70 – 1529 f., 1533 f.
Clement VIII, Pope, 148, 152-157 – 1592 f., 1595
Cleves, 91
Coeworden – 1592
Coligny, Gaspar de, 45, 121 n.2, 211 – 1557, 1569
Coligny, Louise de, 211 f. – 1583
Cologne, 50 n.1, 193, 210 – 1579
Como, 139, 144
Communism, 15 f., 25, 170 n.3, 216. *See also* Kautsky.
Corbeil, 89 – 1590
Cortés, Hernán, 28
Corunna – 1588
Cosmo I, Grand Duke of Tuscany, 143
Coulton, G.G., 8 f., 12, 23 n.2, 74 n.4
Council of Troubles, Tumults, or Blood, 93, 95 f., 100-102, 104, 106, 108, 191 – 1567
Counter Reformation, 20, 25, 144, 148
Coutras – 1587
Covenanters, 30
Cranmer, Thos. – 1533
Creed of Pius IV, 137 – 1564
Creighton, Mandell, 3-5, 84 n.4
Crespy – 1544
Cromwell, Oliver, 14, 24, 57, 88, 190, 196, 216
Cromwell, Thos., 87
Crusades, 139
Cuenca, 60
Culloden, 102
Cumberland, 102

Darnley, Henry, 141 – 1565, 1567
Darwin, Francis, 53 n.2
Davies, R. Trevor, *The Golden Century of Spain*, 16 n., 31 f., 36-39, 40 n1. etc.
Defoe, Daniel, 42 n.1
Delft, 124, 194 – 1576, 1580, 1584
Dendermonde – 1566, 1583
Derby, 102
Deventer – 1591
Dictionary of National Biography, 30 n.1 56 n.1, etc.
Diest – 1583
Dillenburg, 183 – 1533, 1544, 1567 f., 1580
D.L.K., 39
Doesburg – 1586
Dort – 1573, 1575
Douay, 146 – 1579
Dougall, Lily, 5
Dourlans, 89 – 1595
Drake, Francis, 25 – 1586 f., 1595 f.
Dresden – 1560, 1575
Dryden, John, 10 n.1, 30 f.
Duchesne, L., 100
Dunkerque – 1583

Eboli, Princess of, 123
Economics, 16 f., 42, 166 f.
Edward VI, King of England, 14, 166 – 1547, 1553
Egmont, Count of, 77-80, 93, 95, 97, 106, 129, 142, 162, 164 – 1557 f., 1561-1563, 1565-1568
Elincx, Eva, 209
Elizabeth, Queen of England, 25, 34, 36, 45-47, 55 f., 102 f., 108 f., 121, 124, 126, 128 f., 131, 138, 141 f., 146 f., 149, 154, 157 f., 171, 202, 218 – 1533, 1558, 1568 – 1571, 1578, 1581, 1583-1586, 1598
Elizabeth (or Isabel) of Valois, wife of Philip II, 77 n.1, 116, 122, 200, (201) – 1559 f., 1565, 1568
Elizabeth of Austria, 116
Encyclopædia Britannica, eleventh edition, 61 n.1, etc.
England, Dr. Sylvia L., *The Massacre of St. Bartholomew*, 145 n.3
Erasmus, 68, 162, 201 f. – 1536

Ernest, Archduke – 1594 f.
Escovedo, 123 f., 129
Essex, Earl of – 1596
Eugenius, supposed first Archbishop of Toledo, 33
European Civilization: Its Origin and Development, 23 f.
Eymericus, 58
Eyre, Edw., 23

Fabricius of Antwerp, 167 f. – 1564
Fadrique, Don, son of Alva. *See* Frederic.
Fairbairn, A.M., 121 n.1
Farnese, Alexander, later Duke of Parma, 81 f., 91 f., 109 f., 114, 124, 129 f., 163, 169, 175, 179 f., 192 – 1545, 1565, 1578-1592
Farrer, A.J.D., 17 n.
Farinacci, Prospero, 60 f.
Fascism, 22 f., (217), 219 n.
Ferdinand of Aragon, 66 – 1555
Ferdinand I, Emperor, 134, (136), 137 – 1551 f., 1555 f., 1564
Ferdinand II, Emperor, 88, (181)
Feria, Spanish Ambassador in England, 127 f.
Ferrara, Señor, 25
Ferrara – 1598
Finisterre, Cape – 1596
Firth, C.H., 11 n.1
Flanders, 82, 84 n.1, 100, 168, 173 f., 193 – 1529, 1582, 1590
Fleix – 1580
Florence, 143
Florida, 167 n.1
Flushing, 173 – 1585-1587
Foxe, John, 29
Francis I, King of France, 69 – 1533, 1536, 1547
Francis II, King of France – 1558-1560
Frederic (Fadrique) of Toledo, Don, son of Alva, 97, 99, 107 – 1572 f.
Frederick Henry, Stadtholder of Holland, 181, 211
Franco of Spain, 217
Frankfort, Diet at, 209 – 1558
Freemasonry, 34
Friesland, 66 – 1535
Froude, J.A., 7, 42 n.1, 56 n.1

Gachard, *Études et Notices*, etc., 97 n.
Gairdner, Jas., 29 n.
Galileo, 21 f., 155
Gardner, P., 2 n.1
Gelderland, 66, 82, 168, 175, 193, (195 n.2) – 1538, 1578-1580, 1583
Gemblours, 81 – 1578
Geneva, 137, 142, 157 – 1536, 1553, 1564
Gérard, Balthasar, 109, 124, 172, 194 – 1584, 1589
Gertruydenberg – 1589, 1593
Geyl, Pieter, ix, 2 n.1, 68 n.1, etc.
Ghent, 69, 92, 161, 195 – 1539 f., 1559, 1576 f., 1579, 1584, 1588. Pacification of, 81, 174 f., 192, 198 f., 207 – 1576 f.
Gibraltar, 88, 174 – 1563
Goethe, 9
Granvelle, Cardinal, 75, 77, 82 n.1, 124, 128, 164, 188 – 1560-1564, 1579, 1586
Grave – 1586
Gravelines – 1588
Green, J.R., 43 n.3
Gregor, Joseph, 27
Gregory XIII, Pope, 143-147, 188 – 1572, 1585
Gregory XIV, Pope, 152 – 1590 f.
Groningen, 66, 89, 97, 107 – 1568, 1579, 1580, 1594
Grotius, Hugo, 96 n.2, 178
Guadalajara – 1560
"Gueux, Les" – 1566
Guise, members of family of, 20, 24 f., 44, 76 n.2, 92, 144, 146, 150 – 1538, 1553 f., 1556-60, 1562, 1576, 1584 f., 1588 f.
Gwynn, Denis, 22

Haarlem, 71, 89, 99 f., 107 – 1532, 1572 f.
Hague, The, 70, 193 – 1527, 1530, 1570, 1581, 1585
Hainault – 1579
Hallam, Henry, 190. View of the State of Europe during the Middle Ages (ed. 1878), 45 n.5, etc. The Constitutional History of England (ed. 1891), 55 n.3, 56 n.1, etc.
Hapsburg Family, The, 69, 115-118, 125, (132), 134, 163, 218 – 1549, 1551
Harrison, *William the Silent* (1897), 97 n.1, etc.

Haultain, 173
Heemskirk, 173
Hegel, 7
Heiliger Lee, 97, 106 – 1568
Henry II, King of France, 149, 187 f., 205 – 1533, 1547, 1551, 1557, 1559
Henry III, King of France, 121, 130, 149 f. – 1574, 1576, 1585, 1587-1589
Henry of Navarre, later King Henry IV of France, 45, 76, 121, 125 f., 130 f., 150-154, 156, 174, 202 – 1584 f., 1587, 1589-1595, 1597 f.
Henry of Nassau – 1574
Henry VIII, King of England, 14, 108, 136 – 1533, 1534, 1547
Hesdin – 1553
Heussi, Karl, *Kompendium der Kirchengeschichte* (ed. 1909), 50 n.1, etc.
Hinsley, Cardinal, 20
Hitler, A., 217, (219)
Hoorn, Count of, 80, 93, 95, 97, 106, 129, 142 – 1563, 1566 – 1568
Horniman Museum, Forest Hill, 59 f.
Howard, Lord, – 1596
Hughes, P., 25
Huguenots, 20, 25, 45, 76 n.2, 98 f., 103 f., 119, 129, 141, 144-146, 150, 154, 157, 167, 170 n.3, 181, 211, 218 – 1560, 1562 f., 1569 f., 1572, 1576, 1597
Hulst – 1591, 1596
Hume, M. (A.S.), *Philip II of Spain* (1897), 43 n.1, 64 n.1, etc.; *Two English Queens and Philip* (1908), 115 n.1, etc.; and in *Camb. Mod. Hist.*

Ignatius Loyola, 28 – 1556
India, Indians, Indies, 28 f., 42, 47 n.2 – 1556
Innocent VIII, Pope, 50 n.1
Innocent IX, Pope, 152 – 1591
Ireland, Irish, 102, 129, 146, 173 – 1582, 1588
Ireton, Hy, 65 n.1
Isabella of Castile, 26, 66 – 1555
Isabel of Valois. See Elizabeth.
Isabel Clara Eugenia, daughter of Philip II, 87, 113, 116 – 1598
Isabel de Osorio, Philip's mistress, 115, 200

Italy, 22 f., 94, 126, 129, 134 f., 140, 148, 152, 189, 216 f., 224 – 1529, 1542, 1548, 1554, 1556 f., 1559, 1567, 1571. See also Naples, Milan, Rome.
Ivry, 151 – 1590

James, Apostle, 33, 90
James V, King of Scotland – 1538, 1542
James I, King of England, 157
James II, King of England, 14, 30
Japan, 217
Jarnac – 1569
Jauréguy, 172, 196, (225) – 1582
Jeffreys, Judge, 14
Jemmingen, 89, 97, 106, 108, 142 – 1568
Jerusalem, 1554
Jesuits, Society of Jesus, 18, 21, 28, 48, 56 n.1, 61, 83, 144, 146-148, 154-157, 205 – 1540, 1580, 1594
Jews, 26, 36, 41, 45 n.1, 49, 108, 139, 148, 186
John, King of England, 14
John of Austria, Don, 81, 109 f., 114, 123 f., 126 f., 129, 138, 146, 174 f., 186, 193, 196, 198 f. – 1547, 1569-1571, 1576-1578
John of Nassau, brother of William, 210 – 1559, 1577-1579, 1580
Johnson, Samuel, 10 n.1
Joinville – 1584
Jourdan, G.V., 35 f.
Juan de Mariana, 121
Juana, mother of Charles V, (48), 66, (132) – 1555
Jülich, 177
Julius III, Pope, 135 – 1550, 1553, 1555
Justification of William of Orange – 1568
Justin of Nassau, 209 – 1559

Kappel – 1531
Kautsky, Karl, 15 f.
Kidd, B.J., 138 f., 143
Kirk, K.E., 11 n.2
Knox, John – 1572

Lagny, 89 – 1590
Lane-Poole, S., 7 n.
Lea, Henry Charles, 4 f., 38, 43 nn.1 and 2, 51, 53 n.2, 54;

Index

History of the Inquisition of Spain (vols, iii and iv, 1907), 43 n.2, 51 n.3, etc., etc.; and in American Historical Review, q.v.
League, The French Catholic, 146, 150, 152 f. – 1576, 1590
Lecky, W.E.H., History of the Rise and Influence of the Spirit of Rationalism in Europe (2 vols., ed 1872), 52 n.2, etc.
Leicester, Earl of – 1585 – 1587
Leipzig – 1561
Lenin – 217
Leo XIII, Pope, 21
Lepanto, 90 n.2, 138, 200 n.1 – 1571
Lerma, 86 f.
Leyden, 99, 182, 208 – 1573 – 1575
L'Hôpital, 44
Liége, 66 – 1543
Lille – 1579
Lindsay, T.M., *A History of the Reformation* (two vols, Edinburgh, 1907-1908), 61 n.2, 72 n.1, etc.
Lisbon, 113 – 1581 f., 1587 f.
Llorente, Antonio, 27, 50
Loevestein – 1570
Longjumeau, 45 – 1568
Louis XIV, King of France, 2
Louis of Nassau, brother of William, 89, 97-99, 103, 106, 109, 142 – 1565, 1568 f., 1571 f., 1574
Louvain, 97 – 1578
Luther, Martin, 6 – 1529, 1546, 1560
Lutherans, Lutheranism, 37, 45, 69 f., 75, 134, 159, 183, 205 n.1, 207, 214, 224 – 1529 f., 1546 f., 1555, 1567
Luxemburg, 198

Maccarthy, Desmond, 9, 11
Macaulay, T.B., 16, 30 f., 166 n.
Machiavelli, 4, 117 n.2, 130 f., 186
Madrid, 77, 80, 109, 123, 128 – 1567
Maestricht, 81, 84, 89, 109, 113 – 1576, 1579 f.
Malta – 1565
Mandelbaum, M., 1 n.1
Marburg – 1529
Marcellus, Pope – 1555
Margaret of Parma, Philip II's Regent in the Netherlands, (75), 76-79, 81, (128),
164, 189, 191, (194), 206 n. – 1559, (1565 f.), 1567
Maria Manuela of Portugal, 115, (132), 200 f. – 1543, 1545
Mark, de la (William de Lumey), 171 f., 195 – 1571, 1573
Marnix. *See* St. Aldegonde.
Marseilles – 1533
Marxism *See* Communism
Mary the Virgin, 90, 171
Mary of Burgundy, 65 f.
Mary, Ex-queen of Hungary, Charles V's Regent in the Netherlands, 72, (84), (186) – 1531, 1533, 1536, 1553, 1555
Mary Queen of Scots, 20, 30, 37, (103), 141, 146 – 1542, 1548, 1558 f., 1561, 1565, 1567 f., 1587
Mary Tudor, Queen of England, 21, 29 f., 45-47, 115, 127, 135, 166, 218 – 1553-1558
Mason, A.E.W., on Drake, 25
Matthias, Archduke of Austria, 192 – 1577 f., 1580 f.
Maurice, Elector of Saxony, 197, 210 – 1551-1553
Maurice of Nassau, Stadtholder, etc. son of Willima of Orange, 82 f., 87 f., 91, 124, 173 f., 176 f., 181, 210, 215, 225 – 1567, 1585 f., 1591-1594, 1597
Maximilian I, Emperor, 66
Maximilian II, Emperor, (67), (79 f.), 86, (103), 106, (125) – 1551, 1564, (1568), (1575), 1576
Mazarin, Cardinal, 87
Mechlin, 89, 96, 99, 107 – 1560, 1572
Medina Sidonia, 114 – 1588
Melanchthon – 1560
Mendoza, Bernardino de, Philip's Ambassador to Elizabeth, 55, 57, 129 – 1584
Mendoza, Franceso, Spanish Admiral, 91
Menéndez, 167 n.1
Merivale, Chas., 122 n.1
Merriman, R.B., The Rise of the Spanish Empire in the Old World and the New: vol. ii, The Emperor (1925), 47 n.3, etc.; vol. iv, Philip the Prudent (1934), 51 n.1, etc.
Meteren, 96 n.2
Metz – 1553

Meuse – 1572
Mexico, 28 – 1574
Middelburg, 76 n.3 – 1574
Milan – 1540, 1546, 1549, 1554
Millar, Jan, 1548
Miracles, 33
Mirbt, C., Quellen zur Geschichte des Papstums und des römischen Katholizismus (ed. 1924), 141 n.2, 147 n.1, etc.
Modern Historian, The, 13 n.1, etc.
Mohammedans, Moslems, etc., 37, 46, 91 n.1, 182
Mommsen, T., 8
Moncontour – 1569
Mons, 89 – 1572 f., 1578
Montesquieu, 121 n.2
Month, The, 49 n.4, 51 n.1
Montigny, Baron of, 80, 95, 123, 128 f. – 1562, 1566 f., 1570
Mookerheid – 1574
Moors, Moriscos, 37 f., 41 f., 69, 86 f., 113 – 1566 f., 1569 f.
Motley, J.L., 16, 130, 161, 183, 185 f., 199 – *The Rise of the Dutch Republic: a History* (ed. 1874), 72 n.2, etc.; *History of the United Netherlands*, 4 vols. (ed. 1875-1876), 3 n.1, etc.
Motton, Lamph, 70
Mühlberg – 1547
Münster, 71, 74 – 1534, 1535
  Peace of, 88, 91
Mussolini, 7 n., 23, 217 n.1

Naarden, 89, 99, 107 – 1572
Namur, 109 – 1577
Nancy, 65
Nantes, Edict of, 45, 154, 156 – 1598
Naples, 134 f. – 1554
Nassau, House of, 183
Neal, Daniel, 42 n.1, etc.
Neale, J.E., 34; *Age of Catherine de Medici*, 77 n.1, etc.
Nemours, – 1585
Nero, 14, 122 n.1
Neusz, 89, 172 – 1586
Nevers, Duc de, 153 – 1593
Nieuport, 88 – 1583

Nimwegen – 1573, 1591
Noailles – 1553
Noircarmes, 99, 101

Oakeley, H.D., 1 n.1, 8
Oldenbarneveld, 125, 178, 180 f., 215 – 1586 f.
Oman, John, 59 n.6
Orange, 183, 198 – 1561
Orléans, Duke of, 120
Orsini, Cardinal, 144 f.
Ostend, 88 f. – 1588
Oudenarde – 1582
Oudewater, 89, 109 – 1575
Overyssel – 1528
Oxford Magazine, 39

Pacifism, 218 n.2, 220-223
Parry, L.A., *The History of Torture in England* (London, 1934), 55 n.3, etc.
Parsons, Robert, 146 n.1 – 1580
Passau – 1562
Pastor, Ludwig von, *The History of the Popes* (Eng. trans.), 21, 98 n.1, etc.
Paul III, Pope, 32, 71 – 1534, 1537, 1540, 1542, 1547, 1549
Paul IV, Pope (formerly Cardinal Caraffa), 134-136, 139 – 1542, 1554 f., 1557, 1559
Paul V, Pope, 60
Perez, Antonio, 112 n., 123 f.
Perpetual Edict, 199 – 1577
Peru, 41 – 1548, 1573
Philibert of Orange-Châlons, 183 – 1530
Philip I, King of Spain, 66
Philip III, King of Spain, 37, 86-88, 116, 121, (180) – 1598
Philip IV, King of Spain, 88
Philip, Landgrave of Hesse, 210 – 1567
Philip William, son of William of Orange, 97 – 1568, 1596
Picardy – 1568
Pirenne, Henri, *Histoire de Belgique*, viii n.1, 73 n.2, etc.
Pius IV, Pope, 136 f., 139, 198 – 1559, 1564 f.
Pius V, Pope, 46, 56 f., 98, 128, 137-143, 145-147, 198 – 1566, 1569 f., 1572

Index

Pius IX, Pope, 216
Pius XI, Pope, 22 f.
   Plessis-les-Tours – 1589
Poland, 144
Pole, Cardinal Reginald, 135 – 1553 f.
Pope, Popes, 36, 46
Portugal, 115 f., 166, 201 – 1531, 1543, 1581 f., 1589
Porto Bello – 1595
Poullet, Edmond, article "De la répression de l'hérésie," etc., in *Revue Générale*, etc., 18 n.1, 50 n.2, etc., etc.
Powicke, F.M., 24, 47 n.1, 146 n.1
Poynter, J.W., 23 n.2
Protestant (the name) – 1529
Provence – 1545
Prussia, 216 n.1
Putnam, Ruth, *William the Silent, Prince of Orange: the Moderate Man of the Sixteenth Century*, 2 vols, (first published in 1895), ed. 1898, 76 n.1, 82 n.2, etc., etc. *William the Silent, Prince of Orange, 1533-1584* (in series "Heroes of the Nations," 1911), 76 n.1, 82 n.2, etc., etc.

Quakers, 220
Quarterly Review, The, 3 n.3, 84 n.4

Ranke, L. von, *History of the Popes* (Eng. trans. 1847-1851, 3 vols.), 78 n.1, 140 n.2 etc.
Rashdall, H. The Universities of Europe in the Middle Ages, 24
Ratisbon – 1541, 1547
Rea, W.F. 49 n.4, 50 n.1 etc.
Regnans in Excelsis, 141, (146) – 1570
Relics 33
René of Nassau, 183 – 1530, 1544
Renier, G.J. – ix f.
Requesens, 80 f., 109 f., 124, 193 – 1573 f., 1576
Revolution, the French, 181
Rheims, 146
Richard III, King of England, 14
Richelieu, 181
Ridolphi Plot, 142 – 1571 f.
Rochelle – 1573

Roermund, 107 – 1572
Romorantin, 44 – 1560
Rome – 1527, 1557
Roth, Cecil, 27 f., 43 n.3, 59 n.
Rouen, 173 – 1592
Rowse, A.L., 35
Rubens, John, 195, 210 – 1571
Rudolf II, Emperor, 67 – 1576, 1594
Russia, 217

St. Aldegonde, Philip Marnix, Seigneur de, 125, 220
St. Bartholomew, Massacre of, 45, 99, 104, 119, 129, 139 f., 144-146, 187 – 1572
St. Denis – 1593
St. Germain – 1570
St. Juste – 1557
St. Omer, 169
St. Quentin, 113, 135 – 1557
St. Thomas, Isle of, 173
Salamanca, 58 – 1543
Sallust, 7
Sanseverina, Cardinal Santori, 152
Santa Cruz – 1588
Saragossa, 123
Scheldt, River – 1585
Scotland, 102, 141 – 1553, 1588. *See also* James *and* Mary Queen of Scots.
Segovia, 80 – 1565, 1567
Seneca, 122 n.1
Servetus, Michael – 1553
Seville – 1559
Seymour, Edward, 14
Shakespeare, on drinking, 209
Sicily, 135 – 1556
Sidney, Sir Philip – 1586
Simancas, bishop, 58
Simancas, place, 80 – 1570
Sixtus V, Pope, 116, 147-152, 157 – 1585-1587, 1589 f.
Sluys, 82, 88, 174 – 1587
Smerwick, 102 – 1580
Smith, S.F., 51 n.1, etc.
Sonoy, Diedrich, 172, 195, 205, 225 – 1575
Speier, Diet of – 1529

Steenwyk – 1582, 1592
Stewart, C. Poyntz, *The Roman Church and Heresy*, 145 n.3
Study of Theology, The, 11 n.2, etc.
Suarez de Paz, 58
Sultan. *See* Turks.
Sykes, Norman, 142 n.1

Tacitus, 7
Tawney, R.H., 42
Thamar – 1581
Thérouanne – 1553
Thirty Years War, 88, 181, 215
Throgmorton Plot – 1583
Thucydides, 7
Times Literary Supplement, The, 7 n., 19-40, etc.
Tirlemont – 1578
Titelmann, Peter, 77, 188
Toledo, 46, 59
Topcliffe, Richard, 55 f.
Torquemada, 26 f.
Torture, 53-63
Tournai – 1581
Tours – 1580
Toynbee, A.J., 7 n.
Trent, Council of, and Tridentine Decrees, 32, 37, 77, 109, 137 f., 148, 154, 156 f. – 1545, 1547, 1551 f., 1562-1564, 1566
Truce of 1609, 88, 167 f., 180 f.
Tunis, 89 – 1535
Turks, 43 n.3, 47 n.2, 69, 90 n.2, 106, 134 f., 146, 149, 156, 164, 174, 182, 200 – 1565, 1571
Turnhout, 173 – 1597
Tuscany 143
Tyrannicide 120 f., 154

Unwin, G., 17 n.
Urban VII, Pope, 151 – 1590
Urban VIII, Pope, 21
Utrecht, 66, 82, 89, 97, 168, 175, 179, 191, 193, 195 – 1528, 1534, 1559, 1568, 1579 f., 1583. Union of Utrecht, 82, 175, 178, 192 f. – 1579

Valencia – 1598
Valenciennes, 79, 89, 96 – 1561 f., 1567 f.
Valladolid, 119 – 1527, 1556, 1559
Vargas, Juan, 95 n.1
Vasari, 145 f.
Vassy – 1562
Vaucelles, Truce of, 127, 135 – 1556
Venice, 45 n.2, 78 n.1, 143, 150, 155, 166 n.2 – 1547
Venloo – 1586
Vervins, Peace, 154 – 1598
Viglius, 101, 164
Vives, Luis, 56 n.2, 58
Voltaire, 20, 70
Vulgate, 148, 154

Waldenses – 1545
Walsh, Wm. Thos., *Philip II*, 31-36, etc., etc.
Walsingham, Sir F., 47, 146 n.1
Wedgwood, C.V., William the Silent, William of Orange, Prince of Nassau, 1533-1584 (London, 1944), 16 n.1, 76 n.3, etc.
Wesley, John, 181
Westminster Catholic Federation, 19, 23 n.2
Weyer, Johann, 50 – 1563
Whig. *See under* Acton *and* Butterfield.
Winchester – 1564
Witchcraft, 45, 50, 216 n.1 – 1563
Wittlin, Alma, 26 f.
Wood, H.G., 7 f., etc.

Xavier, Francis, 28 f.

Ypres – 1584

Zierickzee – 1576
Zuider Zee, 71, 99
Zutphen, 89, 99, 107 – 1572, 1583, 1586, 1591
Zwingli, H. – 1529, 1531

You may also be interested in:

The Lord Protector

Religion and Politics in the Life of Oliver Cromwell

by Robert S. Paul

Oliver Cromwell stands at the gateway of modern history; his resolute Puritanism formative to concepts of political and religious liberty, the development of democracy, and the individual's duty to resist tyranny. In *The Lord Protector*, Robert S. Paul traces Cromwell's political career, from his early influences and political experience, to the English Civil Wars, his brutal conquest of Ireland and campaigns in Scotland.

Where some historians present Cromwell in extremes, either as a scheming power-hungry tyrant, or as a noble hero, Paul seeks to understand the Lord Protector through the religious context of the seventeenth century, removed from the typical historical readings of his contemporaries. In order to understand Cromwell's career, Paul's investigation focusses his study through the extent to which Cromwell shared the theological beliefs common to his time. This relationship between his religion and political action provides an estimate of Cromwell as a man of faith, statesman and ruler.

> 'Learned, scholarly and accurate. It is of value not only as a study of a great English Protestant and Puritan but in tackling problems of the relations of the church, state, and society which confront us all.'
> **– Gordon Rupp**

Dr Robert S. Paul (1918-1992) was a graduate in the School of Modern History at Oxford and specialised in the study of Cromwell. Paul gained his DPhil from the University, and was later appointed Assistant Director of the Ecumenical Institute at Bossey, Switzerland.

Published 2023

Paperback ISBN: 978 0 7188 9679 9
ePub ISBN: 978 0 7188 9681 2
PDF ISBN: 978 0 7188 9680 5